THE MORAL PICTURESQUE

Studies in Hawthorne's Fiction

THE MORAL PICTURESQUE

Studies in Hawthorne's Fiction

by

Darrel Abel

PURDUE UNIVERSITY PRESS
West Lafayette, Indiana

Book and jacket designed by James McCammack
Illustrations by Donald K. Carter

Published 1988
SECOND PRINTING FEBRUARY 1990

Library of Congress Cataloging-in-Publication Data

Abel, Darrel.
    The moral picturesque: studies in Hawthorne's fiction by Darrel Abel.
       p. xx cm.
    IBSN 0-911198-91-1
    1. Hawthorne, Nathaniel, 1804–1864—Criticism and interpretation.
    I. Title.
    PS1888.A25 1988   87-26843
    813'.3—dc19   CIP

Printed in the United States of America

To my wife Janet
who has given me love, comfort, and
companionship
for more than half a century

TABLE OF CONTENTS

ix   Acknowledgments

1   Introduction

PART ONE
Premises and Theory

9 • CHAPTER 1
The System of Life

19 • CHAPTER 2
Ghostland and the Jurisdiction of Veracity

25 • CHAPTER 3
Our Common Nature

31 • CHAPTER 4
Marbles and Bubbles: "This Troublesome Mortality"

37 • CHAPTER 5
Hawthorne's Qualified Transcendentalism

44 • CHAPTER 6
Illusive Credence

PART TWO
Materials and Techniques

53 • CHAPTER 7
The Play of Imagination

68 • CHAPTER 8
The Stony Excrescence of Prose

76 • CHAPTER 9
Visions That Seem Real

85 · C H A P T E R   10
The Loom of Fiction

108 · C H A P T E R   11
Giving Lustre to Gray Shadows: Prospero's Potent Art

125 · C H A P T E R   12
Metonymic Symbols: Black Glove and Pink Ribbon

142 · C H A P T E R   13
"A Vast Deal of Human Sympathy"

PART THREE
The Scarlet Letter:
"A Drama of Guilt and Sorrow"

163 · C H A P T E R   14
"The Strong Division-Lines of Nature"

180 · C H A P T E R   15
Hester: "In the Dark Labyrinth of Mind"

190 · C H A P T E R   16
Pearl: "The Scarlet Letter Endowed With Life"

207 · C H A P T E R   17
Chillingworth: The Devil in Boston

225 · C H A P T E R   18
Dimmesdale: Fugitive from Wrath

PART FOUR
The Other Major Romances

251 · C H A P T E R   19
The House of the Seven Gables:
"A Long Drama of Wrong and Retribution"

270 · C H A P T E R   20
The Blithedale Romance: "A Counterfeit Arcadia"

298 · C H A P T E R   21
The Marble Faun: "A Masque of Love and Death"

ACKNOWLEDGMENTS

Special thanks go to my friend and colleague Professor G. R. Thompson, whose careful reading and constructive criticism of the first two drafts of this book have greatly helped me to clarify many points of the text and to deal with problems of organizing these disparate pieces. I am grateful also to Verna Emery, managing editor of the Purdue University Press, for her patience and encouragement during the preparation of the book for publication. Professor Kenneth W. Cameron, whose scholarly work has been an inspiration and example, solicited several of the pieces included in this collection, and I here express my gratitude to him. Finally, I thank my wife Janet and my daughter Janet Smith for indispensable help in preparation of the manuscript.

I am grateful to the following journals and presses for permission to reprint these essays:

"*The Blithedale Romance*: 'A Counterfeit Arcadia' ": Originally published under the title "Hawthorne's Skepticism About Social Reform: With Especial Reference to *The Blithedale Romance*" in *The University of Kansas City Review* 19 (Spring 1953): 181–93. Reprinted (revised) by permission of *New Letters*.

"Chillingworth: The Devil in Boston": Originally published in *Philological Quarterly* 32 (October 1953): 366–81. The University of Iowa. Reprinted by permission.

"Dimmesdale: Fugitive from Wrath": © 1956 by The Regents of the University of California. Reprinted from *Nineteenth-Century Fiction*, Vol. 11, No. 2, September 1956, pp. 81–105, by permission of The Regents.

"Ghostland and the Jurisdiction of Veracity": Originally published under the title "Hawthorne, Ghostland, and the Jurisdiction of Veracity" in *American Transcendental Quarterly*

(Fall 1974). © 1974 by Kenneth W. Cameron. Reprinted (abridged) by permission of Kenneth W. Cameron.

"Giving Lustre to Gray Shadows: Prospero's Potent Art": Originally published under the title "Giving Lustre to Gray Shadows: Hawthorne's Potent Art," in *American Literature* 42:3, pages 373–88. Copyright © 1969 Duke University Press.

"Hester: 'In the Dark Labyrinth of Mind' ": Originally published under the title "Hawthorne's Hester" in *College English* (March 1952). Reprinted by permission of the National Council of Teachers of English.

"*The House of the Seven Gables:* 'A Long Drama of Wrong and Retribution' ": Originally published as "Hawthorne's House of Tradition," in *The South Atlantic Quarterly* 52:4, pages 561–78. Copyright © 1953 Duke University Press. Copyright renewed 1981.

"*The Marble Faun:* 'A Masque of Love and Death' ": Originally published in the *University of Toronto Quarterly* (October 1953). Reprinted by permission.

"Marbles and Bubbles: 'This Troublesome Mortality' ": Reprinted by permission from *Studies in Romanticism* 8 (Summer 1969): 193–97. © Boston University, 1969.

"Metonymic Symbols: Black Glove and Pink Ribbon": Originally published in *NEQ* 42 (June 1969): 163–80. Reprinted with permission of the *New England Quarterly.*

"Pearl: 'The Scarlet Letter Endowed with Life' ": Originally published as "Hawthorne's Pearl: Symbol and Character" in *ELH, A Journal of Literary History* 18:1, pp. 50–66. Copyright © 1951 The Johns Hopkins University Press. Reprinted (revised) by permission of The Johns Hopkins University Press.

"The Play of Imagination": Originally published as " 'A More Imaginative Pleasure': Hawthorne on the Play of the Imagination" in *Emerson Society Quarterly* 55:2 (1969): 63–71. Reprinted (revised and enlarged) by permission of Kenneth W. Cameron.

" 'The Strong Division-Lines of Nature' ": Originally published in *American Transcendental Quarterly* 14 (Spring 1972): 23–31. © 1972 by Kenneth W. Cameron. Reprinted by permission of Kenneth W. Cameron.

"A Vast Deal of Human Sympathy": Originally published under the title "A Vast Deal of Human Sympathy: Idea and Device in Hawthorne's 'The Snow-Image,' " in *Criticism* 12:4 (1970): 316–32. Reprinted by permission of Wayne State University Press.

"The artist—the true artist—must look beneath the exterior. It is his gift—his proudest, but often a melancholy one—to see the inmost soul. . . ."—"The Prophetic Pictures"

"I have contrived a certain pictorial exhibition, somewhat in the nature of a puppet show, by means of which I propose to call up the multiform and many-colored Past before the spectator, and show him the ghosts of his forefathers, amid a succession of historic incidents. . . ."—"Main Street"

"Take my arm, gentle reader, and come with me into some street, perhaps trodden by your daily footsteps, but which now has such an aspect of half-familiar strangeness, that you suspect yourself of walking abroad in a dream."
—"Old News"

INTRODUCTION

WHAT DISTINGUISHES HAWTHORNE AS A WRITER, BESIDES THE seventeenth century elegance of his style, are two characteristics. One is his habitual use of a psychological approach to his subjects. He assumed an absolute of archetypal human experiences enacting a providentially directed cosmic drama of which he had uncertain knowledge through sympathy with persons enacting primordial roles. Like his Concord contemporaries, he believed that there was a transcendent Oversoul, but unlike them he did not believe that he could communicate with it directly by intuition or indirectly by what Emerson called the "tuition" of nature. Instead, he looked for truth in a psychological undersoul.

The second distinctive characteristic of his fiction was his use of the mode he called "the moral picturesque." This was a mode of figuration of the archetypal experiences that his psychological preoccupations discovered. When he characterized himself as "a lover of the moral picturesque," (CE 10:439) he attached to the terms *moral* and *picturesque* larger significance than they have in current usage.

Moral did not refer merely to right and wrong behavior, but to all underlying human reality—vital, spiritual, and psychological. This acceptation of the term *moral* is defined in the *Oxford English Dictionary* as "that kind of probable evidence that rests on a knowledge of the general tendencies of human nature, or of the character of particular individuals or classes of men."

1

Picturesque meant strikingly graphic and extraordinary, either in its intense typicality, or its irregularity and variety, or its eccentricity.

These somewhat overlapping categories can be illustrated by Hawthorne's comments on picturesque scenery. *Intense typicality*: "The silver Links of Forth are as sweet and gently picturesque an object as a man sees in a lifetime." (EN, 527) "I never saw anything more picturesque than the prospect from the castle-wall [at Conway, Wales] toward the sea."(EN, 66) *Irregularity and variety*: "The irregularity of old towns and villages is one of their most striking peculiarities. . . . There is a constant unexpectedness; . . . I should think it never could grow tame." (EN, 128–29) The "level streets of Stratford," however, make the effect "quite tame and unpicturesque." (EN, 130) *Eccentricity*: English trees are "more individual and picturesque than American trees," "with more character in their contorted trunks. . . . Our forest trees have a great sameness of character, like our people." (EN, 53) "Men are so much alike in their nature, that they grow intolerable unless varied by their circumstances." (CE 3:150)

His comparison of trees to people is appropriate, for the traits of picturesqueness that he discerned in natural scenes were like the traits of moral picturesqueness that he discerned in human character and behavior.

The moral picturesque was an attempt to express meanings through figures rather than in explicit statement. He did so because much of the meaning he wanted to convey was unconscious and not otherwise expressible. The technical problem involved was how to make notation of fact, the picture, graphic and solid enough to be convincingly real without obscuring intimations of deeper meaning. Thus he wrote, in "The Old Manse," "I resolved at least to achieve a novel that should evolve some deep lesson and should possess physical substance enough to stand alone." (CE 10:5) And in his preliminary jottings for the unfinished romance *The Ancestral Footstep*, he wrote,

> I do not wish it to be a picture of life, but a Romance, grim, grotesque, quaint. . . . It might have so much of the hues of life that the reader should sometimes think it was intended for a picture, yet the atmosphere should be such as to excuse all wildness. In the Introduction, I might disclaim all intention to draw

a real picture. . . . The descriptions of scenery, &c, . . . might
be correct, but there should be a tinge of the grotesque given to
all the characters and events. (CE 12:58)

Henry James erred in his judgment that in Hawthorne's
fiction "the picturesque is a limitation of sensibility that dwells
upon appearances rather than penetrating deeply." James recognized and appreciated Hawthorne's interest in psychology,
but he didn't comprehend Hawthorne's use of the picturesque.
Hawthorne's sensibility penetrated more deeply than his often
banal thought, and his picturesque mode enabled him to cognize
perceptions that were not reducible to explicit statement. His
insights anticipated findings of modern depth psychology, but
he lacked a modern conceptual vocabulary, and he was evidently
unaware of the disjunction between his conventional thought
and his deeper perceptions.

In all his work he was preoccupied with two concerns: how
the ideal appears in the real world, and the distinction and relation of the sexes. He saw in both of these concerns paradoxes of
opposition and affinity. The real and the ideal were antithetic
but at the same time complementary. So also male and female.

He dealt with these paradoxes not as subjects of philosoph-
ical speculation, but as matters for artistic treatment. In fact, he
thought that the problems of relation posed by these paradoxes
were inexplicable, and his sole concern was to present them
vividly and dramatically. That is, he dealt with them as literary
material, not as intellectual problems. His thinking and formulas
of literal reference to such matters were conventional. His distinction as a writer is not in his ideas.

These two concerns are mingled throughout his work, and
it is impossible to disengage either one as a single ordering principle for discussion of his fiction. That consideration and the fact
that the essays that constitute the bulk of material in this volume
were written over a period of about thirty-five years without
forethought of integrating them into a coherent volume have
presented problems of organization of this book. But, as his
work is best approached through consideration of his technical
dispositions and strategies, it has seemed best to put these
pieces together according to their literary more than their thematic concerns and characteristics. Consequently, the chapters

in Part One set forth the overt premises and the deeper and essentially operative principles of Hawthorne's imaginative handling of materials. Part Two describes and illustrates the technical operations and strategies according to which these principles are put into practice in his fiction. Part Three explicates his masterwork, *The Scarlet Letter*, with particular attention to themes and characters, according to these principles and strategies. Part Four examines the remaining three major romances in the same fashion, but with special regard to the social concerns that engaged his attention in *The House of the Seven Gables* and *The Blithedale Romance*, and to showing the central situation of *The Marble Faun* as variously interpretable by the actors in the scene, especially the several artists. Discussion of all four romances points out how the artist presence controls perception of reality.

In all of Hawthorne's work we are sensible of an artist presence, sometimes incarnate in a character, sometimes not. The function of this presence is to observe events, to sympathize with the characters involved in them and thus to try to understand or identify with them, and to give expression and meaning to their actions and roles. Meaning is given by ideas in the artist mind, and amounts to creation of reality, since for Hawthorne all reality is subjectively defined.

In *The Scarlet Letter* the child Pearl is a kind of artist, who sees moral possibilities in the characters with whom her life is involved and tries to bring them into being. The witch Mistress Hibbins is also a kind of artist, who senses darker possibilities in the same characters and tries to bring them to realization. Both the male/female and sense/spirit dilemmas are basic to the plot.

In *The House of the Seven Gables* the same dualities are apparent. The "abortive lover of the Beautiful," (CE 2:216) Clifford, represents the artist imagination oppressed by the gross materialism of his cousin Jaffrey. There is another artist present, the daguerreotypist Holgrave, who "makes pictures out of sunshine" (CE 2:91)—that is, whose envisagements of life are initially only of "broad daylight reality," (CE 10:11) which to Hawthorne means sense-awareness only. But after he is enlightened by what Hawthorne elsewhere calls "the deep intelligence of love," (CE 10:460) his vision is no longer restricted to broad daylight reality. "All these outward circumstances are made less than visionary by the renewing power of the spirit." (CE 10:153) Phoebe, both child and woman, brings out the spiritual awarenesss of both the abortive artist Clifford and the too-realistic artist Holgrave.

In *The Blithedale Romance* the artist observer is the poet Coverdale, who is also accused of cold spectatorial detachment. This occurs so often in Hawthorne's fiction that it is evidently a projection of his feeling that he was himself guilty of what he took to be the besetting sin of artists. The male/female affinity/opposition occurs again in the relationships of Hollingsworth with Zenobia and Priscilla; and the material/spiritual problem again also—especially in the Westervelt/Priscilla subplot.

The Marble Faun is peopled with artists: the sculptor of ideal forms Kenyon, the painter Miriam who projects her own distempered thoughts on canvas, and the copyist Hilda. Each has a different vision of reality from the others, but no one of these visions is complete or certain. And again the male/female and earthly/heavenly dualities are basic.

In all of these fictions the same concerns are prominent, all have a mythic dimension that removes the action into a timeless realm of archetypes, and in all of them it is the artist presence that tries, and fails, to find truth and certitude amidst the confusion of various appearances. For Hawthorne the best endeavor of an artist was to attempt something that was bound to fail; conversely, any artistic attempt that succeeded was by definition a failure, because its accomplishment could only mean that the artist had not aimed high enough. As Andrea del Sarto, the "faultless painter" of Browning's poem says, "a man's reach should exceed his grasp / or what's a Heaven for." But as the same poet wrote, in "Rabbi Ben Ezra," "hence a paradox / That comforts while it mocks— / What I meant to be / And was not comforts me."

The principles for interpretation of Hawthorne's fiction that I have set forth above are not ideas that I had distinctly in mind while I was writing the essays collected in this volume over widely spaced intervals of time. They have emerged only in retrospect, while I was mulling over the problems of integrating these essays into a coherently organized book.

In order to achieve such book unity, and to reduce duplication of material and to bring related topics together, some revision and transfer of materials in previously published essays has been necessary. Specifically, some portions of the essay included as chapter 2 have been incorporated in chapter 7, and a segment of material from what is now chapter 11 has also been transferred to chapter 7. Some material from the essay that is now chapter 2 has been included in chapter 10. Chapters 16 and 20 have been extensively revised since their original journal publication.

Works to which numerous references occur throughout the text of this book are identified parenthetically as follows:

> *Centenary Edition of the Works of Nathaniel Hawthorne* (Columbus, OH: Ohio State University Press, various dates)—CE, Vol., p.
>
> *Complete Works of Nathaniel Hawthorne, Riverside Edition* (Boston: Houghton Mifflin & Co., 1884)—RE, Vol., p.
>
> *The English Notebooks by Nathaniel Hawthorne*, ed. Randall Stewart (New York: Russell and Russell, 1962)—*EN*, p.
>
> *Letters of Hawthorne to William D. Ticknor*, 2 vols. (Newark, NJ: Carteret Book Club, 1910)—LT, Vol., p.
>
> *Love Letters of Nathaniel Hawthorne*, 2 vols. (Chicago: The Society of the Dofobs, 1907)—LL, Vol., p.

PART ONE
Premises and Theory

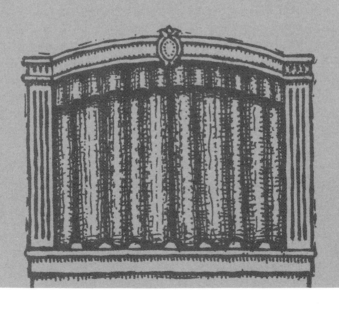

CHAPTER
ONE

The System of Life

Hawthorne envisioned the plenum of reality as a "system of life" that was in fact a system of systems: God's system—ideal, infinite and eternal; nature's system—physical, universal, and temporal; and "the world's artificial system" (CE 10:247)—conventional, social, and traditional.

God's system was perfect and unchanging, and all truth and reality were derived from it. The spiritual influence of God's system was distributed throughout the subordinate systems of nature and society. The three systems together constituted "the golden links of a great chain that entwined [mankind] with an angelic kindred." (CE 11:43) When Ethan Brand renounced his connection with this great chain, he specified each element of the triad: "Mother Earth . . . who art no more my mother"; "mankind, whose brotherhood I have cast off"; and "stars of heaven that shone on me of old, as if to light me onward and upward!—farewell all and forever!" (CE 11:100)

Hawthorne's theory of a system of systems was his version of the venerable, but by his time outmoded, conception of a Great Chain of Being.

> The conception of the plan and structure of the world which, through the Middle Ages and down to the late eighteenth century, many philosophers, most men of science, and, indeed, most educated men were to accept without question [was] the conception of the universe as a "Great Chain of Being," composed of an immense . . . number of links ranging in hierarchical order

from the meagerest kind of existents . . . to the highest possible kind of creature.[1]

Hawthorne's scheme of a system of systems was never elaborated in his writings; rather, it was a set of assumptions to which he made continual implicit reference in his fiction. In fact, he was not interested in social and political or metaphysical concerns on any grand scale. His entire concern was to make literary use of individual destinies as they were worked out within the "framework" of systems: the successes, or usually the failures, of persons functioning in these systems, seen as cases or typical instances.

> [Earth] alone was supposed to have an indigenous population of rational beings whose final destiny was not yet settled. . . . [This] gave it its unique status in the world and a unique share in the attention of Heaven. If it was the only region of corruption it was also the only region of generation; here alone new souls were born, immortal destinies still hung in the balance, and in some sense, the fulfilment of the design of the Creator himself was at stake. If, then, this dim and squalid cellar of the universe was (with one exception) the least respectable place in which humans could have their abode, it was also the only place in which all that was dramatic and stirring was going on.[2]

It was the dramatic and stirring events in the dim and squalid cellar of the universe that preoccupied Hawthorne.

Hawthorne's conception of nature did not, however, see it as dim and squalid, although it contained sinister and gloomy possibilities. Although it was the region of corruption, he most often emphasized that it was the region of generation. Nature's system was continuously regenerative. "Nature renews the scene year after year," (CE 8:395) "converts decay to loveliness." (CE 10:266) In "The New Adam and Eve" he wrote of "the marks of wear and tear, and unrenewed decay, that distinguish the works of man from the growth of nature." (CE 10:249)

There is congeniality between man and nature because nature is man's "true parent." (CE 10:247) In confirming the relationship man makes real one of his potential modes of being. The value of converse with nature was not merely a theory to Hawthorne. His boyhood in the wilderness of Maine seemed to him the happiest period of his life. He thought the best part of his college life was not his studies but his rambles in the woods. His honeymoon in the Old Manse seemed to him a renewal of an interrupted life in nature, a return to Eden: "It is as if the original relation between Man and Nature were restored in my case." (CE 8:332)

Natural good, *being* on a merely natural plane, does not, however, include moral good, which has reference to a higher, distinctively human level of being. Although Hawthorne frequently speaks of "sympathies" between man and nature, such sympathies appear upon examination to be sympathies of man *with* nature, not a reciprocation. Hawthorne's habitual attribution of personality to nature is a metaphor expressive only of man's intimate relation with her, not an attribution of sentience or benignity to her. Nature is unfeeling; she has relations with man which are fixed by her own rigorous and impersonal laws, and has no sentiment toward him, nor does she make any distinction between him—that is, all she knows of him, his natural part—and her other children. Hawthorne makes this point in allusion to events both trivial and tragic. Of an unseasonably late frost that killed his spring garden, he observed, "It is sad that Nature will play such tricks with us poor mortals, inviting us with sunny smiles to confide in her, and then, when we are entirely within her power, striking us to the heart." (CE 8:387) And of the suicide that he later used as a model for Zenobia's in *The Blithedale Romance* he expressed the same sentiment about nature's apathy toward man:

> Nothing comes amiss to Nature—all is fish that comes to her net. If there be a living form of perfect beauty instinct with soul—why, it is all very well, and suits nature well enough. But she would just as lief have that same beautiful, soul-illumined body, to make worm's meat of, and to manure the earth with. (CE 8:272)

He was especially struck by the luxuriance of malignant growths in nature, such as fungi and oak-galls, and frequently remarked in his notebooks how they flourished in the decline and decay of other organisms. So, although he cherished nature as a valuable part of the life of man, he insisted that nature recognizes no moral or spiritual distinctions among her creatures, such dis-

tinctions being referable to higher realities than she has cognizance of.

His sense of the lapse of man's "original relation" with
nature occasionally moved him to extravagant exclamation: "Oh
that I could run wild! that is, that I could put myself into a true
relation with nature, and be on friendly terms with all congenial
elements." (CE 8:358) Of his walks with Ellery Channing during the Old Manse days he wrote, "The chief profit of those
wild days lay in the freedom which we thereby won from all
custom and conventionalism and fettering influences of man on
man." (CE 10:25) As he did not believe in divine presence in
nature, as the Romantic poets did, he did not go to nature for
spiritual communion and sympathy, but only for refreshment
and relief. He asked, "What would a man do, if he were compelled to live always in the sultry heat of society, and could
never bathe himself in cool solitude?" (CE 8:26) "[P]erhaps it is
necessary for the health of the human mind and heart that there
should be a possibility of taking refuge in what is wild, and
uncontaminated by any culture." (EN, 517)

In general men have forfeited too much of their nature to
conventions, he thought. He admired Thoreau above all other
men with whom he became acquainted because Thoreau had
succeeded in maintaining a true relation with nature and resist-
ing the bondage of convention: "[S]o far as he is sophisticated,
it is in a way and method of his own. . . . He . . . seems inclined to lead a sort of Indian life among civilized men." (CE
8:353–54) Hawthorne's assertion of the need for occasional relief
from "the sultry heat of society" was not, however, a denial of
the value of society, whose institutions had "grown out of the
heart of mankind." (CE 10:26) The "sweetest moment" of such
journeying between society and nature was the moment of return to society: "And when, at noontide, I tread the crowded
streets, the influence . . . will still be felt; so that I shall walk
among men kindly and as a brother, but yet shall not melt into
the indistinguishable mass of human-kind." (CE 9:461)

Hawthorne had an anachronistic teleological and anthropocentric conception of the place of creatures in the scheme of
Providence. He wondered about the utility of weeds and noxious
insects. "Perhaps if we could penetrate nature's secrets, we
should find that what we call weeds are more essential to the

well-being of the world than the most precious fruit or grain."
(CE 8:348) "The whole insect tribe, so far as I can judge, are
made more for themselves and less for man, than any other
portion of the creation." (CE 8:248) "The only use of flies
seems to be to amuse children." (CE 8:434)

> Italy beats us, I think, in mosquitoes; they are horribly pun-
> gent little satanic particles. . . . . I wonder whether our health,
> at this season of the year, requires that we should be kept in a
> state of irritation, and so the mosquitoes are Nature's prophylac-
> tic remedy for some disease; or whether we are made for the
> mosquitoes, not they for us. (RE 10:422)[3]

This teleological and anthropocentric view of creation had
most significance in its influence on his imagination of individual
self-consciousness and motivation. A character in "The Intelligence Office" states a theme central to many of Hawthorne's
tales: "I want my place! my own place! my true place in the
world! my proper sphere, which nature intended me for when
she fashioned me thus awry, and which I have vainly sought all
my lifetime!" (CE 10:323)[4]

Hawthorne's comments on man's artificial system are more
explicit, although no more frequent, than his references to God's
and nature's systems. This is so because persons are more intimately and continuously involved in it, and because it controls
their perceptions of and relations with other systems. "It is one
great advantage of a gregarious mode of life that each person
rectifies his mind by other minds, and squares his conduct to
that of his neighbors, so as seldom to be lost in eccentricity."
(CE 9:400) "Most persons are so constituted that they can be
virtuous only in a certain routine." (CE 11:159) Man's system
establishes the routine by which persons manage their lives. It
assigns to each person a "propriety" according to his station and
function in the universal system of created things, in an historic
order, in a socio-political system, and in a domestic system.

In addition to these concepts of system and propriety, Hawthorne regularly used notions of "class," "sphere," and "circle"
to define his imaginations of characters and relationships.

"The Procession of Life" is an essay on his concept of
classes in which he discusses the possibilities of various principles of classification. In "The Procession of Life," after remark-

ing that members of society are customarily "classified by the merest external circumstances," (CE 10:207) and "separated into various classes according to certain apparent relations" so that "we lose sight of those realities by which nature, fortune, fate, or Providence, has constituted for every man a brotherhood," he considers various principles by which we might make out "a true classification of society." (CE 10:208) Some of the classes discussed in this sketch furnished conceptions that aided his imagination of characters in later fictions.

Sphere and *circle* are interchangeable terms in Hawthorne's conceptual vocabulary. "For Hawthorne, every person inhabits a "little sphere of creatures and circumstances in which [he] is the central object." "Each person, in effect, is a perpetual center around which there is a circumference made up of the objects and people which fall within the field of perception."[5] *Sphere* and *circle* are individualizing and enclosing terms rather than classifying terms. They are subjectively determined and vary according to the vicissitudes and the changing states of mind of characters. Thus, the new Adam and Eve are "content with an inner sphere which they inhabit together" before "they feel the invincible necessity of this earthly life" and attempt to puzzle out the meaning of "the objects and circumstances that surround them." (CE 10:248-49) The scarlet letter on Hester's gown "had the effect of a spell, taking her out of the ordinary relations with humanity, and enclosing her in a sphere by herself." (CE 1:54) Wherever she stood, "a small vacant area—a sort of magic circle—had formed itself about her." (CE 1:234) It was a "magic circle of ignominy." (CE 1:246) When, after her brief reunion with Dimmesdale, he rejected her plan for them to flee together, he seemed "remote from her own sphere." (CE 1:239) As a result of her long seclusion, Hepzibah in *The House of the Seven Gables* "gazed forth from her habitual sluggishness . . . as from another sphere," (CE 2:76) and Holgrave tells her that "the lifeblood has been gradually chilling in your veins as you sat aloof, within your circle of gentility." (CE 2:44) At the climax of *The House of the Seven Gables* Holgrave and Phoebe are confined "within the circle of a spell, a solitude in the midst of men." (CE 2:305) In *The Marble Faun* it is supposed that Beatrice Cenci's sorrow "removed this beautiful girl out of the sphere of humanity, and set her in a far-off region." (CE 4:64) Donatello's murder of the Capuchin, prompted by Miriam's glance, had such a "terrible contractile power" "that it seemed as if their new sympathy annihilated all other ties, and that they were released from the chain of humanity; a new sphere, a special law, had been created for them alone." (CE 4:174) Edgar Dryden's comment is accurate:

> The motif of the sphere, then, embodies the basic intersubjective tension which torments Hawthorne's characters. At the same time that it expresses the sense of privacy and separateness which is such an important aspect of the characters' lives, it also points to the fact that "our souls are not our own. We convey a property in them to those with whom we associate, but to what extent can never be known, until we feel the tug, the agony of our abortive effort to resume an exclusive sway of ourselves."[6]

Man's artificial system is both corruptible and ameliorable. The corruption is due to human agency; the amelioration is providential. "We who are born into the world's artificial system can never adequately know how little in our present state and circumstances is natural, and how much is merely the interpolation of the perverted mind and heart of man." (CE 10:247) The new Adam and Eve are puzzled by the gallows: "This mysterious object was the type of mankind's whole system in regard to the great difficulties which God had given to be solved—a system of fear and vengeance, yet followed to the last." (CE 10:255) Hawthorne's animadversions against the love of money are frequent; it is "the mainspring, the very essence of the system that [has] wrought itself into the vitals of mankind, and choked their original nature in its deadly grasp." (CE 10:261)

Such passages indicate that he believed that man's original nature was innocent, but that it had been corrupted by evils perpetuated in the "rusty iron framework" (CE 3:19) of society. In *Our Old Home* he recalled from his consular experience "wrongs that were immense, but for which nobody could be held responsible, and which, indeed, the closer you looked into them, the more they lost the aspect of willful misdoing, and assumed that of an inevitable calamity. It was the fault of a system, the misfortune of an individual." (CE 5:33) In "Main Street" he remarked that the rigidity of daily life "could not fail to cause miserable distortions of the moral nature." (CE 11:67)

In *The Scarlet Letter* dramatic tension results from the discord
between "the dismal severity of the Puritanic code of law" (CE
1:52) administered by rigidly self-righteous men and Hester's
"freedom of speculation" in holding that "the world's law was
no law for her mind." (CE 1:164)

Hawthorne's criticism of the system of human justice is not
a criticism of system as such, but of excessive rigidity in systems.
He regarded systems as necessary and beneficial. Systems grew
out of and expressed all the latent possibilities in the heart of
man, and therefore incorporated evil as well as good.

> The heart, the heart,—there was the little yet boundless sphere
> wherein existed the original wrong of which the crime and misery
> of this outward world were merely types. Purify that inward
> sphere, and the many shapes of evil that haunt the outward, and
> which now seem almost our only realities, will turn to shadowy
> phantoms and vanish of their own accord. (CE 10:403–4)

He thought there was providential influence directing the
general course of social development, and that such influence
became inoperable if the system of society hardened into forms
that inhibited change. The conception of providential superin-
tendence is expressed in a passage in "The Old Manse," describing an impression when returning from a river excursion
with Ellery Channing:

> Once, as we turned our boat to the bank, there was a cloud, in
> the shape of an immensely gigantic figure of a hound, couched
> above the house, as if keeping guard over it. Gazing at this sym-
> bol I prayed that the upper influences might long protect the
> institutions that had grown out of the heart of mankind. (CE
> 10:25–26)

He thought the system of society was in evolution. There
could be no evolution in God's perfect system; there was renovation rather than evolution in the system of nature; but man's
system was in process of continual gradual amelioration according to providential design. Impetus and direction are not given
by man, who lacks sufficient understanding of "the intricate and
unintelligible machinery of Providence." (CE 5:30) "The progress of the world, at every step, leaves some evil or wrong on
the path behind it, to which the wisest of mankind of their own

set purpose could never have found" (RE 12:417) the remedy. In short, he believed that men might meddle with and obstruct the scheme of Providence, or might intelligently recognize and accept providential amelioration, but could do nothing to hasten it by intervention.

The purpose of the providential scheme is to spiritualize mankind. "The wisest people and the best keep a steadfast faith that the progress of mankind is onward and upward, and that the toil and anguish of the path serve to wear away the imperfections of the Immortal Pilgrim." (CE 9:337) He wrote in *The House of the Seven Gables* that "the great system of human progress, which, with every ascending footstep, as it diminishes the necessity for animal force, may be destined gradually to spiritualize us, by refining away our grosser attributes of body." (CE 2:121) The fault of Aylmer in "The Birthmark" was that he undertook the work that was the sole prerogative of Providence. "Man's best-directed effort is a kind of dream, while God is the sole worker of realities." (CE 2:180)

Generally it is in personal difficulties in dealing with man's artificial system that the problems arise that Hawthorne imagines and treats in his fiction. "Amid the seeming confusion of our mysterious world, individuals are so nicely adjusted to a system, and systems to one another and to a whole, that, by stepping aside for a moment, a man exposes himself to a fearful risk of losing his place forever." (CE 9:140) This idea is worked out in every imaginable variation in his stories of outcasts, solitary men, egotists, frustrated seekers, and anxious inquirers at the intelligence office.

NOTES

1. A. O. Lovejoy, *The Great Chain of Being* (New York: Harper Torchbooks, Harper & Row, 1960), 59.

2. *Ibid.*, 102–3.

Some of the many writers who wrote of the Great Chain of Being and were read by Hawthorne are Francis Bacon, Fénelon, Fontenelle,

Goldsmith, Samuel Johnson, Milton, Montaigne, Pascal, Pope, and F. Schlegel. See Marion L. Kesselring, *Hawthorne's Reading. Bulletin of the New York Public Library* 53 (1949).

3. Lovejoy (187) quotes Francis Bacon, "the whole world works together in the service of man"; and Fenelon, "In nature not only the plants but the animals are made for our use." But he points out that this anthropocentric and teleological conception was challenged by other proponents of the Great Chain of Being theory, as being inconsistent with the basic concept: "Not only against this assumption that the rest of the creation is instrumental to man's good but . . . against the premises of the teleological argument generally, the logic of the conception of the Chain of Being worked potently." (187–88) Lovejoy quotes Galileo, Henry More, Descartes, and Leibniz, among others, in opposition to the teleological argument. "The universe, in short, was made in order that all possible forms of being might manifest themselves after their kinds." (189) This was the principle of "plenitude." "It was implied in the principle of plenitude that every link in the Chain of Being exists, not merely and not primarily, for the benefit of any other link, but for its own sake, or more precisely, for the sake of the completeness of the series of forms, the realization of which was the chief object of God in creating the world." (186) Hawthorne evidently did not detect this and other inconsistencies in his thought.

4. "Hawthorne's theme is not limited to the adjustment of the individual to society; he sees as essential the adjustment of the individual to his natural environment, which almost always contains other humans in an organized social system, but which may be only external nature. Therefore the problem of the characters is to discover in their natural environment their particular places, which, to a great extent, depend upon the simplicity or the complexity of the environment itself. Once men and women find their rightful positions, they must confine themselves to the boundaries."—James W. Mathews, "Hawthorne and the Chain of Being," *Modern Language Quarterly* 18 (December 1957):284.

5. Edgar A. Dryden, *Nathaniel Hawthorne: The Poetics of Enchantment* (Ithaca, NY: Cornell Univ. Press, 1977), 60.

6. *Ibid.*, 67–68. The inner quotation is from Hawthorne's sketch "The Village Hall." See also CE 3:194.

TWO

Ghostland and the Jurisdiction of Veracity

Hawthorne shared an epistemological assumption that underlies most major nineteenth-century fiction and that has influenced its technical development. According to Nietzsche, modern philosophy proceeds from "epistemological skepticism."[1] For more than a century this has been the predominant mode of American fiction, although the fact and its significance are perhaps only beginning to be fully appreciated. A rhetorical question put by William James has been repeatedly posed by our major novelists: "Objective evidence and certitude are doubtless very fine ideals to play with, but where on this moonlit and dream-visited planet are they found?"[2] A casual list of representative works suggests how obsessively our major writers have dealt with epistemological quandaries: "Ligeia" and *The Narrative of Arthur Gordon Pym*, "Young Goodman Brown" and *The Marble Faun*, "The Encantadas" and *The Confidence Man*, "Which Was the Dream?" and *The Mysterious Stranger*, "The Turn of the Screw" and *The Sacred Fount*.

Throughout his career, Hawthorne was preoccupied with the lack of "objective evidence and certitude." He wrote in *The English Notebooks* that "Ghostland lies beyond the jurisdiction of

veracity." (EN, 39) His work abounds in such terms as *mystery,*
phantasmagoria, hieroglyphics, chaos, labyrinth, vicissitude, and *rid-*
dle to refer to the character of visible things. His earliest tales
were symbolizations of frustrated search for objective evidence
and certitude and intimated that truth must be sought introspec-
tively, that the only certainties are subjective and imperfectly
communicable. His fondness for such participles as *glimmering*
and *flitting* indicates his mistrust of the reality of objective
evidence.

The epistemological basis of modern philosophy and fiction
is Cartesian. James wrote, "There is but one indefectibly certain
truth, and that is the truth that pyrrhonistic skepticism leaves
standing,—the truth that the present phenomenon of consciousness exists. That, however, is the mere starting-point of knowledge, the mere admission of stuff to be philosophized about."
(725) This gives the writer both his material—the content of
consciousness—and his task—to give meaning to it by his own
forms and fiat.

Nietzsche wrote, "Let us assume that nothing is real except
our world of desires and passions, that we cannot step down to
or step up to any kind of 'reality' except the reality of our
drives—for thinking is nothing but the interrelation and inter-
action of our drives." (42)

As our major novelists have generally suspected that the
object-world is incomprehensible, they have devised fictional
methods of discovering truth and reality in the subject-world.
Eighty years ago William James remarked that "a great empirical
movement toward a pluralistic panpsychic view of the universe
is proceeding." (804) He endorsed the opinion of the "little
known" German philosopher Gustav Theodor Fechner that "the
entire earth on which we live must have its own collective consciousness" compounded of individual experiences: "The more
inclusive forms are in part *constituted* by the more limited forms."
(536,542) In effect, James was noting that modern thought has
got rid of a transcendent spiritual oversoul by substituting for it
a subliminal psychological undersoul.

Although the "panpsychic" world is also "pluralistic," there
must be something normative in human experience, something
deeper than individual consciousness that communicates with

what Emerson called "the sovereign self." That is, there must be archetypal experiences by means of which the "collective consciousness" informs individual minds. These are, according to James, ancestral experiences. He says that *"our fundamental ways of thinking about things are discoveries of extremely remote ancestors, which have been able to preserve themselves throughout the experience of all subsequent time."* (420) They preserve themselves by presenting their forms to the consciousness of living individuals and prompting the reexperiencing of life in those forms. Such ancestral memories, according to James, constitute "a great reservoir in which the memories of earth's inhabitants are pooled and preserved, and from which, when the threshold lowers, or the valve opens, information ordinarily shut out leaks into the minds of exceptional individuals among us." (300)

Since information thus leaks into individual minds from a great reservoir, it would be more accurate to say, not that individual minds summon thoughts, but that they entertain thoughts. Nietzsche wrote, "A thought comes when 'it' will, not when 'I' will." (18) Persons do not so much think thoughts as thoughts think them. "Is Ahab Ahab?" Thoughts are like fish swimming into an inlet of individual consciousness from an oceanic mind. The author needs to invite and entertain such thoughts. The characteristic activity of the authorial mind is, therefore, not the exploration of the object-world, but the exploration of what Melville called "the world of mind" and the objectification of such experience.

Ernst Cassirer says that "instead of defining man as an *animal rationale*, we should define him as an *animal symbolicum*." "No longer in a merely physical universe, man lives in a symbolic universe. . . . Physical activity seems to recede in proportion as man's symbolic activity advances. Instead of dealing with things themselves man is in a sense constantly conversing with himself."[3] That is to say, the "real" human world is a world of fictions dreamed into reality from the "panpsychic universe." Hawthorne and Melville were pioneers in adapting this understanding to the uses of literary fiction in America.

Hawthorne's fictions are what Robert Frost called "tentatives"—various grasps at an ultimately ungraspable beyond. Despite his outmoded formal techniques and vocabulary, they are modern in their multivalence. They conform to the notion of subjective truth described by George Santayana in *The Sense of Beauty*:

> It is conceivable that two different theories should be equally true in respect of the same facts. All that is required is that they should be equally complete schemes for the relation and prediction of the realities they deal with. The choice between them would be an arbitrary one, determined by personal bias, for the object being indeterminate, its elements can be apperceived as forming all kinds of unities.[4]

It is this latitude of choice and indeterminateness that Hawthorne claimed for the Romance as distinguished from the Novel: "The latter form of composition is presumed to aim at a very minute fidelity, not merely to the possible but to the probable and ordinary course of man's experience. The former,—while as a work of art, it must rigidly subject itself to laws, and while it sins unpardonably so far as it may swerve aside from the truth of the human heart—has fairly a right to present that truth under circumstances, to a great extent, of the writer's own choosing or creation." (CE 2:1)

Alfred North Whitehead, in *Process and Reality,* remarks that Kant "was the great philosopher who first, fully and explicitly, introduced into philosophy the conception of an act of experience as constructive functioning, transforming subjectivity into objectivity or objectivity into subjectivity; the order is immaterial in comparison with the general idea."[5] And Frank Kermode, in *The Sense of an Ending,* says that "ever since Nietzsche generalized and developed the Kantian insights, literature has increasingly asserted its right to an arbitrary and private choice of fictional norms."[6] Joyce Carol Oates somewhat more extravagantly says that the "most basic desire of the imagination" is "to be lied to in a realistic manner."[7] Oates also sees Nietzsche as the philosopher who generalized the conceptions that modern fiction relies on: "The falseness of a given judgment does not constitute an objection against it," according to Nietzsche. "The real question is how far a judgment furthers and maintains life." (Nietzsche, 41) To "him the permanent, Being itself, is only a parable, an 'empty fiction.' . . . It is possible for Nietzsche to entertain contradictory thoughts at the same time because he views the intellect as superficial, the creator of values and also their destroyer." (Oates, 155)

One of Hawthorne's contemporary critics complained that *The Marble Faun* began in mystery and ended in mist, and a modern critic has likewise in exasperation characterized him as a literary squid. He was a literary squid only in the sense that he was able to entertain contradictory thoughts at the same time, to achieve what Coleridge remarked as the "magical power" of imagination, which "reveals itself in the balance, or reconcilement of opposite or discordant qualities; of sameness, with difference; of the general with the concrete; the idea with the image; the individual with the representative."[8] Simon Lesser has noticed this as the equivalent in Hawthorne of "what Keats meant by Shakespeare's 'negative capacity'—his willingness to tolerate uncertainty and doubt, to take cognizance of viewpoints directly at variance with ones being proclaimed."[9] Lesser further remarks that "the value systems of great literature are all pervaded by what I like to think of as *a sense of the opposite.*"[10] This was an acceptable mode for an author who thought that objective truth was unascertainable. Any definite presentment of reality could, paradoxically, be truthful only if it were patently fictive.

The ability to entertain contradictory thoughts at the same time accounts for the fact that, as Henry James long ago noted, Hawthorne is "to a considerable degree ironical."[11] Recent critics have begun to explore the hitherto unregarded ironies in the works of some of our great romantic fiction writers—G. R. Thompson in his studies of Poe and Alfred Marks in his studies of Hawthorne, for examples. The ironic dimension of Melville's work has always been evident, and Henry James's ironies are also manifest. Irony in our major writers registers their blank misgivings and questionings of outward things—even of their own presentments of apparent fact.

NOTES

1. Friedrich Nietzsche, *Beyond Good and Evil*, trans. Marianne Cowan (Chicago: "Gateway Editions," Henry Regnery Co., 1955), 60. Subsequent references to Nietzsche, parenthetically identified in the text, are to this work.

2. *Writings of William James*, ed. John J. McDermott (New York: Modern Library, 1967), 725. Subsequent references to James, parenthetically identified in the text, are to this work.

3. *An Essay on Man* (Garden City, NY: Doubleday Anchor Books, Doubleday & Co., 1953), 44.

4. (New York: Dover Publications, 1955), 139.

5. *Process and Reality: An Essay in Cosmology* (New York: Free Press, 1978), 156.

6. (New York: "Galaxy Books," Oxford Univ. Press, 1970), 36.

7. *The Edge of Impossibility* (New York: Vanguard Press, 1972), 167.

8. *Biographia Literaria*, ed. J. Shawcross (Oxford: Oxford Univ. Press, 1907), 2, 1. 14.

9. *Fiction and the Unconscious* (New York: Vintage Books, Random House, 1962), 87.

10. *Ibid.*, 89.

11. *Hawthorne* (New York: Harper and Brothers, 1879), 59. See also chapter 6, "Ironic View," in Arlin Turner, *Nathaniel Hawthorne* (New York: "American Authors and Critics Series," Barnes and Noble, 1961).

CHAPTER
THREE

Our Common Nature

A consequence of the considerable shift of attention from history to psychology in modern literature is that our writers have recently been more engaged with figuring possibilities than with transcribing and interpreting events. Although Hawthorne never freed himself from old-fashioned idealist formulas of statement, his fictional practice was altogether an attempt to discover and express psychological truths—what he called "truths of the heart." It was in recognition of this that Henry James commended him for being interested in "the deeper psychology."[1] Thus, in the preface to the *Snow-Image* volume, he refuted any imputation of egotism by insisting that in his fictions he had been "burrowing, to his utmost ability, into the depths of our common nature for the purposes of psychological romance"; and that he had pursued "his researches in that dusky region as well by the tact of sympathy as by the light of observation." (CE 11:4)

The faculties by means of which he pursued his researches, loosely distinguished in his numerous comments on his own imaginative processes and in his comments on other arts than fiction, are soul or spirit, the five senses, heart, mind or intellect, and will.

Soul and spirit are almost interchangeable terms in Hawthorne's fiction, and it is not possible to make a definite distinction between them; but judging by the contexts in which they most often appear, they are different aspects of an identical faculty, the immortal part of man. The soul is this faculty considered as the receptacle of spiritual communications, wherein man's ideal nature resides and reposes. As Rita K. Gollin says, "Sometimes *spirit* and *soul* are used synonymously; but when they are differentiated, the spirit is the agent of the soul. It voyages forth and stirs the imagination. . . . The spirit is the active element of consciousness that transcends the limits of waking life and the limits of mortality."[2]

Human beings have a dual nature, compounded of body and spirit. "Mankind are earthern jugs with spirit in them." (CE 8:236) The sense organs of the body give several modes of perceiving and participating in the processes of the natural world, but not directly of the spiritual world. "In every human being there is imagination, creative power, genius, which according to circumstances, may either be developed in this world, or shrouded in a mask of dulness until another state of being." (CE 10:319–20)

Body and spirit are disparate, sometimes antagonistic. They are a union but not a unity. Hawthorne seldom mentioned spirit without mentioning in the same context body as something contrasted to or distinct from it. As the two elements of identity in his characters are not fused into a unity, persons live two existences, or alternate between two, sensuous existence being continuous so long as mortal life lasts, with only occasional transport into spiritual awareness, a condition in which ordinary life becomes dreamlike. "Nobody would think that the same man could live two such different lives simultaneously." (LL 1:121) The texture of life is not uniformly woven, but is a patchwork of sensuous and spiritual experience.

The heart is the organ for gaining access to the spiritual truth latent in the soul. Hawthorne habitually referred to the heart as a cavern or orifice opening into "the soundless depths of the human soul." (CE 10:446) The "truth of the heart" has a more permanent character than intellectual truth. "If mankind were all intellect, they would be continually changing, so that one age would be entirely unlike another. The great conservative is the heart, which remains the same in all ages; so that common-places of a thousand years standing are as effective as ever." (EN, 45) The truth of the heart is unchanging because it is communicated through the medium of the soul from the changeless reality of the spiritual world.

The heart as the organ by which one knows truth operates through the power of sympathy. "The sympathy or magnetism among human beings is more subtile and universal than we think; it exists, indeed, among different classes of organized life, and vibrates from one to the other." (CE 2:174) It includes nature, man, and the spiritual world. Hawthorne wrote of his attachment to Salem that it was "mere sensuous sympathy of dust for dust" because so many of his ancestors "have mingled their earthly substance with the soil" (CE 1:9) there. He said, "I never stood in an English crowd without being conscious of hereditary sympathies"; (CE 5:4) and London satisfies "that mysterious yearning—the magnetism of millions of hearts operating upon one—which impels every man's individuality to mingle itself with the immensest mass of human life within its scope." (CE 5:214–15) Of several incidents of this magnetism in his fiction, perhaps the most striking are Clifford's impulse in *The House of the Seven Gables* to reestablish his lapsed social relation by attempting to throw himself from the arched window into the busy street, and his frantic journey on the railroad that was to him an emblem of the current of human progress.

This magnetism is so universal that Hawthorne asked about a wolf, a bear, and a hyena, "Are there any two living creatures who have so few sympathies that they cannot possibly be friends?" (CE 9:127) He wrote of a sick monkey in the London Zoo that it appealed for sympathy to the spectators; (EN, 209) and he said of birds that "all these winged people, that dwell in the vicinity of homesteads, seem to partake of human nature, and possess the germ, if not the development, of mortal souls." (CE 10:155–56) Men have estranged themselves from communion with both nature and spirit by insulating themselves within their artificial system, but by reanimating their diminished sympathies they can gain insight into truth. Pearl in *The Scarlet Letter,* Phoebe in *The House of the Seven Gables*, Priscilla in *The Blithedale Romance*, and Donatello in *The Marble Faun* are characters who have retained enough of their primal innocence to sympathize and communicate with existences throughout the entire system of life.

Failure or denial of sympathy is calamitous, for it is moral death when one's heart no longer "partake[s] of the universal throb." (CE 11:99) Gervayse Helwyse in "Lady Eleanore's Mantle" reminds the Lady Eleanore of "the chain of human sympathies—which whoso would shake off must keep company with the fallen angels." (CE 9:280) Such characters are numer-

ous in Hawthorne's fiction, among them Ethan Brand and the
Wandering Jew in "The Virtuoso's Collection." Almost as disastrous is being enclosed in a circle of sinful sympathy by crime
or knowledge of crime, a possible danger for every mortal, since
Hawthorne shared the Calvinist conviction that there is "evil
latent in every human heart." (CE 8:29)

To communicate effectually with his readers, an author
needed not only to sympathize with them but to have them
sympathize with him. Hawthorne apparently felt that in his early
career there had been a lack of sympathy on both sides that had
made him less productive than he might otherwise have been.
Although he wrote that "the dark seclusion—the atmosphere
without any oxygen of sympathy—in which I spent all the years
of my youthful manhood—have enabled me to do almost as well
without it as with it," (EN, 256) he nevertheless, in the Preface
to *Twice-Told Tales*, attributed what he supposed to be a scanti-
ness of achievement to the lack of sympathy: "To this total lack
of sympathy, at the age when his mind would naturally have
been most effervescent, the Public owe it . . . that the Author
can show nothing for the thought and industry of that portion of
his life, save these forty sketches, or thereabouts." (CE 9:3–4)

He did not, however, attribute the lack of sympathy altogether to his readers, but acknowledged that it was largely the
effect of his own reclusive disposition. "It is this involuntary
reserve, I suppose, that has given the objectivity to my writings.
And when people think that I am pouring myself out in a tale or
essay, I am merely telling what is common to human nature, not
what is peculiar to myself. I sympathize with them—not they
with me." (LL 2:80) In "The Old Manse" he wrote,

> I have appealed to no sentiment or sensibilities save such as are
> diffused among us all. So far as I am a man of really individual
> attributes I veil my face; nor am I, nor have I ever been, one of
> those supremely hospitable people who serve up their own
> hearts, delicately fried, with brain sauce, as a tidbit for their
> beloved public. (CE 10:32–33)

The artist character is central to all Hawthorne's work, and
the artist was to him above all a person with insight into motives
and with ingenuity in portraying them. He is enabled to understand novel and revealing behavior in other persons by a process

of introspection and reflection. He shares a common nature with the rest of mankind, and through "tact" he approaches and participates in the experience of other persons, although liable to intrude and violate if he lacks reverence. Through "sympathy" he understands—that is, what he sees as actual in the behavior of others he feels as potential in himself. As an artist with a good conscience he can assert that, "My conscience . . . does not reproach me with betraying anything too sacredly individual to be revealed by a human spirit to its brother or sister spirit." (CE 10:32)

He felt that there was a line to be drawn between the private self and the community, that sympathy should have its limits. The crucial question was where the line should be drawn, and he suspected that he had withdrawn too far from the circle of human sympathy in his early years and had been in danger of becoming cold-hearted, as he indicated in his sketch "The Journal of a Solitary Man." This situation, however, would be preferable to a too entire disclosure of the self. "It would be a very foolish thing, to expose his whole heart—his whole inner man—to the view of the world." (CE 8:49) "We may prate of the circumstances that lie around us, and even of ourself, but still keep the inmost Me behind its veil." (CE 1:4) He wrote to his friend and publisher William Ticknor from Liverpool about the poems of Julia Ward Howe, "What a strange propensity it is in these scribbling women to make a show of their hearts, as well as their heads, upon your counter, for anybody to pry into that chooses." (LT 1:29–30) And again, "Mrs. Howe's genius does not appear to be of the dramatic order. In fact, she has no genius or talent, except for making public what she ought to keep to herself—viz., her passions, emotions and womanly weaknesses. 'Passion Flowers' were delightful, but she ought to have been soundly whipt for publishing them." (LT 2:50)

Hawthorne's excessive reserve justified the witticism of Henry James, Sr., that his demeanor in society was that of a rogue in a company of detectives. He was morbidly shy, although capable of some degree of intimacy with such friends as Horatio Bridge, Thoreau, Ellery Channing, Melville, and Ticknor. But he complained even of his infant daughter Una's too intent gaze that "there seems to be a want of delicacy in dwelling upon one's face so remorselessly; it seems to embarrass the

springs of spiritual life and the movement of the soul." (CE
8:414) And he wrote of a statue of Wilberforce in Westminster
Abbey, "I really felt as if the statue were impertinent, staring
me in the face with that knowing complication of wrinkles; and
I should have liked to fling a brick-bat right at the nose, or to
have broken off the foot that dangled over its knee." (EN, 595)

His hypersensitivity to the dilemmas of persons trying to
maintain the "sanctity" of self, the "holy of holies," while at
the same time sustaining a vital relation with community, preoccupied his imagination.

It is a misfortune to live entirely according to the inclinations of either the heart or the senses. Since one lives in "two
such different worlds simultaneously," (LL 1:121) the mind or
intellect operates to bring them into some degree of compatabil-
ity. The mind is not directly engaged with reality, as the senses
are with the natural world and the heart through the medium of
the soul is with the spiritual world, but mediates between the
heart and the senses, and exercises judgment in composing data
furnished by both. When the mind is concerned only with
knowledge of the physical world, its product is science, which
Hawthorne thought inferior to the kind of knowledge that he
called poetry, his term for all imaginative construction.

The will is, like the intellect, and unlike the primary faculties of sense and heart, a secondary and managing faculty. It
gives direction and energy to attempts to organize the inchoate
visions of possibility that appear in the haunted chamber of the
mind. The imagination is not a single faculty; rather, it is a
cooperative activity of the faculties of spirit, sense, heart, mind,
and will in composing the contents of consciousness into presentments that are apparently factual and suggestively truthful.

NOTES

1. *Hawthorne* (New York: Harper and Brothers, 1879), 63.
2. *Nathaniel Hawthorne and the Truth of Dreams* (Baton Rouge, LA:
Louisiana State Univ. Press, 1979), 42. Subsequent references to
Gollin, parenthetically identified in the text, are to this work.

CHAPTER

FOUR

Marbles and Bubbles: "This Troublesome Mortality"

*Plotinus thanked God, that his soul was not tied to an
immortal body. —Coleridge,* Aids to Reflection

$\mathbb{A}$ subject of frequent macabre
speculation with Hawthorne was burial customs, especially
methods of disposing of dead bodies. An entry in *The American
Magazine of Useful and Entertaining Knowledge* notes a method of
"converting animal substances to stone." "It is confidently believed, that dead persons may thus be preserved for ages, with
precisely the aspect that they wore, when Death laid his hand
upon them." Thus, dead persons might be artificially petrified
and erected in graveyards as their own tombstones. The piece
ends with a fervent wish that "never may we—the writer—stand
amid that marble crowd!" "Our clay must not be baulked of its
repose. We are willing to let it moulder beneath the little hill-
ock, and that the sods should gradually settle down, and leave
no traces of our grave. We have no yearnings for the grossness of
this earthly immortality."[1]

It was perhaps not so much a horror of death itself as disapproval of an unnatural denial of death that accounts for Hawthorne's fascination by such macabre possibilities. Specifically,

the horror of such unnatural arrest of the process of the body's decay was that it signified man's moral confusion—his placing a higher value on his mortal than on his immortal part. Hawthorne did not fear that body might be bruised to pleasure soul, but that soul might be slighted to preserve body:

> "I desire not an earthly immortality. . . . Were man to live longer on the earth, the spiritual would die out of him. The spark of ethereal fire would be choked by the material, the sensual. There is a celestial something within us that requires, after a certain time, the atmosphere of heaven to preserve it from decay and ruin." (CE 10:489)

Therefore, "Death is the very friend whom, in his due season, even the happiest mortal should be willing to embrace." (CE 10:489)

A frequent theme of Hawthorne's tales is the necessity of casting off the slough of sense before it extinguishes spirit. The body manures Nature's garden, while the soul returns to its celestial home. What is material decays into Nature's process to form the stuff of other bodies, a conception very like Whitman's: "And as to you Corpse I think you are good manure, but that does not offend me, / I smell the white roses sweet-scented and growing."[2] The refuse of factories, something outside of Nature and therefore in a way horrible to Hawthorne, "seems to be the only sort of stuff that Nature cannot take back to herself, and resolve into the elements, when man throws it by." (EN, 462) Even the most innocent have a pure intuition that their incarnation in physical form is an alienation from their spiritual home. Thus, the New Adam and Eve have a sense of "the soul's incongruity with its circumstances. They have already learned that something is to be thrown aside. The idea of Death is in them, or not far off." (CE 10:267)

Hawthorne's horror of overvaluing the mere physical remains of life is most explicit in his sketch "Chippings with a Chisel." He remarked ironically of Wigglesworth, the tombstone-carver:

> His sole task and office among the immortal pilgrims of the tomb—the duty for which Providence had sent the old man into the world as it were with a chisel in his hand—was to label the dead bodies, lest their names should be forgotten at the resurrection. (CE 9:409)

Such preoccupation with dead bodies was morbid, he thought:

> The weight of these heavy marbles, though unfelt by the dead corpse of the enfranchised soul, presses drearily upon the spirit of the survivor, and causes him to connect the idea of death with the dungeon-like imprisonment of the tomb, instead of with the freedom of the skies. Every gravestone . . . is the visible symbol of a mistaken system. Our thoughts should soar upward with the butterfly—not linger with the exuviae that confined him. (CE 9:418)

The appropriation of the butterfly as emblem of psyche or soul lends force to the climactic scenes of "The Artist of the Beautiful" in which "this spiritualized mechanism, this harmony of motion, this Mystery of Beauty" (CE10:469) is rudely snatched and crushed in the grip of "a young child of strength . . . moulded out of the densest substance which earth could supply." (CE 10:468–69) Induration as symbol of extinction of spirit is indicated in the fate of Ethan Brand, whose heart turned to marble, and of Richard Digby, the Man of Adamant, whose figure petrified into the awful likeness of "a statue, chiselled by human art." (CE 11:169)

Hawthorne's preoccupation with this idea persisted in the latter phase of his career, in the four romances. It is evinced in the graveyard scenes in the opening and closing pages of *The Scarlet Letter*; in the elaborate description of Judge Pyncheon's corpse in *The House of Seven Gables*; in the vivid description of Zenobia's drowned body, "the marble image of a death-agony," (CE 3:235) in *The Blithedale Romance*; and in numerous references to tombs and mouldering relics in *The Marble Faun*.

In Italy he was amazed and oppressed at the sight of heaped-up human bones in the catacombs, and turned his attention to a concern exactly the opposite to that of Wigglesworth the tombstone-carver: not how to make reliquiae as solid and enduring as possible, but how to annihilate them as quickly as possible. After visiting a columbarium, he noted that

> All difficulty in finding space for the dead would be obviated by returning to the ancient fashion of reducing them to ashes,—the only objection, though a very serious one, being the quantity of fuel that it would require. But perhaps future chemists may discover some better means of consuming or dissolving this troublesome mortality of ours. (RE 10:116)

A few months after he wrote this notebook entry, he entertained a fancy less scientific:

> how delightful it would be, and how helpful towards our faith in
> a blessed futurity, if the dying could disappear like vanishing
> bubbles, leaving, perhaps, a sweet fragrance diffused for a min-
> ute or two throughout the death-chamber. This would be the
> odor of sanctity! And if sometimes the evaporation of a sinful
> soul should leave an odor not so delightful, a breeze through the
> open windows would soon waft it quite away. (RE 10:193–94)

Such a fancy had occurred to Hawthorne earlier: for example, in his comment in *The House of the Seven Gables* on the death
of Judge Pyncheon, with its terrible suggestion that the Judge's
dying out of mortal life is sheer annihilation, there being no
spirit left in him to diffuse a sweet fragrance at parting from
its exuviae, but only a foul corruption deliquescing into swift
decay:

> It may be remarked . . . that, of all the events which constitute a
> person's biography, there is scarcely one . . . to which the world
> so easily reconciles itself as to his death. . . . [T]here is only a
> vacancy, and a momentary eddy, . . . and a bubble or two,
> ascending out of the black depth and bursting at the surface. As
> regarded Judge Pyncheon, . . . the public, with its customary
> alacrity, proceeded to forget that he had ever lived.[3] (CE 2:309)

This bubble passage is meaningful in view of the earlier
account, in the chapter "The Arched Window," of Clifford's
blowing soap-bubbles, "an amusement, as Hepzibah told
Phoebe apart, that had been a favorite one with her brother
when they were both children":

> Behold him, therefore, at the arched window, with an earthen
> pipe in his mouth! Behold him, with his gray hair, and a wan,
> unreal smile over his countenance, where still hovered a beautiful
> grace, which his worst enemy must have acknowledged to be
> spiritual and immortal, since it had survived so long! Behold him,
> scattering airy spheres abroad, from the window into the street!
> Little impalpable worlds were those soap-bubbles, with the big
> world depicted, in hues bright as imagination, on the nothing of
> their surface. It was curious to see how the passers-by regarded
> these brilliant fantasies, as they came floating down, and made
> the dull atmosphere imaginative about them. Some stopped to
> gaze, and, perhaps, carried a pleasant recollection of the bubbles

onward as far as the street-corner; some looked angrily upward, as if poor Clifford wronged them by setting an image of beauty afloat so near their dusty pathway. A great many put out their fingers or their walking-sticks to touch, withal; and were perversely gratified, no doubt, when the bubble, with all its pictured earth and sky scene, vanished as if it had never been.[4] (CE 2:171)

This passage is built upon a contrast of emblems which frequently recur in Hawthorne's work. The arched window is his figure for the artist's station vis-à-vis ideal and real as well as composed and observed life. It is the "abortive artist" Clifford's Hall of Fantasy. The arch relates ideal and real for the artist as Hawthorne was later to remark that the broken arches of Furness Abbey do: "they translate the sweep of the sky to our finite comprehensions." (EN, 158) Hawthorne regularly used the adjective *dusty* to suggest mortality; and *highway* or *pathway* to designate the mundane routine of human life.[5] Thus worldly persons, passers-by on the dusty pathway, recognize various degrees of reality in the artist's bright imaginations: some are briefly pleased by them; others are angry at the interposition of such airy spheres; still others, contemptuous of what cannot abide the gross test of touch, palpate the impalpable to demonstrate its unreality, destroying it as the child of strength destroyed the artist's butterfly. Such a one was Judge Pyncheon, a character who, in Thoreau's phrase, valued only the grossest of groceries. He looked up and cried contemptuously, "What! Still blowing soap-bubbles!" (CE 2:159) The question between Clifford and the Judge (as between Hawthorne and the world which appeared to undervalue his bright imaginations) was: Whose bubbles are finally more real, the "airy spheres" of the artist or the "solid unrealities" of the Judge, whose life ends like a bubble "ascending out of the black depth" and bursting into nothingness.

NOTES

1. "Preservation of the Dead," *Hawthorne as Editor*, ed. Arlin Turner (Baton Rouge, LA: Louisiana State Univ. Press, 1941), 90. Although Hawthorne admired "ideal" statues such as that of the Venus

di Medici, which he saw in the Uffizi Gallery in Florence, he thought portrait busts disagreeable because the image they preserved of an actual person appeared to him to be a kind of petrification of a mortal identity: "[I]t is an awful thing, indeed, this endless endurance, this almost indestructibility, of a marble bust!" (CE 4:118)

2. "Song of Myself," Section 49. Hawthorne makes similar use of the imagery of white roses in *The House of the Seven Gables*.

3. The narrator in "The Celestial Railroad" during his sojourn in Vanity Fair, notes that it is a common thing there for a person "suddenly to vanish like a soap bubble, and be never more seen of his fellows; and so accustomed were the latter to such little accidents that they went on with their business as quietly as if nothing had happened." (CE 10:202)

4. See Roy R. Male, *Hawthorne's Tragic Vision* (New York: Norton Library, 1964), 137.

5. See, e.g., "David Swan" and "The Toll-Gatherer's Day" in *Twice-Told Tales*.

FIVE

Hawthorne's Qualified Transcendentalism

Hawthorne's literary theory was what M. H. Abrams has described as "the transcendental theory," which "specifies the proper objects of art to be Ideas or Forms which are perhaps approachable by the world of sense, but are altogether trans-empirical, maintaining an independent existence in their own ideal space, and available only to the eye of the mind."[1]

There has hitherto been confusion and controversy concerning whether and how far Hawthorne was a transcendentalist. The principal cause of this confusion is his frequent statement of belief in the transcendental theory as defined by Abrams, but a contributing cause is his arm's-length association with American Transcendentalist contemporaries. The explanation of this difficulty is that he was a transcendentalist but not a Transcendentalist. In his essay "The Old Manse" he emphatically rejected identification with Emersonian Transcendentalists. He called the disciples of Emerson "hobgoblins of flesh and blood," "young visionaries and gray-headed theorists," "uncertain, troubled, earnest wanderers, through the midnight of the moral world." "I . . . admired Emerson as a poet of deep beauty and austere tenderness, but sought nothing from him as a philosopher." (CE 10:30–31) It is appropriate here to cite two of Hawthorne's most perceptive critics. Floyd Stovall says that "although Hawthorne and Melville were not, strictly speaking, transcendentalists, they were products of the same Puritan culture that produced Emerson and Thoreau, and they were, like them, persevering students of the mysteries of the soul." [2] Arlin Turner says that Hawthorne

> found much in Transcendental thought to attract him—its radicalism, for example; its stress on soul, on the individual, on self-reliance and independence, and its corollary denial of materialism, the senses, and the conventions of society; its view that consequences are inevitable and that good may come from evil, or apparent evil, and evil from good; and perhaps most important of all, its questioning of the nature of reality and its concern with such concepts as symbol, shadow, and substance.
>
> The Transcendentalists, that is to say, were discussing the same matters which interested Hawthorne, and again and again he paralleled both their ideas and their phrasing: "the true unreality of earthly things"; "the grosser life is a dream, and the spiritual life is a reality. . . ."

Nevertheless,

> It becomes clear that Hawthorne was at home with both Transcendental thought and language, but he can by no means be called a Transcendentalist.

What, according to Turner, distinguished Hawthorne from the Transcendentalists was that they denied the reality of evil. "Hawthorne could agree that in the divine scheme of things good and evil may be indistinguishable, but his observation of human nature taught him that people believe in the reality of evil and feel real guilt."[3] It was of course this conviction, even obsession, with the reality of evil that accounts for Hawthorne's sharp satire against Transcendentalism in "The Celestial Railroad." But I think that when he identified himself in the prefatory comment to "Rappacini's Daughter" under the *nom de plume* of M. de l'Aubépine as a writer who "seems to occupy an unfortunate position between the Transcendentalists . . . and the great body of pen-and-ink men who address the intellect and sympathies of the multitude," (CE 10:91) he is calling attention to a broader distinction than Turner notices. He was not merely concerned with the "evil latent in every human heart," but with the psychological probings of which this was merely one aspect.

What distinguished Hawthorne from his Transcendentalist contemporaries, in short, was that, although he fully accepted their ontology, he admitted their epistemology in theory only, and employed it in his fiction not at all, for it was oriented in the wrong direction. The objects of his art were transcendental ideas and forms, but his approach to them was distinctive.

Coleridge remarked that "under strong sensuous influence, we are restless because invisible things are not objects of vision."[4] This has always been a problem for transcendentalists, who have usually posited two ways of envisioning the invisible. One is by direct intuition of spiritual reality, "Truth with a big *T*." Emerson declared that such Truth is accessible through revelations of "primary reason." He wrote in "Self-Reliance" that "all persons have their moments of reason, when they look into the region of absolute truth."

A second, more available transcendentalist epistemology consisted of what Emerson called "later tuitions," operating through "correspondences" between ideas latent in the soul and Ideas emanating from the World Soul and symbolized in nature. He wrote in "Nature":

1. Words are signs of natural facts.
2. Particular natural facts are symbols of particular spiritual facts.
3. Nature is a symbol of spirit.[5]

So, according to Emersonian Transcendentalism, one could know Truth by "interrogation" of nature. He said that "the noblest ministry of nature is to stand as the apparition of God." It is a sufficient account of that Appearance we call the world that God will teach a human mind, and so makes it a receiver of a certain number of congruent sensations." "Nature is thoroughly mediate."[6]

Hawthorne's epistemology was transcendentalist insofar as he accepted both intuition as a primitive human faculty and nature as a symbol of spirit. The qualification is the *insofar*. For he did not consider intuition to be a reliably available faculty for knowing spiritual truth, nor did he believe nature to be thoroughly mediate; so they were not practicable epistemologies for an artist of the beautiful.

He occasionally referred to intuition as an endowment of exceptionally delicate or frail persons. "Children possess an unestimated sensibility to whatever is deep or high, in imagination or feeling, so long as it is simple, likewise." (CE 7:4) "Often, in a young child's ideas and fancies, there is something which it requires the thought of a lifetime to comprehend." (CE 6:20) Of Ernest, in "The Great Stone Face," he wrote, "[T]he boy's tender and confiding simplicity discerned what others could not see." (CE 11:29) This primitive gift of intuition retained by unsophisticated persons could detect falsity as well as discover truth. Of the witch's phantom in the tale "Feathertop" he wrote: "[O]f all the throng that beheld him, not an individual appears to have possessed enough insight to detect the illusive character of the stranger except a little child and a cur dog." (CE 10:240)

Delicate maidens in Hawthorne's fiction have the same gift of spiritual intuition. Thus, Coverdale remarks to Priscilla in *The Blithedale Romance*, "[Y]ou have spiritual intimations respecting matters which are dark to us grosser people" (CE 3:142)—a gift exploited by the cynical materialist Westervelt in a parable of what Hawthorne saw as the subjugation of spiritual to material values in western civilization.

Men have such sensitivity only when their physical vitality is enfeebled, so their spiritual awareness is less obscured by it. Thus, "[O]ld men have a kind of susceptibility to moral impressions, and even . . . a receptivity to truth, which often appears to come to them after the active time of life is past." (CE 5:230) During the illness of Coverdale in *The Blithedale Romance*, he was convinced that

> there is a species of intuition—either a spiritual lie, or the subtle recognition of a fact—which comes to us in a reduced state of the corporeal system. The soul gets the better of the body, after wasting illness, . . . Vapors then rise up to the brain, and take shapes that often image falsehood, but sometimes truth. (CE 3:46)

So, although he admitted a latent faculty of spiritual intuition in fallen mankind, Hawthorne thought that most persons, himself included, were too corporeal to intuit ideal truth, and that what they took to be "spiritual intimations" (CE 3:142) were often "shapes that image falsehood." Therefore he could not admit what sometimes seemed to be spiritual intimations as a resource for his fiction.

He also mistrusted the other Transcendentalist epistemology, interpretation of nature as a set of intelligible symbols of divine meaning. Coleridge wrote, "A man may look at glass or through it, or both. Let all earthly things be to thee as glass to see heaven through!"[7] And Emerson wrote that "for the wise man . . . the universe becomes transparent, and the light of higher laws than its own shines through it."[8]

Transcendentalists did, however, acknowledge the difficulty of "recalling the drowsed soul from the dreams and phantom world of sensuality to *actual* reality"[9]—that is, to the transcendent realm of Ideas. Man's fallen nature, they conceded, has made him a prisoner of sense, with impaired capability of interpreting the divine hieroglyphics. Emerson's disciple Christopher P. Cranch wrote in his prose poem "Correspondences":

> All things in nature are beautiful types to the soul that will
>   read them.
> Nothing exists upon earth but for unspeakable ends.
> Every object that speaks to the senses was meant for the spirit;
> Nature is but a scroll—God's handwriting thereon.
> Ages ago, when man was pure, ere the flood overwhelmed him,
> While in the image of God every soul yet lived,
> Everything stood as a letter or word of a language familiar,
> Telling of truths which *now* only the angels can read.
> Lost to man was the key to those sacred hieroglyphics—
> Stolen away by sin—till with Jesus restored.
> Now with infinite pains we here and there spell out a letter;
> Now and then will the sense feebly shine through the dark.
>
> ———
>
> Yet is the meaning the same as when Adam lived sinless in Eden.
>
> ———
>
> O thou spirit of truth! visit our minds once more!
> Give us to read, in letters of light, the language celestial
> Written all over the earth—written all over the sky.
>
> ———

Hawthorne shared the transcendentalist belief that nature is a symbol of spirit. Symbolic representation is necessary because the spiritual world is not directly accessible to the senses:

"no corporeal perception can take cognizance" (CE 10:170) of
it. "[I]s it merely the defect in my own eyes, which cannot
behold the spiritual?" (LL 1:65) he asked. "[E]verything has its
spiritual meaning, which to the literal meaning is what the soul
is to the body." (RE 11:330) "I am half convinced that the
reflection is indeed the reality, the real thing which Nature
imperfectly images to our grosser sense. At all events, the dis-
embodied image is nearest to the soul." (CE 8:360) "Knowing
such images to be insubstantial, they assumed the ideality which
the soul always craves in the contemplation of earthly beauty."
(CE 8:321) But this assumption of ideality amounts, after all,
only to a half-conviction that he can behold the spiritual through
contemplation of earthly beauty.

For him, nature was not "transparent,"—"glass to see
heaven through"; it was materially dense and opaque—what he
called in *The Scarlet Letter* "that wild heathen Nature . . . never
subjugated by human law, nor illumined by higher truth." (CE
1:203) In nature as Hawthorne perceived it, its own laws were
more evident and operative than Emerson's "higher laws," and
nature was not thoroughly mediate but compellingly immediate.
So he could not "go to the god of the wood / To fetch his word
to men," as Emerson did. Persons were more likely to project
their moods and thoughts, often distempered, *on* nature than to
find mysteries "figured in the flowers." The only spiritual refreshment Hawthorne sought in nature was not a communication
from the Oversoul but a freeing of his own individual spirit from
the oppression of conventions and society. This distinction has
been ably discussed by David B. Kesterson, who concludes that
for Hawthorne "[N]ature is an amoral realm as juxtaposed to
moral human life," and that Hawthorne "used nature as a link
between him[self] and the natural world."[10]

Nevertheless, although for Hawthorne nature was not prac-
ticably mediate with the divine, it did bear ambiguous imprints
of its divine origin, but these were as undecipherable as the
veins on the gigantic rock in "Roger Malvin's Burial," which
"seemed to form an inscription in forgotten characters." (CE
10:338)

Hawthorne did, however, utilize symbols he saw in nature—not as communications of divine Ideas, but as a way of
expressing his own ideas. The correspondences he saw in nature

were figures for his own thoughts; he used them analogically, as a set of objective correlatives to express his ideas. He also found intuitions a valuable resource for ideas to be figured in his fictions, but his were not intuitions of divine Ideas but of the secrets hidden in men's bosoms. The "dusky region" of "subtile and universal" sympathies that exists "among different classes of organized life, and vibrates from one to the other" was for Hawthorne the realm of accessible truth; and his intuitions were intuitions of this subliminal undersoul, not of the transcendent Oversoul intuited by his Transcendentalist contemporaries.

NOTES

1. *The Mirror and the Lamp* (New York: Oxford Univ. Press, 1953), 36.
2. *American Idealism* (Norman, OK: Univ. of Oklahoma Press, 1943), 64.
3. *Nathaniel Hawthorne* (New York: "American Authors and Critics Series," Barnes & Noble, 1961), 86, 87, 88.
4. *Biographia Literaria*, ed. J. Shawcross (Oxford: Oxford Univ. Press, 1907), 1, 6.112–13.
5. *Emerson's "Nature": Origin, Growth, Meaning*, ed. M. M. Sealts, Jr. and A. R. Ferguson (New York: Dodd, Mead and Co., 1969), 15.
6. *Ibid.*, 30, 23, 20.
7. *Table Talk and Omniana* (London: "Bohn's Popular Library," George Bell and Sons, 1884), 396. R. H. Fogle has remarked "the pervasive influence of Coleridge's theoretical criticism upon Hawthorne's literary theory, and even upon his imagination and sense of unity."—"Art and Illusion: Coleridgean Assumptions in Hawthorne's Tales and Sketches," in *Ruined Eden of the Present*, ed. G. R. Thompson and Virgil Lokke (West Lafayette, IN: Purdue Univ. Press, 1981), 109.
8. *Emerson's "Nature": Origin, Growth, Meaning*, 18.
9. *Aids to Reflection* (London: "Bohn's Popular Library," George Bell and Sons, 1913), 273.
10. "Nature in the Life and Works of Nathaniel Hawthorne," *Dissertation Abstracts*, 26:1023 (1965).

SIX

Illusive Credence

Hawthorne's transcendentalist literary theory led him to view the local and temporary passages of actual life as symbolic scenes in an ongoing cosmic drama. Like his "unfortunate friend P.," in "P.'s Correspondence," a persona of himself, he beheld "spectral scenes and characters with no less distinctness than a play upon the stage, and with somewhat more of illusive credence." (CE 10:361) God's continually developing plot actualized in time ideas that transcended time, and had for him what he called "the mysterious glory that has surrounded theatrical representations ever since my childhood." (EN, 115)

When he visited Scotland in the summer of 1857, he wrote admiringly in his journal of the prospect from the ramparts of Stirling Castle that it is

> one of the most splendid scenes, morally and materially, that this
> world can show. Indeed, I think there cannot be another such
> landscape as the Cärse of Stirling, set in such a frame as it is—
> the highlands . . . surrounding it to the westward and northward;
> and in other directions some range of prominent objects to shut
> it in; and the plain itself so worthy of the richest setting, so
> fertile, so beautiful, so written over and over again with histories.
> The silver links of the Forth are as sweet and gently picturesque
> an object as a man sees in a lifetime. I do not wonder that
> Providence made great things to happen on this plain.
> . . . Bannockburn could not have been fought upon a meaner
> plain; nor the field of Wallace's victory; and if any other great
> historic act still remains to be done, in this country, I should
> imagine the Cärse of Stirling as the future scene of it. (EN, 527)

This passage occurs in a context of historical reminiscences stirred by the author's journeying through a vicinity long familiar to his imagination of historic events and personages but only now seen with his bodily eye. The language and the transcendent sweep of vision in the passage make the world a stage, history an epochal drama, God a divine showman, and providence the plot of God.

Such a transcendent sweep of vision robs the here and now of substance and intrinsic meaning. If there is any far-off divine event toward which the whole creation moves, it is beyond the reach of human intelligence. The narrator's guide through the "Hall of Fantasy" remarks:

> "We cannot tell what mighty truths may have been embodied in act through the existence of the globe and its inhabitants. . . . Perhaps it may be revealed to us after the fall of the curtain over our catastrophe; or not impossibly, the whole drama; in which we are involuntary actors, may have been performed for the instruction of another set of spectators. I cannot perceive that our comprehension of it is at all essential to the matter." (CE 10:182)

If one could extend the span of consciousness to include a succession of generations or epochs in one act of vision, he would see that the repetition of human character types obliterates the identities of individual lives, as Hawthorne intimated in *The House of the Seven Gables* and the three "torso" romances of his last years. The roles that characters play, although they seem to themselves unique and personal, are traditional and typical. The title character of *Septimius Felton* expresses this thought:

> "We may find that the world is the same always, and mankind the same; so that by and by we shall discover that the same old scenery serves the world's stage in all ages, and that the story is the same, though none but [immortals] can be aware of it, and that the actors and spectators would grow weary of it; were they not bathed in forgetful sleep, and so think themselves new made in each successive lifetime. As dramatists and novelists repeat their plots, so does man's life repeat itself." (RE 11:411)

This conception removes significant action from the realm of time and history into that of eternity. In the various modes of retaining memory or record of human experience, essential truth emerges when the quotidian facts that invest it have lost

their significance. Thus Hawthorne wrote of "a few old news-
papers and still older almanacs" that it was

> as if I had found bits of a magic looking-glass. . . . It is the age
> itself that writes newspapers and almanacs, which, therefore,
> have a distinct purpose and meaning at the time, and a kind of
> intelligible truth for all time. . . . Genius, indeed, melts many
> ages into one, and thus effects something permanent, yet still
> with a similarity of office to that of the ephemeral writer. A work
> of genius is but the newspaper of a century, or perhaps a hundred
> centuries. (CE 10:20–21)

He thought that "tradition is just as good as truth," (CE 8:513)
that it "sometimes brings down truths that history has let slip."
(CE 2:17) "[Legends] get to be true, in a certain sense, and
indeed in that sense may be called true throughout, for the very
nucleus, the fiction in them, seems to have come out of the
heart of man in a way that cannot be imitated of malice afore-
thought." (RE 11:326) Even "ancient superstitions, after being
steeped in human hearts and embodied in human breath, and
passing from lip to ear in manifold repetition, through a series
of generations, become imbued with an effect of homely truth."
(CE 2:124)

Viewed in the time-frame of history or as fleetingly embodied creatures in the sweep of eternity, all characters are feather-
tops, and all authors, whether God, Hawthorne, or Mother
Rigby, are creators who deck lay figures with garments of
illusion.

Hawthorne called *The Scarlet Letter* a "drama of guilt and
sorrow." (CE 1:253) In *The House of the Seven Gables* Holgrave
speaks to Phoebe of the events he witnesses as an act in "the
drama which, for almost two hundred years, has been dragging
its slow length over the ground where you and I now tread."
(CE 2:216) In *The Blithedale Romance* Coverdale says that his own
part in the action

> resembled that of the Chorus in a classic play, . . . Destiny, it
> may be,—the most skilful of stage-managers,—seldom chooses
> to arrange its scenes, and carry forward its drama, without secur-
> ing the presence of at least one calm observer. It is his office to
> give applause when due, and sometimes an inevitable tear, to
> detect the final fitness of incident to character, and distill in his

long-brooding thought the whole morality of the performance. (CE 3:97)

He expects, and finally longs for "a sufficiently tragic catastrophe" (CE 3:79) as an appropriate close to the tragedy.[1] *The Marble Faun* is characterized as "a masque of love and death" (CE 4:397) and "the firmest substance of human happiness" is said to have "just reality enough to bear up the illusive stage-scenery amid which we tread." (CE 4:161–62)

Hawthorne wrote in *Our Old Home*, "The shades of the mighty have no substance; they flit ineffectually about the darkened stage where they performed their momentary parts, save when the poet has thrown his creative soul into them, and imparted a more vivid life than they were able to manifest to mankind while they dwelt in the body." (CE 5:267) To Hawthorne there was little difference between historical personages and fictional ones, both being actors in some author's drama. Of Archer and Aimwell in *The Beaux Stratagem*, who ogled the ladies in Lichfield Cathedral Close, he wrote, "The creatures have as positive a substance as the sturdy old figure of Johnson himself. They live, while realities have died." (CE 5:130) That is to say, reality is not in the figure, whether actual or fictional, but in the idea that the figure vividly presents.

With such a view of life as role-playing, Hawthorne saw his own life and his friends' lives in intensely dramatic terms. Thus he followed the career of Franklin Pierce with a playgoer's interest in the impending peripeties of a protagonist's fate more than with a friend's sympathy: "Should he fail, what an extinction it will be! He is in the intensest blaze of publicity." "If he loses the election, in one little month he will fall out of sight and never come up again. He is playing a tremendous game, and for a tremendous stake."[2] When Franklin Pierce was elected president, Hawthorne commented, "When I look at it one way, it strikes me as absolutely miraculous; in another, it came like an event I had all along expected." (RE 10:504)

A personal life is a role-enactment in God's show. People enact roles, not fatally, but voluntarily—at least initially. Thus Hawthorne solved the Calvinist problem of fate and free will. Although his characters sometimes declare their sense that they are acting through "a dark necessity," they acknowledge also an

initial choice of which there are necessary if unforeseen consequences. Having assumed a role, one must play it out, for he is
then involved in the plot of God. The plot of God has primordial
and typical roles which characters undertake to play, enacted by
successive generations of persons until God's idea becomes fully
realized. If some persons abort their roles, the ideas unacted or
imperfectly enacted nevertheless await actors who will perform
them.

Persons are thus "spectres," as Hawthorne often calls
them; the ideas they enact are the realities. The literary artist
summons up shapes from history and from the life that he sees
around him. His gift is that of unifying perception and vivifica-
tion rather than of pure invention or combination. He is perforce
limited to revivals and enhancements of such scenes of life as
direct observation and research bring to his notice. Hawthorne's
significant travel experiences came too late to contribute much
to his fiction except *The Marble Faun*. Ransacking the pages of
old annals and histories gave him more. Aware of the insufficiency of his knowledge and of the unreliability of perceptions,
he mistrusted his own shows, offering them with diffidence,
questioning their credibility.

To stage his dramas Hawthorne created the fiction of a
realm between the finite temporal world of human affairs and
the infinite eternal world of the spirit. He meant it to be a "Faery
Land, so like the real world, that, in a suitable remoteness, one
cannot well tell the difference, but with an atmosphere of
strange enchantment, beheld through which the inhabitants
have a propriety of their own. This atmosphere is what the
American romancer needs." (CE 3:2) Thus he wrote in a note
of his intention in the unfinished tale "Alice Doane's Appeal,"

> By this fantastic piece of description . . . I intended to throw a
> ghostly glimmer round the reader, so that his imagination might
> view the town through a medium that should take off its every-
> day aspect, and make it a proper theatre for so wild a scene as
> the final one. (CE 11:274)

He wrote in the "Custom-House" introduction to *The Scarlet Letter* that his intention was to establish "a neutral territory
somewhere between the real world and fairy-land." (CE 1:36)
Terence Martin has remarked that "Hawthorne's neutral terri-

tory has only a metaphorical existence; but as a metaphor with ontological pretensions, it held a great attraction for him."[3] When writing *The Marble Faun*, he hoped to use Italy as he had used Brook Farm, "as affording a sort of poetic or fairy precinct, where actualities would not be so terribly insisted upon as they are, and must needs be, in America." (CE 4:3) Miriam's studio in *The Marble Faun* is such a fairy precinct:

> One of those delightful spots that hardly seem to belong to the actual world, but rather to be the outward type of the poet's haunted imagination, where there are glimpses, sketches and half-developed hints of beings and objects grander and more beautiful than we can find anywhere in reality. (CE 4:41)

A problem for the romancer in staging his dramas was whether the showman did not become a manipulator of puppets instead of reserving to the characters he had imagined the typical roles he had envisioned, and the motives and elements of apparent self-determination belonging to their individual proprieties. Did the showman assume to himself the powers of providence to his characters, and determine rather than merely reveal their appropriate destinies? The painter of "The Prophetic Pictures" is guilty of this. "He stood like a magician, controlling the phantoms which he had evoked." (CE 9:182)

NOTES

1. See Maurice A. Crane, "The Blithedale Romance as Theatre," *Notes & Queries* 5 (February 1958): 84–86.

2. Horatio Bridge, *Personal Recollections of Nathaniel Hawthorne* (New York: Harper, 1893), 133.

3. *Nathaniel Hawthorne* (New Haven, CT: Twayne, 1965), 40.

PART TWO

Materials and Techniques

The Play of Imagination

I

To Hawthorne, a child playing with a toy was exercising that faculty which Coleridge designated the secondary imagination, "which struggles to idealize and unify. It is essentially *vital*, even as all objects (as objects) are essentially fixed and dead."[1] A child is not yet enthralled in the stale bonds of custom; so any object not unmistakably one of the full-sized and finished utensils of adult use, if it shows traits of possible function and form, prompts imaginings of some reality toward which it yearns and toward which the child can help it by his sympathy: "A perfect plaything is far less effective with a child than an imperfect one. A plaything should be suggestive, and the more work it leaves the imagination to do, the better will the child be occupied and satisfied." (CE 8:428)

To thus arouse imagination into activity, the plaything cannot be a kind of physical thing-in-itself which contains its own value and manifests its own meaning. Instead, it must be an apparent index of meaning and value beyond itself, which prompts imagination to summon up ideas latent in the mind. It must leave completion to the viewer, and must wear some marks of its imperfection in order to subsist in the natural world. Aylmer's Georgiana "bore a crimson stain upon the snow" (CE 10:38) of her cheek. The Snow-Image fashioned by Violet

and Pansy bore on its neck "the delicate print of Violet's fingers." (CE 11:22) The Venus di Medici, which Hawthorne
greatly admired, was improved rather than injured, he thought,
by the discoloration of the marble, which made her "an inmate
of the heart, as well as a spiritual existence." (RE 10:291)

He admired the Venus because she effectually kindled his
idea of womanhood:

> I do not, and cannot, think of her as a senseless image, but as
> a being that lives to gladden the world, incapable of decay and
> death; as young and fair to-day as she was three thousand years
> ago, and still to be young and fair as long as a beautiful thought
> shall require physical embodiment. (RE 10:302)

Therefore he felt affection for her "not as if she were one
woman, but all womanhood in one." (RE 10:291)

His conception of her being all womanhood is explicitly
Platonic. Immediately after looking at the Venus in the Uffizi
Gallery in Florence, he visited the Museum of Natural History,
where, looking at the anatomy of the natural woman, he contrasted it with the beauty of the ideal woman:

> It is good to have the wholeness and summed-up beauty of
> woman in the memory, when looking at the details of her system
> as here displayed; for these last, to the natural eye, are by no
> means beautiful. But they are what belong only to our mortality.
> The beauty that makes them invisible is our immortal type,
> which we shall take away with us. (RE 10:303)

Not only did great art-things carry the imagination from naturalistic details to the immortal type; they also set images of pure
types in the mind instead of the crass ones which people might
form from their meager experience without them. He remarked,
for example, that sailors may never have found out "what woman
is, though they may have encountered a painted spectre which
they took for her." (CE 5:230)

The proper intention of the artist, Hawthorne thought, is
"to attain to the ideal which Nature has proposed to herself in
all her creatures, but has never taken pains to realize." (CE
10:466) He thought that any endeavor that aims at distorting
rather than attaining to Nature's ideal was inartistic and monstrous. In the British Museum he remarked that the Egyptian
rooms were "full of monstrosities and horrible uglinesses," for

"the Egyptians controverted Nature in all things, only using it as a groundwork to depict the unnatural upon." (EN, 243) (What would he have thought of Cubist painting or the sculptures of Giacometti?)

But the artist cannot attain to Nature's ideal by a mere copying of Nature. Since Nature imperfectly embodies the ideal, a mere copying of Nature would be a faulty copy of a faulty copy, just as Plato's painter imitating the carpenter's bed is thereby at a further remove from God's bed. The artist must work from the idea, not from the observed object.

Nor should the artist attempt to take Nature's imperfect creatures in hand to improve them, for "our great creative Mother" (CE 10:42) Nature "permits us, indeed, to mar, but seldom to mend, and, like a jealous patentee, on no account to make." (CE 10:42) (It is plain what Hawthorne would have thought of genetic engineering.) Aylmer, the idealistic scientist of "The Birthmark," who seeks to improve "Nature's fairest work," instead destroys it. The more enlightened Artist of the Beautiful, in his attempt to "spiritualize machinery," succeeds because he does not seek to mend Nature's creature nor to make a static copy of it, but to make it a vitalized emblem of his idea. The scientist's experiment fails because he can comprehend and value only what he can finger and peep at, what is fixed and definite and capable of physical embodiment. The artist's effort succeeds because, although the physical embodiment of his idea is wantonly destroyed, he has attained to an envisagement of the ideal, and it is imagination of that, not the artifact that represents it, that is of value.

Although the best works of art are those that best express an idea, this best expression does not consist in elaboration and finish. Hawthorne's remarks about the sculptor Kenyon's studio in *The Marble Faun* are apparently an analogue of the process of his own art. First,

> some hastily scrawled sketches of nude figures[2] on the whitewash of the wall. These . . . are probably the sculptor's earliest glimpses of ideas that may hereafter be solidified into imperishable stone, or perhaps may remain impalpable as a dream. Next there are a few very roughly modelled little figures in clay or plaister [sic] exhibiting the second stage of the idea as it advances toward a marble immortality; and then is seen the exquisitely

designed shape of clay, more interesting even than the final marble, as being the intimate production of the sculptor himself,
moulded throughout with his loving hands, and nearest to his
imagination and heart. (CE 4:114)

A sculptor's success in fully realizing his idea would prove
that his work is not ideal enough.

"[T]his final despair, and sense of short-coming, must always be
the reward and punishment of those who try to grapple with a
great or beautiful idea. It only proves that you have been able to
imagine things too high for mortal faculties to execute. The idea
leaves you an imperfect image of itself, which you at first mistake
for the ethereal reality, but soon find that the latter has escaped
out of your closest embrace." (CE 4:378–79)

This danger is even more present in painting, for "there is
something radically artificial and deceptive in painting with
which minds in the primal simplicity cannot sympathize." (CE
10:256) "Sculpture, in its highest excellence, is more genuine
than painting, and might seem to be evolved from a natural
germ, by the same law as a leaf or flower." (CE 10:257) A
sculptor's "material, or instrument, which serves him in the
stead of shifting and transitory language, is a pure, white, un-
decaying substance. It insures immortality to whatever is
wrought in it." (CE 4:135) Hawthorne took sculpture to be art
par excellence because he thought its medium had a simplicity
and chasteness which could not beguile the artist into play with
the medium at the expense of concentration on his idea, and
because he thought the idea of a sculptured figure could be
taken in more instantaneously and directly and absolutely free
of supporting circumstance than the idea of any other kind of
art-thing, although he confessed that the ideas of some sculptures baffled his understanding. The artificiality and deception
of painting increase as the painter elaborates his conception and
"cover[s] up the celestial germ." (RE 10:398) He preferred
sketches by Raphael and Michelangelo to their finished pictures,
because looking at their drawings is "like looking into their
brains, and seeing the first conception, before it took shape
outwardly." (EN, 414) In the finished painting "the glory of
their pristine idea" "inevitably became overlaid with their own
handling of it." (RE 10:27) In their preliminary sketches "the

artist seemed to have bestirred himself at the pinch of the moment, snatching up whatever material was nearest, so as to seize the first glimpse of an idea that might vanish in the twinkling of an eye." (CE 4:137) "There is an effluence of divinity in the first sketch" (CE 4:138) which is obscured in the elaboration. "The charm lay partly in their very imperfection; for this is suggestive, and sets the imagination at work; whereas the finished picture . . . leaves the spectator nothing to do." (CE 4:138)

Hawthorne often objected to the hard enamel of too much finish, just as he often hinted that a too glossy appearance in persons was a sign of falseness. He complained of the "mighty Italian masters" that they "were not human; nor addressed their work to human sympathies, but to a false intellectual taste, which they themselves were the first to create." (CE 4:336) The divine effluence did not flow through them, and the connoisseur who appreciated them for their technical excellence was misled by factitious things as much as was the bland and blasted virtuoso of the "Virtuoso's Collection," who said, "[G]ive me what I can see, and touch, and understand, and I ask no more." (CE 10:496)

> They substituted a keen intellectual perception, and a marvellous knack of external arrangement, instead of the live sympathy and sentiment which should have been their inspiration. And hence it happens, that shallow and worldly men are among the best critics of their works;[3] a taste for pictorial art is often no more than a polish upon the hard enamel of an artificial character. (CE 4:338–39)

Because it is the imperfectness of the art-thing that enlists the aid of the imagination to perfect its idea, things in ruins and fading things have the same suggestive capability as rude unfinished things. He wrote of the fading portrait of old Colonel Pyncheon in *The House of the Seven Gables* that "in such cases the painter's deep conception of his subject's inward traits has wrought itself into the essence of the picture, and is seen after the superficial coloring has been rubbed off by time." The result is that the "character of the man seemed to be brought out in a kind of spiritual relief." (CE 2:58–59) In England he thought that the broken arches of Furness Abbey "suggest a

greater majesty and beauty than any human work can show—
the crumbling traces of the half-obliterated design producing
somewhat of the effect of the first idea of anything admirable,
when it dawns upon the mind of an artist or poet—an idea
which, do what he may, he is sure to fall short of." (EN, 157)

Two of Hawthorne's early tales illustrate his belief that the
locus of value was beyond the art-thing, not in it. "A Select
Party" tells of an entertainment given by a Man of Fancy to an
assemblage of distinguished personages in a castle in the air in
the realm of Nowhere. To "people of the lower world" this
castle in the air

> was unreal, because they lacked the imaginative faith. Had they
> been worthy to pass within its portal, they would have recognized
> the truth, that the dominions which the spirit conquers for itself
> among realities become a thousand times more real than the
> earth whereon they stamp their feet, saying, "This is solid and
> substantial; this may be called a fact." (CE 10:58)

Only in the dominions that the spirit conquers is the idea
of a work of art fully beheld:

> Along the walls, illuminated by the mild intensity of the moon-
> shine, stood a multitude of ideal statues, the original conceptions
> of the great works of ancient or modern art, which the sculptors
> did but imperfectly succeed in putting into marble; for it is not
> to be supposed that the pure idea of an immortal creation ceases
> to exist; it is only neccessary to know where they are deposited
> to take possession of them. (CE 10:69)

Not only ideal works of sculpture are located in those dominions which the spirit conquers; ideal works of all kinds are
there:

> In the alcoves of another vast apartment was arranged a splendid
> library, the volumes of which were inestimable, because they
> consisted not of actual performance, but of the works which the
> authors only planned, without ever finding the happy season to
> achieve them. . . . The shelves were crowded; for it would not
> be too much to affirm that every author has imagined and shaped
> out in his thought more and far better works than those which
> actually proceeded from his pen. (CE 10:69)

Another tale, "The Hall of Fantasy," describes a halfway
house between the castle in the air which is the realm of the

purely ideal and the "mud and mire" of ordinary life. The Hall of Fantasy

> occupies in the world of fancy the same position which the Bourse, the Rialto, and the Exchange do in the commercial world. All who have affairs in that mystic region, which lies above, below, or beyond the actual may here meet and talk over the business of their dreams. (CE 10:173)

It is occupied by a feat of imaginative levitation: "Artists are lifted by the ideality of their pursuits a little way off the earth." (CE 4:155) That is, it is the community of artistic imagination, which, although it is removed from the actual, is not the ideal:

> Standing in this Hall of Fantasy, we perceive what even the earth-clogged intellect of man can do in creating circumstances which, though we call them shadowy and visionary, are scarcely more so than those which surround us in actual life. (CE 10:184)

"What even the earth-clogged intellect of man can do"—this is the humanistic realm which a person's imagination ought to inhabit as comfortably as his physical sensibility inhabits the natural world: "It may be said, in truth, that there is but half a life—the meaner and earthlier half—for those who never find their way into the hall." (CE 10:179)

Such tales are hyperbolic charades telling the author's conception of what art is by telling where and when it is. Art is neither in the realm of the actual nor in the realm of the ideal, but in the Hall of Fantasy which imagination hypostasizes in yearning from one to the other.

II

An author uses his fictive personages—whether figures sketched from life or purely imaginary "snow-images"—as plastically as the child uses her doll. Hawthorne observed persons and described them in his notebooks in order to use them as lay figures; that is, as a graphic or factual thesis for his imagination's antithesis to encounter.

To do this, he divested them of much of their actuality when he transferred them into imagined situations, in order to equip them with appropriate traits and actions. Such observed figures were what Henry James described as "disponible" characters. The developments the author imagined for them when they were observed were drastically revised when he imagined situations in which they could be assigned roles suited to the ideas they represented to him.

As preliminary to fictional re-creation, an observed person had to be reduced in his mind to some such "pasteboard figure" as that manipulated by the Showman in "Main Street" or as the wooden puppet in "Little Annie's Ramble." "Though made of wood, a doll is a visionary and ethereal person, endowed by childish fancy with a peculiar life; the mimic lady is a heroine of romance, an actor and a sufferer in a thousand shadowy scenes." (CE 9:125) A "miraculous Jewess" (EN, 321) that Hawthorne saw at a dinner given by the Lord Mayor of London in 1856 served as lay figure for the author's imagination of the painter Miriam in *The Marble Faun*, who described the lay figure in her studio in similar terms.

Although his notebook descriptions were carefully detailed, Hawthorne's literary intention was not to present observed characters realistically, but to seize on the ideas that persons represented to him in order to invest them with appropriate fictional identities and histories.[4] Thus, in his North Adams notebooks of 1838 he described in detail the appearance and behavior of "a strange fellow in the bar room," and noted that, "This character might be wrought into a strange portrait of something sad, terrific, and laughable." (CE 8:121)

A typical example of his imagination's seizing on an idea of a character is this:

> I saw a tall old lady in black, who seemed to have just alighted from a train. She caught my attention by a singular movement of the head, not once only, but continually repeated, and at regular intervals, as if she were making a stern and solemn protest against some action that developed itself before her eyes, and were foreboding terrible disaster, if it should be persisted in. Of course, it was nothing more than a paralytic or nervous affliction; yet one might fancy that it had its origin in some unspeakable wrong, perpetrated half a lifetime ago in this old gentlewoman's presence, either against herself or somebody she loved still better. Her features had a wonderful sternness, which, I presume, was

caused by her habitual effort to compose and keep them quiet, and thereby counteract the tendency to paralytic movement. The slow, regular, and inexorable character of the motion—her look of force and self-control, which had the appearance of rendering it voluntary, while yet it was so fateful—have stamped this poor lady's face and gesture into my memory; so that, some dark day or other, I am afraid she will reproduce herself in a dismal Romance. (CE 5:141)

Several things are noteworthy in this paragraph: (1) Like many other remarkable portraits in the notebooks, it refutes the notion that Hawthorne's descriptions and characterizations were general because he lacked a gift of precise notation. (2) Again like many passages in his work, it shows that his "hawk-eye" (CE 8:92) was on the watch for real characters to suggest ideas for his fiction (his denial that Zenobia was modeled on Margaret Fuller was partly a fib to avoid embarrassment, and partly justified by the fact that it was not the real Margaret but the idea she represented to him that he portrayed). (3) Above all, it is the *idea* that he seizes in a chance-met person, not the fact. (4) But he is aware that his impression is capable of another "naturalistic" explanation that he feels bound to notice as an alternative to his "romantic" interpretation. (5) Finally, it was not merely the old lady's oddity that stamped her face and gesture into his memory, but the kind of oddity she had—one which suggested a struggle of fate with inclination, and the inescapable effect of some long-past misfortune.

In such passages the author is not only closely observant of figures, but he is also clearly aware of realistic and probable interpretations that he puts aside in order to give range to his imagination, which would be inhibited by minute fidelity to observation. This explains his embarrassment when he used as lay figures persons recognized as prototypes of his fictional characters. He hardly knew how to respond to probing questioners who saw a resemblance between Margaret Fuller and Zenobia, or to such literal-minded gadflies as Martin Tupper, who "asked me whom I meant by Zenobia in the Blithedale Romance, and whether I had drawn my own character in Miles Coverdale." (EN, 299)

Undoubtedly he had used his own character as lay figure in imagining Coverdale, as he did in imagining characters in some of his tales, and as he did in using his daughter Una as lay figure for the character of Pearl in *The Scarlet Letter* and his wife Sophia as lay figure for the character of Phoebe in *The House of the Seven Gables*. He could not deny unmistakable resemblances, but to acknowledge identifications would point readers' understanding in the wrong direction, away from his imaginative conceptions.

What is important to note in all such passages is that Hawthorne is more interested in the vital action of the mind, in the play of imagination, than in either the datum or the formal product of such action. The "thing" is palpably specious, whether a doll made of wood, a poor puppet made all for show, or a figment based on observation. The insistence upon the speciousness of the imagination's plaything satisfied two requisites of his fiction: his idealistic metaphysic, which sought to avoid the despotism of the eye characteristic of persons under strong sensuous influence who suppose that reality is fully contained, and contained only, in things that they can finger and peep at; and the corollary esthetic that throws off the despotism of the senses by unfixing the fixities and definites that are Fancy's counters.

III

Such unfixing is done by various means. Perfect mimicry or deceitful aping of reality are pointless to the idealist, for they lead entirely into fixities and definites as the be-all and end-all of reality; so Hawthorne stressed in imagination's playthings the palpable woodenness of the doll or the exceeding pliability of the poor puppet. Further, the patent imperfection and surrogate character of the plaything vis-à-vis the "real" object that it imitates instill a notion of the real object itself as a plaything and surrogate: a mimic lady and a real lady are similar not only in figure but also in contingency—in being merely formal facts that draw their life from ideas beyond themselves.

Another means of suggesting this surrogate character is miniaturization, a shrinking of the proportions of the actual. This is evidently true of the doll; a more striking example is given in one of the entries in Hawthorne's notebooks in 1842 in which he remarks, of a toy ship which a boy was sailing on the Boston Frog Pond, that in it there is something that kindles the imagination more than the reality would. If we see a real, great ship, the mind grasps and possesses, within its real clutch, all there is of it; while here, the mimic ship is the representative of an ideal one, and so gives a more imaginative pleasure. (CE 8:233–34)

This comment reminds us of many passages in which Hawthorne remarked "how much more beautiful reflection is than what we call reality" and stated his half-conviction that "the reflection is indeed the reality—the real thing which Nature imperfectly images to our grosser sense." (CE 8:360) The mimic ship on the Frog Pond by its miniaturization works the same effect that the reflection does by disembodiment; that is, it makes it impossible to see the thing as containing its reality and value in itself, and necessitates reference to an idea of something beyond itself of which it is merely a figure. Apparently, the miniaturization of the artist's work in the tale "The Artist of the Beautiful," together with its obvious inutility and artificiality, are intended to effect the same purpose—to obviate any possibility of using or valuing the work for what it is in itself.

IV

Hawthorne regarded art as an activity of the imagination in realizing truths of the heart more than as an activity of the intellectually directed skills of the artist in furnishing products or relics of such activity.

Art is not a transcription of reality; it does not even require that any "outward change" be wrought in actual things: it is above all an act of faith. One of Hawthorne's story-tellers says to his child-auditors, "Faith is the soul's eyesight," and therefore, "People, when deprived of sight, often have more vivid ideas of things than those who possess the perfect use of their eyes." (CE 6:229) And elsewhere, emphasizing that it is in the imagination, not in the realm of physical things, that men realize the grand and beautiful, he says,

After all, the utmost force of man can do positively little towards making grand things, or beautiful things; the imagination can do so much more, merely on shutting one's eyes, that the actual effect seems meager. (EN, 75)

It is imagination that changes fact, not fact that changes imagination. A fact too definitely seen can block imagination of an idea, but an idea intensely believed in can create somewhat of a visible fact from the most tenuous of materials.

Hawthorne thought that every work of art or literature that had the effect he desiderated was a kind of reaching out to the imagination of the spectator or reader; that in fact it was not completed, and could not be completed, by the author, but reached completion only in its achieved effect in the auditor's imagination. His most frequent and explicit comments on this were recorded while viewing statuary in Italy, but the principle applies to all the arts. Of Michelangelo's statue of Lorenzo di Medici he wrote,

> He wrought the whole statue in harmony with that small part of it which he leaves to the spectator's imagination, and if he had erred, at any point, the miracle would have been a failure; so that, working in marble, he has positively reached a degree of excellence above the capability of marble, sculpturing the highest touches upon air and duskiness. (RE 10:334)

He wrote of the statue of the Dying Gladiator, "Like all works of the highest excellence, . . . it makes great demands upon the spectator. He must make a generous gift of his sympathies to the sculptor, and help out his skill with all his heart, or else he will see little more than a skillfully wrought surface. It suggests far more than it shows." (RE 10:98) On a later visit he said of the Venus di Medici and the Dying Gladiator, "Marble beauties seem to suffer the same occasional eclipses as those of flesh and blood." (RE 10:495) The Venus now seemed

> little more than any other piece of yellowish white marble. How strange that a goddess should stand before us absolutely unrecognized, even when we know by previous revelations that she is nothing short of divine! It is also strange that, unless when one feels the ideal charm of a statue, it becomes one of the most tedious and irksome things in the world. Either it must be a celestial thing or an old lump of stone, dusty and time-soiled, and tiring out your patience with eternally looking just the same. Once in a while you penetrate through the crust of the old sameness, and see the statue forever new and immortally young. (RE 10:499)

He said, "We looked at the Faun, the Dying Gladiator, and other famous sculptures; but nothing had a glory around it, perhaps because the sirocco was blowing." (RE 10:495)

Such comments are like his saying of *Twice-Told Tales* that "The book, if you would see anything in it, requires to be read in the clear, brown, twilight atmosphere in which it was written; opened in the sunshine, it is apt to look exceedingly like a volume of blank pages." (CE 9:5)

He made similar comments on painting, remarking on the need "of helping out the painter's art with the spectator's own resources of sensibility and imagination" to such a degree that "you can never be sure how much of the picture you have yourself made." "Let the canvas glow as it may, you must look with the eye of faith, or its highest excellence escapes you." (CE 4:335) Although the sensibility to which the artist or author's imagination is addressed may sometimes be dull and unresponsive, "a work of art is entitled to credit for all that it makes us feel in our best moments; and we must judge it by the impression it then makes, and not by the coldness and insensibility of our less genial moods." (RE 10:303)

Hawthorne's frequent appeals in his prefaces to the "known and unknown friends" who constituted his limited public were in fact an acknowledgment that their imagination must be adjuvant to his own in giving life to his creations.

An interesting point in Hawthorne's theory of the necessary cooperation of the auditor with the art-thing in making art vital is that the artist himself does not fully grasp his idea; in fact, that there is no certain idea to be grasped, only a mere general capability in the art-thing of generating ideas. Thus, he says of Michelangelo's painting of the Three Fates:

> I . . . cannot satisfactorily make out what he meant by them. . . . But, as regards the interpretation of this, or of any other profound picture, there are likely to be as many interpretations as there are spectators. . . . Each man interprets the hieroglyphic in his own way; and the painter, perhaps, had a meaning which none of them have reached; or possibly he put forth a riddle without himself knowing the solution. . . . [It] is a great symbol, proceeding out of a great mind; but if it means one thing, it seems to mean a thousand, and, often, opposite things. (RE 10:332)

I see no reason why we are not justified in applying this statement as well to Hawthorne's own work, in view of his frequent complaint that his work seemed to have shaped itself against his own conscious intention. He was as much an interested witness of the shaping of his imagined situations as his readers are.

> Literally, the process of composition is, in one degree or another, a movement toward meaning. . . . The writer, no matter how clear his idea or strong his intuition of the projected work, can never know what it will "be" or "mean" until the last word is in place—for every word, every image, every rhythm participates in the "being," and the "being" is, ultimately, the "meaning." And the reader is made to share in this process.[5]

Hawthorne saw as many suggestions of possible meaning in his fictions as his readers do, and this explains his reluctance to certify any single interpretation. "Young Goodman Brown" and *The Scarlet Letter* were to him as "phantasmagoric" when viewed from different premises or under various lights and conditions as they are to his readers, although commonly some centrally positioned though questionable character has, in a strictly putative sense, "authority," as Henry James conferred authority, for example, on the governess in "The Turn of the Screw."[6] Thus, in *The Scarlet Letter,* and perhaps in "Young Goodman Brown," the Puritan community has such authority, acknowledged even by persons who in regard to the Puritan system are delinquents and doubters, although their whole being rebels against orthodoxy.

NOTES

1. *Biographia Literaria*, ed. J. Shawcross (Oxford: Oxford Univ. Press, 1907), 1, 8. 298.

2. Although Hawthorne sometimes made no objection to nude figures, he usually sounds like Anthony Comstock or Mrs. Grundy when writing about nude sculpture and painting, and was always embarrassedly seeking rationalizations of his prudishness. He wrote, "I am weary of naked goddesses, who never had any real life or warmth in the painter's imagination—or, if so, it was the impure warmth of the

unchaste women who sat or sprawled for them." (EN, 561) Henry G. Fairbanks says, however, that, "Though often alleged to have condemned nude painting and sculpture, Hawthorne preserved a saner judgment in the midst of alien masterpieces than most provincials with his Puritan background."—*The Lasting Loneliness of Nathaniel Hawthorne* (Albany, NY: Magi Books, 1965), 129. This is faint praise.

    3. Hawthorne wrote that he could not

> understand what the enjoyment of a connoisseur is. He is not usually, I think, a man of deep poetic feeling, and does not deal with the picture through his heart, nor set it in a poem, nor comprehend it morally. If it be a landscape, he is not entitled to judge it by his intimacy with Nature; if it be a picture of human action, he has no experience or sympathy of life's deeper passages. (EN, 559)

    4. For example, historic personages such as those identified in Alfred S. Reid's source studies.

    5. Robert Penn Warren, "Hawthorne Was Relevant," *Nathaniel Hawthorne Journal 1972* (Dayton, OH: National Cash Register Co., 1973), 89.

    6. For extended discussion of the epistemological and technical problems involved in such narration, see my explication of James's "The Turn of the Screw," in *American Literature* (Great Neck, NY: Barron's, 1963), 3:301–18.

EIGHT

The Stony Excrescence of Prose

I

Hawthorne thought that facts are the "garb" of truth: "Facts, as we really find them, whatever poetry they may involve, are covered with a stony excrescence of prose, resembling the crust on a beautiful sea-shell, and they never show their most delicate and divinest colors until we shall have dissolved away their grosser actualities by steeping them long in a powerful menstruum of thought." (CE 5:135–36)

In his fiction he aimed at verisimilitude, but not at a literal transcription of apparent reality, which, if densely particularized, would have made it impossible to see the forest for the trees. So in his observations of fact he faced a problem: "Human nature craves a certain materialism, and clings pertinaciously to what is tangible, as if that were of more importance than the spirit accidentally involved in it." (RE 12:88)

To satisfy the human craving for a certain materialism, accurate and vivid notation of fact was required. He was a keen observer, as his lifelong habit of keeping detailed notebooks shows. His friend Horatio Bridge wrote that,

> His mental sight was both panoramic and microscopic; and he
> looked at persons and things with a discerning and discriminating
> eye, whether the object of his attention were a friend or a
> stranger—a tree or a flower—a hill or a pebble.[1]

He advised Bridge about keeping the journal published in 1845
as *Journal of an African Cruiser* and edited by Hawthorne:
"Think nothing too trifling to write down, so it be in the small-
est degree characteristic. You will be surprised on re-perusing
your journal what an importance and graphic power these little
particulars assume."[2]

As Jean Normand says,

> Hawthorne . . . needed to see and feel the same things as other
> people, to appreciate things according to their market value,
> their weight, their usefulness, . . . to look at people as his con-
> temporaries and fellow-countrymen, not merely as they appeared
> to him in the vistas of allegory or as figures in a pastoral.[3]

He was aware of the fact that his preoccupation with the
"moral" element of his fiction might make the "picturesque"
too thin. He wrote in *Our Old Home* of his boyhood fondness for
reading the works of Samuel Johnson that, "considering that my
native propensities were toward Fairy Land, . . . it may not have
been altogether amiss, in those childish and boyish days, . . . to
feed on the gross diet that he carried in his knapsack." (CE
5:122)

II

Hawthorne was engaged with what Emerson called "the
lubricity of all facts." He thought the visible world was as little
capable of definitive and entire comprehension as Ghostland.
Several things contributed to making perceived reality a phantasmagoria: changing subjective states of sensibility and sense-
awareness in the observer, the complexity of things within the
field of vision, the changeability of appearances of things seen
at different times and under different conditions, and the various
aspects of things viewed from changed distances and perspectives. "There is a vast variety of shape, of light and shadow, and
incidental circumstance, even in what looks so monotonous at
first as a green hill." (EN, 519) "Every new aspect of the moun-

tains, or view from a different position, creates a surprise in the mind." (CE 8:104) "It is wonderful how many aspects a mountain has; how many mountains there are in every single mountain! . . . When I think I have described them all, I remember quite a different aspect, and find it equally true, and yet lacking something to make it the whole or an adequate truth." (EN, 524) His recognition of the lubricity of facts prompted a complaint: "Every day of my life makes me feel more and more how seldom a fact is accurately stated. . . . Is truth a fantasy which we are to pursue forever and never grasp?" (RE 9:232)

An observer could do little or nothing to manage the subjective states that conditioned perception, but objective conditions were manageable to some degree. Although the complex and changeable visible reality could not be comprehended in a single view, some of its aspects could be perceived in successive views.

Many of his notebook entries comment on the complexity of scenes:

> The forest bordering the stream produces its effect by a complexity of causes—the old and stern trees, with stately trunks and dark foliage—as the almost black pines—the young trees, with lightsome green foliage—as sapling oaks, maples, poplars, etc,—then the old decayed trunks that are seen lying here and there all mouldered, so that the foot would sink into them. The sunshine falling capriciously on here and there a branch within the forest verge, while it leaves nearer trees in shadow, leads the imagination into the depths. But it soon becomes bewildered there. (CE 8:126)

In such passages the produced effect, the leading of the imagination, and the eventual bewilderment constitute a metaphor of the author's imaginative observation.

Of all the conditions that affected perception various atmospheric conditions and changes of light and shadow were most important. "There seems to be a sort of illuminating quality in new snow." (CE 8:305) "The transparency of the air at this season [February] has the effect of a telescope, in bringing objects apparently near while it leaves the scene all its breadth." (CE 8:303) "A misty atmosphere idealizes all nature." (CE 8:364) "It is wonderful what a difference sunshine makes; it is like varnish bringing out the hidden veins in a piece of rich wood." (CE 8:218) "This is a very windy day . . . and the lights shift with a magical alternation." (CE 8:309) "The gray but transparent evening rather shrouded than obscured the scene, leaving its stronger features visible, and even improved the medium through which I viewed them." (RE 12:17)

The transforming effect of light in spiritualizing the scene especially interested him. While staying in the Old Manse he wrote,

> In the light of a calm and golden sunset [the Concord River] becomes lovely beyond expression. . . . Each tree and rock, and every blade of grass, is distinctly imaged, and, however unsightly in reality, assumes ideal beauty in the reflection. The minutest things of earth and the broad aspect of the firmament are pictured equally without effort and with the same felicity of success. (CE 10:7)

Visiting Edinburgh in 1857, he wrote,

> The sun was setting, and gilded the Old Town with its parting rays, making it absolutely the most picturesque scene that I have ever beheld. The mass of tall, ancient houses, heaped densely together, looked like a Gothic dream; for there seemed to be towers, and all sorts of stately architecture, and spires ascended out of the mass; and above the whole was the Castle, with a crown of gold on its topmost turrent. . . . The last gleam faded from the windows of the old town, and left the mass of buildings dim and indistinguishable; to reappear on the morrow in squalor. . . . The change symbolized the difference between a poet's imagination of life in the past—or in a state which he looks at through a colored and illuminated medium and the sad reality. (EN, 536)

His practice in viewing reality was like his practice in writing romance as he described it in "Howe's Masquerade": "striving to throw a tinge of romance and historic grandeur over the realities of the scene." (CE 9:255)

III

Hawthorne's most comprehensive figure for representing the complexity and variety of reality-as-perceived combines the figures of mosaic and fountain. An example of this figure is the fountain in the Pyncheon garden in *The House of the Seven Gables* that fascinated the hypersensitive Clifford: "He had a singular propensity . . . to hang over Maule's well, and look at the constantly shifting phantasmagoria of figure produced by the agitation of the water over the mosaic-work of colored pebbles at the bottom." (CE 2:153–54) In "The Hall of Fantasy" he wrote, "It is impossible to conceive what a strange vivacity is imparted to the scene by the magic dance of this fountain, with its endless transformations, in which the imaginative beholder may imagine what he will." (CE 10:174) This comment indicates how large was the subjective element in Hawthorne's perception of reality. It was the primary element of perception, and the observed scene was subdued to it.

As imaginative beholder he used various strategies for observing the endless transformations of the visible scene. Chief of these were viewing things through various conditions of atmosphere and light, viewing them from various points of view, and distancing himself from them.

One's local station and limited faculties prevented any comprehensive view of whatever reality was apparent, so to get a more adequate idea of a prospect one needed to change the position from which it was viewed. His comments on differences of impression of objects seen from various points of view specify the vantage point together with statement of the impression produced: "The view from the top of [Browne's Hill] is of very wide extent and variety. . . . [Human activity] looks not so important when we can get so high up as to comprehend several men's portions in it at one glance. It gave me an idea of neighborhood, which I should not have had otherwise." (CE 8:274)

His interest in distancing as a strategy of perception was constant. One of the most striking examples occurs in the North Adams notes taken in 1838 and later utilized in "Ethan Brand." "The village viewed from the top of a hill to the westward, at sunset, has a peculiarly happy and peaceful look; it lies on a level, surrounded by hills, and seems as if it lay in the hollow of a large hand." (CE 8:101–2) In "Ethan Brand" his imagination augmented this "as if" to "The village, completely shut in by the hills, . . . looked as if it rested peacefully in the hollow of the great hand of Providence." (CE 11:101)

Distancing was a device to reveal spiritual meaning in vistas by rendering less distinct the particulars of the scene so that a general idea emerged. "[S]ublime and beautiful facts are best understood when etherealized by distance." (CE 5:138) Distance also unified the scene in a manner similar to the Aristotelian principle that beauty requires "a certain magnitude."[4] As the perception of magnitude is relative, it depends on the range and degree of the observer's visual acuity, so Hawthorne achieved the requisite magnitude by stationing himself at a proper distance from the set of things to be viewed. "I had an excellent view of Graylock and the adjacent mountains, at such a distance that they were all brought into one group, and comprehended at one view. . . . As I drew nearer home, they separated, and the unity of effect was lost." (CE 8:143) Of the sculptures on the tower of Whitnash church in England, he wrote that they show "how a general impression overcomes minor details"; (EN, 129) and of St. Peter's cathedral in Rome, "At any nearer view the grandeur of St. Peter's hides itself behind the immensity of its parts." (CE 4:107) In all such observations it was the general impression he sought, although he was interested in how a multitude of details combined to create such a general impression.

IV

He thought that both first impressions and repeated observations were important for attaining the best possible view of things: "It is singular how many errors one makes in his first hasty sketch and narrative of observation and travel, but yet there is a truth in these earliest impressions, perhaps more vivid than anyone better acquainted with the subject could attain." (EN, 479) This is evidently so because the first view is not defined by a settled impression from previous acquaintance. Nevertheless, "I find it impossible to know accurately how any prospect . . . looks, until after a second view, which essentially corrects the first." (EN, 171)

These apparently conflicting statements are reconciled by the belief that any view is only partial and occasional; so no views, no matter how intense and frequent, can exhaust the reality:

> How strange is the gradual process with which we detect objects
> that are right before the eyes. Were we to sit here . . . a lifetime,
> objects would still be presenting themselves as new, though there
> would seem to be no good reason why we should not have de-
> tected them all at the first moment. (CE 8:247)

And it was essential to note appearances while observation was
recent, for "the hues of recollection fade as quickly as the colors
of a dead dolphin." (EN, 134)

V

He frequently despaired of describing things with the ac-
curacy that he wished for, and after writing a long description in
his notebooks, he wrote, "I hate what I have said." (RE 10:279)
And another entry concluded that

> all attempts at describing scenery—especially mountain scen-
> ery—are sheer nonsense. For one thing, the point of view being
> changed, the whole description that you made up from the pre-
> vious point of view is immediately falsified. And when you have
> done your utmost, such items as those setting forth a scene in a
> play . . . —this dry detail brings the matter before the mind's
> eye more effectively than all the art of word-painting. (EN, 183)

This is so because the incompleteness of the description sets
the imagination to work, and because the right selection of details produces the essential impression.

He disliked too close acquaintance with historic fact, which
might inhibit his imagination. On looking at the scene of Concord Fight near the Old Manse, he remarked, "I have never
found my imagination much excited by this or any other scene
of historic celebrity." (CE 10:10) After visiting Shakespeare's
house, he wrote, "I felt no emotion whatever in Shakespeare's
house—not the slightest—nor any quickening of the imagination." "I think I can form, now, a more sensible and vivid idea
of him as a flesh-and-blood man; but I am not quite sure that
this latter effect is altogether desirable." (EN, 132)

He advised Horatio Bridge about keeping the journal to be
published as *Journal of an African Cruiser:*

I would advise you not to stick too accurately to the bare fact, either in your description, or in your narrative; else your hand will be cramped, and the result will be that want of freedom that will deprive you of a higher truth than that which you strive to attain. Allow your fancy pretty free license, and omit no heightening touches because they did not chance to happen before your eyes. If they did not happen, they at least ought.[5]

Occasionally during his European travels he noted with evident approval facts that indicated that the Romantic poets did not stick too accurately to the bare fact. At the Castle of Chillon he remarked, "The prisoner of Chillon could not possibly have seen the island to which Byron alludes." (RE 10:540) And on seeing a stuffed albatross, "I do not think that Coleridge could have known the size of this fowl, when he caused it to be hung around the neck of his Ancient Mariner." (EN, 588)

The most that Hawthorne could hope to achieve in his descriptions was to furnish by many and varied observations a panorama of reality that by its complexity and variety would suggest the plenitude of the spiritual world.

When necessary facts were not retrievable, as was the case with the supposed documents of Mr. Surveyor Pue which "authorized and authenticated" the "main facts" (CE 1:32) of *The Scarlet Letter*, he fabricated them, to give "authenticity" to the "outline" (CE 1:33) of his story.

NOTES

1. *Personal Recollections of Nathaniel Hawthorne* (New York: Harper, 1893), 64.

2. *Ibid.*, 93.

3. *Nathaniel Hawthorne: An Approach to an Analysis of Artistic Creation*, trans. Derek Coltman (Cleveland: The Press of Case Western Reserve Univ., 1970), 120.

4. Aristotle's *Theory of Poetry and Fine Art*, trans. S. H. Butcher, 4th edition (New York: Dover Books, 1951), 31.

5. Bridge, 63.

CHAPTER
NINE

Visions That Seem Real

I

In a passage of "The Old Manse" Hawthorne wrote of "inducing a magic sleep" in those who enter the precincts of the Old Manse. The world, he wrote,

> has gone distracted through a morbid activity, and, while preternaturally wide awake, is nevertheless tormented by visions, that seem real to it now, but would assume their true aspect and character were all things once set right by an interval of sound repose. This is the only method of getting rid of old delusions and avoiding new ones. (CE 10:29)

The visions that seem real are fixed appearances of things that he repeatedly mentions, often with irony, as "broad daylight reality," which obscure essential ideas. He used two strategies for discerning aspects and character of things other than those apparent as broad daylight reality. One was to so change conditions of perception that the appearance of the daylight reality was altered. This strategy accounts for his fondness for viewing and describing things in a misty atmosphere or a dim light, and for the use of all such veiling effects in his fiction, for veils partly reveal and partly conceal. He said of Manchester Cathedral that "the Gothic architects seem first to imagine beautiful and noble things, and then to consider how they may best be partially

screened from sight. A certain secrecy and twilight effect belong
to their plan." (EN, 454) His other strategy was to escape daylight reality by exploring the realm of dream and daydream.

In the first of these strategies he attended to changes of
ambiance or atmosphere or light that had the effect of suppressing usually visible details of things and of making conspicuous
features and general impressions usually obscured, as in this
entry in the *American Notebooks:* "Towards the dimness of evening, a half-length figure appearing at a window:—the blackness
of the background and the light upon the face cause it to appear
like a Rembrandt picture." (CE 8:259) The method is described
in a simile in the sketch "A Select Party":

> To each of these pillars a meteor was suspended. . . . Such,
> however, was the intensity of their blaze that it had been found
> expedient to cover each meteor with a globe of evening mist,
> thereby muffling the too potent glow and soothing it into a mild
> and comfortable splendor. *It was like the brilliancy of a powerful yet
> chastened imagination—a light which seemed to hide whatever was un-
> worthy to be noticed and give effect to every beautiful attribute.* (My
> italics) (CE 10:58)

Certain places, such as Gallows Hill in Salem or a deserted
seashore, like the precincts of the Old Manse, have the desired
effect of suppressing ordinary perception and giving prominence
to features that alter vision, or suggesting associations that induce it. Gallows Hill, by its blighted and God-and-man-forsaken
appearance, summons associations of its dreadful past. In "Footprints on the Seashore," Hawthorne wrote of the deserted seashore, "There is magic in this spot. Dreams haunt its precincts,
and flit around me in broad daylight, nor require that sleep shall
blind me to real objects ere these be visible." (CE 9:459) In
Italy he wrote:

> I must fairly confess that the Italian sky, in the daytime, is
> bluer and brighter than our own, and that the atmosphere has a
> quality of showing objects to their advantage. It is more than
> mere daylight; the magic of moonlight is somehow mixed up with
> it, although it is so transparent a medium of light. (RE 10:283)

Ordinarily, while one's senses are awake, "the inward eye"
is closed. Attaining insight into Ghostland requires refraction of
the conditions of visibility. What Hawthorne called "the moon-

light of romance" (CE 10:337) delivers us from visions that seem real. Daylight or sunlight, "morning or noontide visibility," (CE 8:283) stands for mundane quotidian views of reality, and the magic of moonlight reveals other possibilities. The shifting of light in his work indicates an alteration of perception and therefore of reality, since for him to be perceived is to be.

II

His second strategy for freeing himself from what Coleridge called "the despotism of the eye" was by recourse to reverie and dream. He thought that profound truths were revealed in dreams; also that some dreams were delusive "shapes that often image falsehood," (CE 3:46) and some were horrible possibilities glimpsed in the dreamer's unconscious. "Truth often finds its way to the mind close muffled in robes of sleep, and then speaks with uncompromising directness of matters in regard to which we practice an unconscious self-deception in our waking moments." (CE 10:40)

Psychology has made dream events surreal continuities of waking consciousness by recognizing the inseparable subjectivity of all human experience. Nietzsche wrote, "What we experience in dreams belongs in the end as much to the total economy of our psyche as any real experience." "Things begun in the dark continue in the light."[1] The dark is all that lies in and beyond the vague borderland of consciousness in both the internal and external worlds, at the farthest reach of illumination afforded by what Henri Bergson called "the luminous nucleus that we call the intellect."[2] The light is the world of event and history; the dark is the world of dimly imagined unenacted possibility.

Hawthorne exploited the brief period of waking from sleep during which he seemed to have twinned vision into both worlds, the actual world and Ghostland.

> What a singular moment is the first one, when you have hardly begun to recollect yourself, after starting from midnight slumber! By unclosing your eyes so suddenly, you seem to have surprised the personages of your dreams in full convocation round your bed, and catch one broad glance at them before they can flit into

obscurity. Or, to vary the metaphor, you find yourself, for a single instant, wide awake in that realm of illusions, whither sleep has been the passport, and behold its ghostly inhabitants and wondrous scenery, with a perception of their strangeness, such as you never attain while the dream is undisturbed. The distant sound of a church clock is borne faintly on the wind. You question yourself, half seriously, whether it has stolen to your waking ear from some gray tower that stood within the precincts of your dream. (CE 9:304)

Clearly in this passage Hawthorne declares that on the border between sleep and waking it is as if he were seeing the invisible.

His dreams were abnormally compelling and vivid, so that he came near to confusing the persons and events in dreams with actuality. He once wrote to Sophia,

Do you never start so suddenly from a dream that you are afraid to look around the room, lest your dream-personages (so strong and distinct seemed their existence a moment before) should have thrust themselves out of dream-land into the midst of realities? (LL 1:27)

Such experiences were available material for his romances because they conveyed glimpses of strange possibilities, because they were distinct enough, and because they had enough resemblance to actual character and event that they could combine with observation and thus have both the significance of dream and the verisimilitude of waking life.

III

In the sketch "Graves and Goblins" Hawthorne imagined a ghostly visitant who whispered truths to him in dreams and daydreams, and who soliloquized thus:

"I steal into his sleep, and play my part among the figures of his dreams. I glide through the moonlight of his waking fancy, and whisper conceptions, which, with a strange thrill of fear, he writes down as his own. I stand beside him now, at midnight, telling these dreamy truths with a voice so dream-like, that he mistakes them for fictions of a brain too prone to such." (CE 11:297)

What is perhaps Hawthorne's most interesting analysis of the process of dreaming occurs as an incidental analogy to an account of mediumistic trance in a séance that he attended in Florence in 1858. He begins with explicit statement of the subjective origin of such manifestations. Admitting that the apparent spiritual manifestations were facts to his understanding, he said that "they seem not to be facts to my intuitions or deeper perceptions. My inner soul does not in the least admit them." (RE 10:394) "I should judge that these effusions emanated from earthly minds, but had undergone some process that had deprived them of solidity and warmth." (RE 10:395) He then went on to explain their mechanism as that of a dream:

> The whole matter seems to me a sort of dreaming awake, in that the whole material is, from the first, in the dreamer's mind, though concealed at various depths below the surface; the dead appear alive, as they always do in dreams; unexpected combinations occur, as continually in dreams; the mind speaks through the various persons of the dream, and sometimes astonishes itself with its own wit, wisdom, and eloquence, as often in dreams; but, in both cases, the intellectual manifestations are really of a very flimsy character. (RE 10:395–96)

To this account of the process of a dream should be added a detail from an 1842 entry in the *American Notebooks:* that despite the inconsistency, eccentricities, and apparent aimlessness of a dream, there is "nevertheless a leading idea running through the whole." (CE 8:240) That is, a dream does have its own kind of coherence—not that of rational concatenation of motive and event usual in logical discourse and plotted narrative, but that of "a leading idea," a nucleus of association that aggregates and aligns its elements. The same kind of coherence is evident in reverie: "The discursive structure of the reverie expresses Hawthorne's understanding of how the mind drifts along its levels of consciousness, one idea drawing another in its wake, while a single strong emotion dominates the stream of association."[3]

Of one of the characters speaking through the trance medium at the Florence séance, Hawthorne remarked that she "is the only personage who does not come evidently from dreamland; and she, I think, represents that lurking skepticism, that sense of unreality, of which we are often conscious, amid the most vivid phantasmagoria of a dream." (RE 10:396) That is, he supposed that some element of waking consciousness accompanies dreams and submits them to rational judgment; just as he thought that a dreamlike aspect was often present in waking experience enhancing its meaning.

He always mistrusted supposed direct revelations from the spiritual world, and took them to be projections from the dreamer's unconscious. He tried to discourage Sophia's interest in spiritualism, and said that mesmerism was "a new science" or "an old humbug." (CE 3:5) If mediumistic revelations were from a beyond, the beyond was a psychological undersoul, not a spiritual Oversoul.[4]

IV

Hawthorne's fantasy life was so strong that he had difficulty in maintaining a sane balance between the life within and the life without. "He feared that dreams drew him apart from life into a world of shadow."[5] He wrote, "A dreamer may dwell so long among fantasies, that the things without him will seem as real as those within." (CE 9:427) He thought that he had become "a hermit in the depths of my own mind," (CE 9:311) during the "Haunted Chamber" period of his young manhood; that he was "a man who had wandered out of the real world and got into its shadow, where his troubles, joys, and vicissitudes were of such slight stuff that he hardly knew whether he lived or only dreamed of living." (CE 9:311)

"Although we come to take it for granted, the ability to discriminate between fantasy and fact is one of the most significant of all psychic achievements."[6] For Hawthorne, who said that his "natural propensity was toward Fairy Land," fantasies were abnormally engrossing. Thus he wrote in "Footprints on the Seashore," "I know these girls to be flesh and blood, yet, glancing at them so briefly, they mingle like kindred creatures with the ideal beings in my mind." (CE 9:457–58) This confusion may have been partly a result of his having been at this stage of his young manhood obsessed with fantasies engendered by his puritanically suppressed eroticism; but the tendency to confuse fantasy with reality persisted throughout his life; and it required a strong exercise of judgment to maintain the distinction, especially if retrospection or conditions of atmosphere aided the illusion. Thus, in "The Custom-House," he wrote, "The life of the Custom-House lies like a dream behind me. . . . Soon, likewise, my old native town will loom upon me through the haze of memory . . . as if it were no portion of the real earth, but an overgrown village in cloudland." (CE 1:44) After leaving Brook Farm he wrote that it "already seems like a dream behind me." (RE 9:237) And in *Our Old Home* he wrote of the Liverpool consulship, "All that phase of my life immediately assumed so dreamlike a consistency that I despaired of making it seem solid or tangible to the public." (CE 5:33) Allowing for some degree of exaggeration in such statements, it is still evident that his sense of reality was abnormally weak and his fantasizing unusually strong.

In fact, his fantasy life was so strong that his real life seemed an actualization of a life prefigured in his fantasy. His love letters to Sophia are as much a romance as any other he ever wrote, although more sketchily presented because they were simply a scenario for a romance he was enacting as he wrote it. This was a lifelong romantic drama in three acts. Act I was that of the hero spell-bound, under the influence of the spiteful East Wind, which symbolized for him all adverse external influences. Act II was that in which the hero is released from his enchantment by love, the life-giving touch of the West Wind.[7] Act III was his adventures in the actual world, in which he was always aware that they were essentially symbolic actions, more significant as signs of what he believed in and worked for than as events in the actual world.

NOTES

1. *Beyond Good and Evil,* trans. Marianne Cowan (Chicago: "Gateway Editions," Henry Regnery Co., 1955). 101.

2. *Creative Evolution,* trans. Arthur Mitchell (New York: Henry Holt and Co., 1910), xiii.

3. Rita K. Gollin, *Nathaniel Hawthorne and the Truth of Dreams* (Baton Rouge, LA: Louisiana State Univ. Press, 1979), 142.

4. He was strongly averse to Sophia's dabbling in spiritualism, and admonished her.

> [I] beseech thee to take no part in [these] magnetic miracles. . . . Supposing that this power arises from the transfusion of one spirit into another, it seems to me that the sacredness of an individual is violated by it; there should be an intrusion into thy holy of holies. . . .
>
> . . . I have no faith that people are raised into the seventh heaven, or to any heaven at all, or that they gain any insight into the mysteries of life beyond death, by means of this strange science. Without distrusting that the phenomena which thou tellest me of have really occurred, I think that they are to be accounted for as the result of a physical and material, not of a spiritual, influence. . . . And what delusion can be more lamentable and mischievous, than to mistake the physical and material for the spiritual? (LL 2:62)

He wrote of spiritualists, "These enthusiasts, who adopt such extravagant ideas, appear to me to lack imagination, instead of being misled by it, as they are generally supposed to be." (EN, 154) He thought spiritualism and mesmerism were related phenomena, and was distrustful of both. Mesmerism is considered in *The House of the Seven Gables* as an hereditary faculty of the Maules, who "were half believed to inherit mysterious attributes. . . . Among other good-for-nothing properties and privileges, one was especially assigned to them,—that of exercising an influence over people's dreams." Although he was skeptical about this good-for-nothing privilege, it is a central device of the story; but he concludes, "Modern psychology, it may be, will endeavor to reduce these alleged necromancies within a system, instead of rejecting them as altogether fabulous." (CE 2:26)

Spiritualism is likewise a central affair in *The Blithedale Romance* in the chapters "Zenobia's Legend" and "The Village Hall." Hawthorne writes,

> If these phenomena have not humbug at the bottom, so much the worse for us. What can they indicate, in a spiritual way, except that the soul of man is descending to a lower point than it has ever before reached while incarnate? . . . To hold intercourse with spirits of this order, we must stoop and grovel in some element more vile than earthly dust. These goblins, if they exist at all, are but the shadows of past mortality, outcasts, mere refuse-stuff, adjudged unworthy of the eternal

world, and, on the most favorable supposition, dwindling gradually into nothingness. (CE 3:199)

Hawthorne did, in fact, believe in the possible existence of spirits of
a celestial nature, but disbelieved in the possibility of communicating
with them. In Italy, in a discussion with the sculptor Hiram Powers,

> We reasoned high about other states of being; and I sug-
> gested the possibility that there might be beings inhabiting
> this earth, contemporaneously with us, and close beside us,
> but of whose existence and whereabout we could have no
> perception, nor they of ours, because we are endowed with
> different sets of senses; for certainly it was in God's power to
> create other beings who should communicate with nature by
> innumerable other senses than those few which we possess.
> (RE 10:376)

His skepticism about mesmerism and spiritualism was consistent with
his skepticism about the visionary pretensions of the Transcendentalists. He wrote, "for my part, I am inclined to put faith in what is
tangible." (EN, 374)

  5. Gollin, 63.

  6. Simon O. Lesser, *Fiction and the Unconscious* (New York: Vintage Books, Random House, 1962), 6.

  7. "Thou only hast taught me that I have a heart—thou only hast
thrown a light deep downward, and upward, into my soul. Thou only
hast revealed me to myself. . . . Indeed, we are but shadows—we are
not endowed with real life, and all that seems most real about us is but
the thinnest substance of a dream—till the heart is touched. That
touch creates us—then we begin to be—thereby we are beings of
reality, and inheritors of eternity." (LL 1:225) For discussion of the
East Wind / West Wind symbolism, see pp. 155–56 below.

CHAPTER

TEN

The Loom of Fiction

I

THE MUSING SPIRIT

Hawthorne's formula for gestation of an imaginative work resembled the Wordsworthian process of emotion recollected in tranquility:

> In youth, perhaps, it is good for the observer to run about the earth—to leave the track of his footsteps far and wide—to mingle himself with the action of numberless vicissitudes; and, finally, in some calm solitude, to feed his musing spirit on all that he has seen and felt. (CE 9:205)

This ruminative process of conversion of experience into usable material for his imagination to work on was apparently a deep psychological assimilation. He said, "I am slow to feel—slow, I suppose, to comprehend; and, like the anaconda, I need to lubricate any object a great deal, before I can swallow it and actually make it my own." (EN, 182) "By long brooding over our recollections, we subtilize them into something akin to imaginary stuff, and hardly capable of being distinguished from it." (CE 3:104–5)

For this stage of lubrication and musing he needed to be "abstracted." (LL 2:49) He said that "the sense of perfect seclusion . . . has always been essential to my power of producing anything." (LL 2:49) "I need monotony . . . and an eventless exterior life, before I can live the life within." (RE 10:311) In

1840, when his days were spent in measuring coal and salt in the Boston Custom House, he wrote,

> How inestimable are the quiet hours of a busy man—especially when that man has no native impulse to keep him busy, but is continually forced to do battle with his own nature, which yearns for seclusion . . . and freedom to think, and dream, and feel. (LL 1:213–14)

His imaginative capability was often suspended by external circumstances that compelled his attention so insistently that he could not live the life within. Sometimes these were invigorating and delightful experiences that gave him a refreshed sense of participation in the system of life and were a seedtime for his soul. Such were his fluvial excursions with Ellery Channing and Thoreau while he was living in the Old Manse, his pleasure in working in the garden there, and above all his enjoyment of the burgeoning of nature in the spring, the lushness of summer, and the mist and mellow fruitfulness of autumn.

In the summer of 1843, while the Hawthornes were living out the idyll of the first year of their marriage in the Old Manse, Sophia wrote to a friend, "As he naturally hates to produce, it becomes a great trial when all outward things are demanding his presence." And he wrote, in "Buds and Bird Voices," of how springtime in the Old Manse enticed him:

> [F]orth into infinite space fly the innumerable forms of thought and fancy that have kept me company in the retirement of this little chamber during the sluggish lapse of wintry weather; visions, gay, grotesque, and sad; pictures of real life, tinted with Nature's homely gray and russet; scenes in dreamland bedizened with rainbow hues which faded before they were well laid on, all these vanish now, and leave me to mould a fresh existence out of sunshine. (CE 10:148)

More often, however, than these invigorating and eventually fruitful intervals when he was drinking pure organic pleasure from nature, he was so much depressed by anxieties about his personal affairs or so engaged with uncongenial work that he was unable to write.

> When the heart is full of care, or the mind much occupied, the summer, and the sunshine, and the moonlight, are but a gleam and glimmer—a vague dream, which does not come within us,

but only makes itself imperfectly perceptible without. (CE 8:252)

Thus, in 1839, while he was working in the Boston Custom House, he wrote to Sophia that

> my thoughts sometimes wander back to literature, and I have momentary impulses to write stories. But this will not be, at present. The utmost that I can hope to do, will be to portray some of the characteristics of the life which I am now living, and of the people with whom I am brought into contact, for future use. (LL 1:81)

Even this he found seldom possible: "My fancy is rendered so torpid by my ungenial way of life, that I cannot sketch off the scenes and portraits that interest me." (LL 1:197–98) "Never was I so stupid as to-night;—and yet it is not exactly stupidity, either, for my fancy is bright enough, only it has, just at this time, no command of external symbols." (LL 1:110)

Later, at Brook Farm, he complained, "My mind will not be abstracted. I must observe, and think, and feel, and content myself with catching glimpses of things which may be wrought hereafter." (LL 2:49)

In the Custom-House sketch introductory to *The Scarlet Letter* he recorded that while he was Surveyor of Customs at Salem his "wretched numbness" of imagination was unrelieved even by "the invigorating charm of Nature, which used to give such freshness and activity of thought, the moment that I stepped across the threshold of the Old Manse."

> I cared not, at this period, for books; they were apart from me. Nature,—except it were human nature,—the nature that is developed in earth and sky, was, in one sense, hidden from me; and all the imaginative delight, wherewith it had been spiritualized, passed away out of my mind. A gift, a faculty, if it had not departed, was suspended and inanimate within me. (CE 1:26)

> It was a folly, with the materiality of this daily life pressing so intrusively upon me, to attempt to fling myself back into another age; to insist upon creating the semblance of a world out of airy matter, when, at every moment, the impalpable beauty of my soap-bubble was broken by the rude contact of actual circumstance. (CE 1:37)

He felt the same torpor during his Liverpool consulship; but wrote hopefully to his friend and publisher William Ticknor near the end of his term there: "In Italy, perhaps, I shall begin to be a literary man again; for I feel some symptoms already." (LT 2:42) And later, in *Our Old Home*, he utilized sketches from an English journal that he said were

> intended for the side-scenes, and backgrounds, and exterior adornment, of a work of fiction [evidently one of the "abortive romances"] of which the plan had imperfectly developed itself in my mind, and into which I ambitiously proposed to convey more of various modes of truth than I could have grasped by a direct effort. . . . [But] the present, the Immediate, the Actual, has proved too potent for me. It takes away not only my scanty faculty, but even my desire for imaginative composition." (CE 5:3–4)

II

NECESSARY EXTERNAL CONDITIONS

Certain external conditions were requisite or favorable for Hawthorne's gestation of imaginative work. Most important were phenomena of light and shadow.[1] Changes of light not only brought out changed saliences in the visible scene, but also prompted corresponding ideas to emerge into consciousness.

Ideas thus emerging into distinctness are what he called, in "The Wives of the Dead," "picturesque effects" (CE 11:196)— material that had reached the condition of assimilation where it was utilizable for romance. A passage in this tale is an analogue of this stage of imaginative preparation. It describes forms starting out of obscurity in the light of a lantern carried through darkness. The lantern is equivalent to the awakened and directed attention of the author, and the surrounding shadow in which indistinct forms are brought into visibility and prominence by its light is equivalent to the medley of inchoate stuff to which the author must give form. "His lantern glimmered along the street, bringing into view indistinct shapes of things, like order glimmering through chaos, or memory roaming over the past." (CE 11:196)

A more explicit figure for the way the "light of the mind" brings figures out of obscurity is in one of Hawthorne's American notes:

> How exceeding bright looks the sunshine, casually reflected from a looking-glass into a gloomy region of the chamber, distinctly marking out the figures and colors of the paper hangings, which are scarcely seen elsewhere. It is like the light of the mind thrown on an obscure subject. (CE 8:157)

He regularly used the conventional Romantic metaphor of a mirror to represent the reflective action of the imagination, but not to mirror reality; rather, to give the illusion of receiving ideas of things stripped of "the stony excrescence of prose." His mirror figure, like Coleridge's, stresses the passive element of imagination. Coleridge wrote, "In our perceptions we seem to ourselves merely passive to an external power, whether as a mirror reflecting the landscape, or as a blank canvas on which some unknown hand paints it."[2] In "The Haunted Mind" Hawthorne wrote of the condition of vision "when the mind has a passive sensibility, but no active strength; when the imagination is a mirror, imparting vividness to all ideas, without the power of selecting or controlling them." (CE 9:306)

As daylight, "ordinary noontide visibility," provides "visions that seem real" instead of the imaginative daydreaming requisite to romance, it was necessary to exclude it to allow images from the realm of reverie and dream to emerge and be merged with enough of graphic specification to achieve the moral picturesque effect. "Set loose by glimmering light, the mind can move through the dream or daydream to make juxtapositions and identifications not bounded by ordinary logic or the limitations of time or space."[3]

An agency for transforming vision was moonlight. "The magic of moonlight" always means in Hawthorne's fiction a significant change in the apparent aspects of reality. There are transforming changes of light, usually moonlight scenes, in all of his major romances and in many of his tales. In "My Kinsman, Major Molineux," he wrote of the transforming effect of moonlight, "creating, like the imaginative power, a beautiful strangeness in familiar objects," to give "something of romance to a

scene, that might not have possessed it in the light of day." (CE
11:221)

The conception is the same as Coleridge's:

> The moonshine, the imaginative poesy of Nature, spreads its
> soft shadowy charm over all, conceals distances, magnifies
> heights, and modifies relations; and fills up vacuities with its own
> whiteness, counterfeiting solid substance; and where the dense
> shadows lie, makes solidity imitate hollowness; and gives all ob-
> jects a visionary hue and softness. Interpret the moonlight and
> shadows as the peculiar genius and sensibility of the individual's
> own spirit.[4]

Hawthorne's often-quoted account of the conditions effectual in setting his imagination to work, in the "Custom-House"
introduction to *The Scarlet Letter*, is strikingly similar:

> Moonlight, in a familiar room, falling so white upon the carpet,
> and showing all its figures so distinctly,—making every object
> visible, yet so unlike a morning or noontide visibility,—is a me-
> dium the most suitable for a romance-writer to get acquainted
> with his illusive guests. . . . —all these details, so completely
> seen, are so spiritualized by the unusual light, that they seem to
> lose their actual substance, and become things of intellect. Noth-
> ing is too small or trifling to undergo this change, and acquire
> dignity thereby. . . . —whatever, in a word, has been used or
> played with, during the day, is now invested with a quality of
> strangeness and remoteness, though still almost as vividly present
> as by daylight. Thus, therefore, the floor of our familiar room has
> become a neutral territory, somewhere between the real world
> and fairy-land, where the Actual and the Imaginary may meet,
> and each imbue itself with the nature of the other. (CE 1:35–36)

It was essential to Hawthorne's imagination that the actual
and imaginary should thus fuse. The further complex description of conditions of visibility suitable for a romance-writer specifies both terms:

> The somewhat dim coal-fire throws its unobtrusive tinge
> throughout the room, . . . This warmer light mingles itself with
> the cold spirituality of the moonbeams, and communicates, as it
> were, a heart and sensibilities of human tenderness to the forms
> which fancy summons up. Glancing at the looking-glass, we be-
> hold—deep within its haunted verge—the smouldering glow the
> the half-extinguished anthracite, the white moonlight on the

floor, and a repetition of the gleam and shadow of the picture, with one remove farther from the actual, and nearer to the imaginative. Then, at such an hour, if a man, sitting alone, cannot dream strange things, and make them look like truth, he need never try to write romances. (CE 1:36)

This passage specifies all the elements of Hawthorne's imaginative requirements: solitude, magical light, a mirrored reflection that brings one nearer to the ideal, the inducing of a dreamlike state, and making strange things look like truth.

III

ACTIVE STRENGTH

The condition of vision "when the mind has a passive sensibility, but no active strength" (CE 9:306) furnishes materials for the romancer, but these must be given construction by another operation of the imagination. Active strength, the power of selecting and controlling ideas, is required to compose indistinct shapes of things into moral picturesque dramas. Even when the imagination is bright and reflective, what it registers can be utilized only by an accompanying creative energy and intention:

A projected tale . . . , in order to produce a sense of reality in a reader's mind, must be conceived with such proportionate strength by the author as to seem, in the glow of fancy, more like truth, past, present, or to come, than purely fiction. (CE 9:225)

"It is requisite for the ideal artist to possess a force of character that seems hardly compatible with its delicacy." (CE 10:454) The power of selecting and controlling his fancies must be strong or they will control him rather than he them. Hawthorne wrote of Clifford, in *The House of the Seven Gables*, that "his fancy—reviving faster than his will and judgment, and always stronger than they—created shapes of loveliness that were symbolic of his native character, and now and then a stern and dreadful shape that typified his fate." (CE 2:154)

"The descent is easy from ambiguity to meaninglessness," as Santayana says.[5] The author's power of selecting and controlling ideas that his passive sensibility entertains is indispensable to literary creation. The task of the writer is to transform what is subjective, nebulous, and private into something objective, formal, and public. He must predicate something of the indeterminate materials experienced and imagined; "we can only see beauty in so far as we introduce form." (Santayana, 146)

Here Santayana points to what he regards as equally necessary gifts of the artist. He is superior to the layman in his greater awareness of the interest attaching to indistinct shapes of things.

> It is the free exercise of the activity of apperception that gives so peculiar an interest to the vague, the incoherent, the variously interpretable. The more this effect is appealed to, the greater the wealth of thought is presumed in the observer, and the less mastery is displayed by the artist. A poor and literal mind cannot enjoy the opportunities for reverie and construction given by the stimulus of indeterminate objects. (Santayana, 131)

But, although the artist must be able to perceive and render experience in its rich complexity, it will not do for him to leave it vague and incoherent. His mastery is displayed in giving airy nothings a local habitation and a name. "[T]he artist who is not artist enough, who has too many irrepressible talents and too little technical skill, is sure to float in the region of the indeterminate. He sketches and never paints; he hints and never expresses; he stimulates and never informs." (Santayana, 131) This criticism might reasonably be made of some passages of Hawthorne's fiction.

The imaginative writer is thus a creator of meaning and reality. Ernst Cassirer says, in *An Essay on Man*, that "like all other symbolic forms art is not the mere representation of a ready-made, given reality. It is one of the ways leading to an objective view of things and human life. It is not an imitation but a discovery of reality."[6] "Fiction is for finding things out," Frank Kermode says.[7] "It is not that we are connoisseurs of chaos, but that we are surrounded by it, and equipped for coexistence with it only by our fictive powers." (Kermode, 64) He says also that "literary fictions belong to Vaihinger's category of 'the consciously false'." (The reference is to Hans Vaihinger's *The Philosophy of As If*.) "I see no reason why we cannot apply to literary fictions what Vaihinger says of fictions in general, that they are mental structures. The psyche weaves this or that thought out of itself; for the mind is inventive; under the compulsion of necessity, stimulated by the outer world, it discovers the store of contrivances hidden in itself." (Kermode, 40) It is in this sense that Kermode says that fictions are for finding things out; what they find out is not the form of the world but the form-giving possibilities of the mind.

IV

WORKING FROM THE INNERMOST GERM

When the processes preliminary to composition had been completed—when sensibility and recollection had provided him with utilizable "picturesque effects," (CE 11:196) when the requisite external conditions were present, and when active strength enabled him to select and control materials for his fiction,—Hawthorne was ready for the actual task of composition.

His theory of composition was what has been called the "organic theory." Roy R. Male has noted that he agreed with Melville and the Transcendentalists

> that the full complexity of human life is best approached through metaphor, symbol, and myth; that mechanical, mathematical, and static concepts are incapable of grasping the rhythmic unity of living things; and that man and his artistic achievements must be considered as an integral part of this unity.[8]

This statement puts succinctly the entirety of Hawthorne's literary theory; but the part that especially concerns his notion of the process of actual composition is that he believed that "artistic achievements must be considered as an integral part" of "the rhythmic unity of living things." Wordsworth wrote that beauty, an expression of the ideal, whether in nature or in art, "Comes not by casting in a formal mould, / But from its own divine vitality." This was Hawthorne's belief as well, and for him the moment of inspired creativity came when his individual effort merged with the rhythmic unity of living things. He wrote, "The reason of the infinite superiority of Nature's work over man's is, that the former works from the innermost germ, while the latter works merely superficially." (CE 8:158)

So he frequently declared his admiration of achieved works of art in organic similes. He wrote that "the multitudinous gray pinnacles and towers" of Salisbury Cathedral "ascend toward Heaven with a kind of natural beauty, not as if man had contrived them, just as the spires of a tuft of grass do." (EN, 356) Westminster Hall is a "great stone flower, growing out of the institutions of England." The sculpture in Lincoln Cathedral is so exquisite "that you might think it, not art, but petrified nature." (EN, 469) Thatched cottages near Leamington "seem like something made by nature, or put together by instinct, like birds' nests." (EN, 122) The town of Assisi in Italy "seems like a stony growth out of the hillside. . . . How came that flower to grow among these wild mountains?" (RE 10:244) In Perugia he wrote, "On another side of the square rose the medieval front of the cathedral, where the imagination of a Gothic architect had long ago flowered out indestructibly." (CE 4:312)

Literary creation was for him likewise a process of germination, ripening and flowering. He had first to identify amidst the medley of incipient ideas in his haunted mind a viable germ. He wrote in his notes. "[S]ometimes I had the glimmering of an idea, and endeavored to materialize it in words." (CE 8:370) And again, "This forenoon, I . . . caught an idea by the tail, which I intend to hold fast, though it struggles to get free." (CE 8:373) He wrote of the illegible characters of an ancient manuscript in *Septimius Felton* that they were without meaning, "like the misty and undefined germs of thought as they exist in our minds before clothing themselves in words." (RE 11:336)

The misty and undefined germs of thought had to harden into definition and semblance of fact to be usable, and "hard and dusty facts" (CE 4:46) had to blur their definition and reduce their substance and opacity, before the two kinds of material could interfuse and blend into the stuff of romance. When this had happened, when the Actual and the Imaginary had combined so that each could imbue itself with the nature of the other, he could undertake the conscious and rationally directed process of clothing his ideas with words.

When he was a weigher in the Boston Custom House, Hawthorne wrote to his prospective bride Sophia Peabody,

> I sometimes wish that thou couldst be with [me] on board my salt vessels and colliers; because there are many things of which

thou mightst make such pretty descriptions; and in future years, when thy husband is again busy at the loom of fiction, he would weave in these little pictures. (LL 1:197–98)

In composing his fictions he drew upon a *fond* of materials consisting of fancies, thoughts, reveries, and dreams; and of factual observations, impressions, and recollections of things read about, seen and experienced, all suspended in a kind of medley of incipient forms in his conscious and preconscious mind. Only a slight portion of this material was available to be organized into fiction:

> And now how narrow, scanty, and meagre, is this record of observation, compared with the immensity that was to be observed within the bounds that I had prescribed to myself. How shallow and small a stream of thought, too,—compared with the broad tide of dim emotions, ideas, associations, which are flowing through the haunted regions of imagination, intellect, and sentiment, sometimes excited by what was around me, sometimes with no perceptible connection with them. (CE 8:250)

Although at this stage the fancy teems with indistinct shapes of things, the faculties of will and intellect must act to define and develop them—will to choose and urge development of a leading idea or dominant impression, intellect to judge and select congruent materials. It was the mind's eye, not the optic nerve, that he hoped to activate, and suggestion was more effectual for this than graphic detail. His "discerning and discriminating eye" focused more on truth of impression than on surface details:

> Correct outlines avail little or nothing, though truth of coloring may be somewhat more efficacious. Impressions, however, states of mind produced by interesting and remarkable objects, these, if truthfully and vividly recorded, may work a genuine effect, and, though but the result of what we see, go further toward representing the actual scene than any direct effort to paint it. Give the emotions that cluster about it, and, without being able to analyze the spell by which it is summoned up, you get something like a simulacre of the object in the midst of them. (CE 5:259)

At this point in the process of composition, when it has passed through an initial dreamlike stage and the secondary stage of conscious clothing of his germinal ideas in words, the author's imagination had to be excited or "kindled" in a manner that seemed to him to be the addition of an external power, to quicken and enliven his characters and animate his scenes. It was at this point that the author's imagination began to operate as an integral part of the rhythmic unity of living things. Intellect and will do not suffice for romantic creation, although they would for such fiction as Trollope's, which Hawthorne admired and sometimes wished he were disposed to write. At this stage of tentative composition, the author had to be seized and assisted by what he considered to be a creative power beyond himself, or his productions would be like the lifeless work of the woodcarver in "Drowne's Wooden Image" before he received "the divine, the life-giving touch." (CE 10:311)

The author had to initiate the process of creation, and toil patiently and hopefully until the moment of inspiration came. He wrote, "Sometimes my ideas were like precious stones, requiring toil to dig them up, and care to polish and brighten them; but often a delicious stream of thought would gush out upon the page at once, like water sparkling up on the desert." (CE 11:174) While the Hawthornes were living in the Old Manse, Sophia wrote to her mother,

> I can comprehend the delicacy and tricksiness of his mood when he is evolving a work of art. He waits upon the light in such a purely simple way that I do not wonder at the perfection of each of his stories. Of several sketches, first one and then another came up to be clothed upon with language, after their own will and pleasure. It is real inspiration, and few are reverent and patient enough to wait for it as he does. [9]

The artists in his fictions were similarly inspired in their best creations: the sculptor Kenyon in *The Marble Faun* said of his statue of Cleopatra

> It is the concretion of a good deal of thought, emotion, and toil of brain and hand. . . . But I know not how it came about at last. I kindled a great fire within my mind, and threw in the material, . . . and, in the midmost heat, uprose Cleopatra, as you see her. (CE 4:127)

Once he had seized his idea, the germinative process began. It could be assisted but not hastened by conscious thought. He wrote to Ticknor from Liverpool in 1855, "There is the germ of a new romance ripening in my mind, which will be all the better for ripening slowly." (LT 1:75) The most striking example of this germinating process in Hawthorne's fiction is the writing of *The Scarlet Letter*. The proto-germ of the romance was probably a passage in Felt's *Annals of Salem* describing the enforced wearing of such a letter as punishment for adultery. This prompted his imagination of an actual letter,

> a certain affair of fine red cloth, much worn and faded. There were traces about it of gold embroidery, which, however, was greatly frayed and defaced; so that none, or very little, of the glitter was left. It had been wrought, as was easy to perceive, with wonderful skill of needlework. . . . This rag of scarlet cloth, . . . on careful examintion, assumed the shape of a letter. It was the capital letter A. . . . It had been intended, there could be no doubt, as an ornamental article of dress; but how it was worn, or what rank, honor, or dignity, in by-past times, were signified by it (so evanescent are the fashions of the world in these particulars) I saw little hope of solving. . . . Certainly, there seemed to be some deep meaning in it, most worthy of interpretation, and which, as it were, streamed forth from the mystic symbol, subtly communicating itself to my sensibilities, but evading the analysis of my mind. (CE 1:31)

This fictive letter, imagined from the hint in Felt's *Annals*, was richly invested with historical fact and appropriate fiction in the romance. Charles Feidelson says, "*A*, a single letter, the most indeterminate of all symbols, the first letter of the alphabet, the beginning of all communication, Hester's emblem represents a potential point of coherence within a manifold historical experience."[10] In the same parchment-wrapped package tied with faded red tape that Hawthorne fabled as found in a heap of rubbish in a corner of his office in the Salem Custom-House were imaginary documents written by his colonial predecessor, Mr. Surveyor Pue, giving "a reasonably complete explanation of the whole affair." "It should be borne carefully in mind, that the main facts of the story are authorized and authenticated by the document of Mr. Surveyor Pue." (CE 1:32) "I have allowed myself . . . nearly or altogether as much license as if the facts had been entirely of my own invention. What I contend for is the authenticity of the outline." (CE 1:33)

It cannot be known when the proto-germ in Felt's *Annals* began to germinate. The earliest record of his borrowing of Felt's *Annals* from the Salem Athenaeum Library is dated September 21, 1833. An entry in the American Notebooks eleven years later, in the summer of 1844, shows that the misty and undefined proto-germ lodged in his mind by the reading of Felt had taken on definition enough to become viable: "The life of a woman, who by the old colony law, was condemned always to wear the letter *A*, sewed on her garment, in token of her having committed adultery." (CE 8:254) His term as Surveyor in the Salem Custom-House from April 1846 to June 1849 must have had much to do with the ripening process. It is almost a certainty that he attempted to imagine, and a possibility that he attempted to write, the romance during this period, for he again consulted Felt's *Annals* in January 1849, more than five months before his dismissal from the Surveyorship. It is therefore probable that a passage in the "Custom-House" refers to such an abortive attempt:

> My imagination was a tarnished mirror. It would not reflect, or only with miserable dimness, the figures with which I did my best to people it. The characters would not be warmed and rendered malleable, by any heat that I could kindle at my intellectual forge. They would take neither the glow of passion nor the tenderness of sentiment, but retained all the rigidity of dead corpses, and stared me in the face with a fixed and ghastly grin of contemptuous defiance. "What have you to do with us?" that expression seemed to say. "The little power you might once have possessed over the tribe of unrealities is gone! You have bartered it for a pittance of the public gold." (CE 1:34)

In *Yesterdays With Authors* Hawthorne's publisher, James T. Fields, tells that when he visited Hawthorne in Salem in "the winter of 1849, after he had been ejected from the custom-house," he found him "in a very desponding mood." When by an inspired guess Fields had surprised the admission that Hawthorne had a manuscript, written during the autumn following his dismissal, "hidden away somewhere," he was allowed to take it back to Boston to read. "On my way up to Boston I read the germ of 'The Scarlet Letter'; before I slept that night I wrote him a note aglow with the marvellous story he had put into my hands." It is clear from Fields' account that the romance must then have been in a transition phase, as he refers to it as "the germ of 'The Scarlet Letter,' " and says, "At my suggestion he . . . altered the plan of the story." This must have been a considerable alteration, for he had intended to make it only "one of several short stories," but "I persuaded him, after reading the first chapters of the story, to elaborate it, and publish it as a separate work."[11] This encouragement was the spark needed to kindle Hawthorne's imagination, for by early February of 1850 he had finished writing *The Scarlet Letter.*

All this is an oftener than twice-told tale, but its repetition here best illustrates the protracted process of Hawthorne's composition.

V

CREATIVE WORDS

Such subjectively originated fiction as Hawthorne's requires a suitable conception of the nature and function of language, of names of things. The reference of words and figures is not to things in the world but to things in the mind. As Ernst Cassirer says,

> The name of an object lays no claim upon its nature; it is not intended to be *physei on*, to give us the truth of a thing. The function of a name is always limited to emphasizing a certain aspect of a thing, and it is precisely this restriction and limitation upon which the value of the name depends. . . . In the act of determination we select, out of the multiplicity and diffusion of our sense data, certain fixed centers of perception.[12]

He says that the primitive use of language was to try to command nature—to use language as magic. But:

> When man first began to realize that . . . nature was inexorable not because it was reluctant to fulfill his demands but because it did not understand his language his discovery must have come to him as a shock. . . . All hope of subduing nature by the magic word had been frustrated. But as a result man began to see the relation between language and reality in a different light. The magic function of the word was eclipsed and replaced by its semantic function. (144)

That is, by its fictive and creative function. Names give definition to our "necessary fictions." As William James says, "By these *whats* we apperceive all our *thises*."[13] " 'Things' have no

other nature than thoughts have, and we know of no things that
are not given to somebody's experience." (154) Denomination
accomplishes the condensation and concentration that Cassirer
says are implied in any work of art.

The "power of selecting and controlling" (CE 9:306) the
ideas that throng the haunted mind of the artist, as Hawthorne
says, is exercised through such creative naming; but the uncertainty and tentativeness of the names he bestows on his characters suggest how partial and elusive are the identities thus
indicated. Many have no surnames and have given names
suggestive of a particular historical and social setting, as Dorcas
and Josiah. Some have generic names: Goodman Brown. Some
have punning names that call attention to the fact that they are
personified ideas: Sylph Etherege (ether edge). Some have
names that show them to be embodiments of a particular trait:
Gathergold. Some have symbolic names: Pearl. Some have
names that recall protonyms with significant associations:
Phoebe. Some have uncertain or possibly various names, such
as the bewildered stripling in "My Kinsman, Major Molineux,"
"one of whose names was Robin." (CE 11:209) Some have assumed names that are not their true ones; in *The Scarlet Letter*
Roger Chillingworth's true name is never revealed; he has assumed the name Chillingworth to hide his identity. In *The House
of the Seven Gables* Holgrave's name is really Maule, and Phoebe
is "not a Pyncheon." (CE 2:74) In *The Blithedale Romance* Zenobia's name is merely "her public name." (CE 3:8)

The ambiguity about names and thus about identities is of
considerable importance in some of Hawthorne's fiction. In *The
Blithedale Romance* Zenobia's father, "a man whom we shall call
Fauntleroy; a man of wealth, and magnificent tastes, and prodi-
gal expenditure," (CE 3:182) after the loss of his wealth and
after social disgrace, took the name of Moodie, "skulked in
corners, and crept about in a sort of noonday twilight, making
himself gray and misty, at all hours, with a morbid intolerance
of sunshine." (CE 3:185) In this changed phase of character and
identity he made a second marriage "to a forlorn, meek-spirited,
feeble young woman, a seamstress," (CE 3:185) who became
the mother of pale wraithlike Priscilla. In *The Marble Faun* the
true identity and history of the young woman "whom her friends
called Miriam" (CE 4:7) are never fully revealed.

> She resembled one of those images of light, which conjurors evoke and cause to shine before us, in apparent tangibility, only an arm's length beyond our grasp; we make a step in advance, expecting to seize the illusion, but find it still precisely so far beyond our reach. (CE 4:21)

She "was plucked up out of a mystery, and had its roots still clinging to her. She was a beautiful and attractive woman, but based, as it were, upon a cloud, and all surrounded with misty substance, so that the result was to render her spritelike in her most ordinary manifestations." (CE 4:23) The supposed revelation of her name and identity near the conclusion of the romance is in fact no revelation at all.

> She revealed a name . . . that, only a few years before, had been familiar to the world, in connection with a mysterious and terrible event. The reader—if he think it worth while to recall some of the strange incidents which have been talked of, and forgotten, within no long time past—will remember Miriam's name. (CE 4:430)

This shiftiness about names indicates that a too definite label hides the full and variable reality of a person; also, as in Miriam's case, with the public invited to make their own identifications according to whatever recent strange incidents they may chance to recall, that traits are not uniquely individual and fixed to a particular name, but are so universal that personal names are too restricting and limiting in a fiction in which ideas are intended to be more interesting and real than personalities.

Hawthorne frequently lamented the inadequacy of language to convey the amplitude and profundity of meaning that he hoped to suggest in his fiction. There are "subtle intimations for which language has no shape." (CE 11:360) Language is "but little better than the croak and cackle of fowls, and other utterances of the brute creation." (CE 8:294) In fact, he sometimes suggested that there was a sort of ur-language that preceded the development of verbal communication of which vestiges still remained as a resource of primitive and unsophisticated persons. Thus the faunlike Donatello, in *The Marble Faun* could converse with animals: "there was a charm—a voice, a murmur, a kind of chant—by which he called the woodland inhabitants, the furry people and the feathered people, in a language that they seemed to understand." He uttered "a sort of modulated breath, wild, rude, yet harmonious." (CE 4:247)

> The sound was of a murmurous character, soft, attractive, persuasive, friendly. The sculptor fancied that such might have been the voice and utterance of the natural man, before the sophistication of the human intellect formed what we now call language. In this broad dialect—broad as the sympathies of nature—the human brother might have spoken to his inarticulate brotherhood that prowl the woods, or soar upon the wing, and have been intelligible to such an extent as to win their confidence. (CE 4:248)

In this fancy, which anticipates W. H. Hudson's conception of Rima the bird-girl in *Green Mansions*, Hawthorne is perhaps not so much advancing a seriously intended linguistic theory as he is reverting to his favorite idea that man has become too much estranged from the system of nature and retains too little of his primal innocence.

He did, however, evidently believe that just as there are elements of consciousness that cannot emerge into the definiteness of thought, so are there capabilities of vocal communication that convey meanings too deep for words. The voices of Phoebe and Hepzibah in *The House of the Seven Gables* convey meaning in their tones and cadences as well as in the purport of their words. Hawthorne often suggested that the speaking voice communicated more ample and deeper meaning through its tones and cadences than through the denotations of words, which because they were definitive were also restrictive. This theory of language accorded with his assumption of the organic constitution of reality; for tones and cadences spoke, not from and to individual intellectual comprehensions, but through the "rhythmic unity of living things."

Thus in *The Scarlet Letter*, commenting on Dimmesdale's appeal on behalf of Hester in the opening scene,

> The young pastor's voice was tremulously sweet, rich, deep, and broken. The feeling that it so evidently manifested, rather than the direct purport of the words, caused it to vibrate within all hearts, and brought the listeners into one accord of sympathy. (CE 1:67)

And in the climactic confession scene,

> A listener, comprehending nothing of the language in which the preacher spoke, might still have been swayed by the mere tone and cadence. Like all other music, it breathed passion and pathos, and emotions high and tender, in a tongue native to the human heart, however educated. (CE 1:243)

The "indistinguishable words . . . if more distinctly heard, might have been only a grosser medium, and have clogged the spiritual sense." (CE 1:243)

A problem that accompanied every stage of composition for Hawthorne was how to find a language both intelligible and richly suggestive that would express more than "the direct purport of the words." To give his ideas too literal definition would strip them of the aura of suggestion that he thought conveyed their amplest significance. The problem was that touched upon by Coleridge in *Biographia Literaria*:

> The poet must likewise understand and command what Bacon calls the *vestigia communia* of the senses, that latency of all in each, and more especially as by a magical *penna duplex*, the excitement of vision by sound and the exponents of sound. . . . Such may deservedly be called the *creative words* in the world of imagination.[14]

There are many oxymoronic and synesthetic expressions in Hawthorne's work that indicate his intention to suggest the latency of all in each: "glimmering shadows," "gray but transparent evening," "The voice of solitude." He wrote in *The House of the Seven Gables* of croaking voices like Hepzibah's, "The effect is as if the voice had been dyed black." (CE 2:135) In the tale "The Canterbury Pilgrims," he wrote that the poet,

> gave himself up to a sort of vague reverie, which he called thought. Sometimes he watched the moon. . . . Lastly, he looked into the spring, and there the light was mingling with the water. . . . He listened to that most ethereal of sounds, the song of crickets, coming in full choir upon the wind, and fancied that, if moonlight could be heard, it would sound just like that. (CE 11:125)

To convey as many "subtle intimations" (CE 11:360) as possible in language, Hawthorne necessarily had recourse to symbolism. "An idea, in the highest sense of that word, cannot be conveyed but by a symbol," as Coleridge said.[15] One of Coleridge's notebook entries suggests that the symbol is an expressive link between innate idea and transcendent truth:

> In looking at objects in Nature while I am thinking, as at yonder moon dim-glimmering through the dewy window-pane, I seem rather to be seeking, as it were *asking* for, a symbolical language for something that already and forever exists, than observing anything new. Even when the latter is the case, yet still I have an obscure feeling as if that new phenomena were the dim awakening of a forgotten or hidden truth of my inner nature.[16]

One of Hawthorne's characters says, "You know that I can never separate the idea from the symbol in which it manifests itself." (RE 12:67) That the idea "manifests itself" indicates that for Hawthorne it may be induced but is not produced by thought.

Simon O. Lesser has discussed the symbolic language of fiction: "For the most part the images register upon our minds *as images*. . . . Untranscribed [into explicit statement], the images are not only understandable, but possessed of more vividness and immediacy than is usually attached to words."[17] "In some instances, . . . fiction is *inescapably* non-discursive; the meaning or full meaning cannot be reduced to conceptual terms." (157) Lesser says that the distinction between the terms *image* and *symbol* is mistaken:

> When the images of fiction have great richness of meaning, it is customary to refer to them as symbols. By now it should be apparent that there is no sharp line of demarcation between a symbol and any other image. Though the designation of certain images of fiction as symbols represents a partial recognition of a highly significant resource of fiction, it is not without unfortunate consequences. It has tended to distract attention from the fact that *in general* the language of fiction functions symbolically. (157–58)

Hawthorne's deliberate use of suggestive but inconclusive and symbolic language caused wrongheaded readers to complain of the ambiguity of his fictions. Apparently in order to appease such readers, he tried in his four major romances to combine allegory with symbolism. The allegory was to satisfy their demand for explicable meaning, and the symbolism, the more significant element, to exercise the imagination. Charles Feidelson says that "the symbolistic and allegorical patterns in Hawthorne's books reach quite different conclusions; or, rather, the symbolism leads to an inconclusive luxuriance of meaning, while allegory imposes the pat moral and the simplified character."[18] This is true. The deprecatory tone of his statement in the preface to *The House of the Seven Gables* "that the Author has provided himself with a moral" because it is the fashion to do so plainly implies a distaste for such explicitness. When "romances do really teach anything, or produce any effective operation, it is usually through a far more subtle process than the ostensible one." (CE 2:2)

He deplored the necessity of adding an explanatory paragraph to *The Marble Faun*. "It was one of the essential excellencies that it left matters in a fog." He said that he explained "such incidents and passages as may have been left too much in the dark" only "reluctantly, because the necessity makes him sensible that he can have succeeded but imperfectly, at best, in throwing about this Romance the kind of atmosphere essential to the effect at which he aimed." (CE 4:463) He wrote to a critic who had complained of the ambiguity of the plot,

> As for what you say of the plot I do not agree that it has been left in an imperfect state. The characters come out of obscurity and vanish into it again, like the figures on the slide of a magic lantern; but, in their transit, they have served my purpose, and shown all that it was essential for them to reveal. Anything further, if you consider it rightly, would be an impertinence on the author's part toward the reader.

Given Hawthorne's sense of a transcendental "beyond" that makes actual happenings so mysterious, the business of the artist is not to solve riddles but to propound them and to dramatize possible solutions. Seekers frequently confront each other in respect to a common focus of attention on an object or situation, each offering a different solution from the others to the problem it poses, but none certified by the author.

> What our criticism of Hawthorne needs is a better appreciation of the *confidence* of Hawthorne's art, an art neither facile nor

optimistic, but able to reconcile its tendency toward obvious explicitness—the simple ideas—with the toleration of a wide range of uncertainties. In the combining of these, Hawthorne's fiction finds its maturity and its complexity.[19]

NOTES

1. Hawthorne's employment of such effects has been definitively discussed in Richard Harter Fogle's classic study *Hawthorne's Fiction: The Light and the Dark* (Norman, OK: Univ. of Oklahoma Press, 1952).

2. *Biographia Literaria*, ed. J. Shawcross (Oxford: Oxford Univ. Press, 1907), 1, 5. 88.

3. Rita K. Gollin, *Nathaniel Hawthorne and the Truth of Dreams* (Baton Rouge, LA: Louisiana State Univ. Press, 1979), 217. Subsequent references to Gollin, parenthetically identified in the text, are to this work.

4. *Biographia Literaria* (Princeton, NJ: Princeton Univ. Press, 1983), 1: 156.

5. *The Sense of Beauty* (New York: Dover Publications, 1955), 144. Subsequent references to Santayana, parenthetically identified in the text, are to this work.

6. (Garden City, NY: Doubleday Anchor Books, Doubleday & Company, 1953), 183.

7. *The Sense of an Ending* (New York: "Galaxy Books," Oxford Univ. Press, 1970), 39. Subsequent references to Kermode, parenthetically identified in the text, are to this work.

8. *Hawthorne's Tragic Vision* (New York: Norton Library, 1964), 20–21.

9. Rose Hawthorne Lathrop, *Memories of Hawthorne* (Boston and New York: Houghton Mifflin, 1897), 70–71.

10. "The Scarlet Letter," in *Hawthorne Centenary Essays* ed. Roy Harvey Pearce (Columbus, OH: Ohio State Univ. Press, 1964), 37.

11. (Boston: J. R. Osgood, 1879), 49, 50, 51.

12. *An Essay on Man*, (Garden City, NY: Doubleday & Company, 1953), 173. Subsequent references to Cassirer, parenthetically identified in the text, are to this work.

13. *Writings of William James*, ed. John J. McDermott (New York: Modern Library, 1967), 235. Subsequent references to James, parenthetically identified in the text, are to this work.

14. ed. J. Shawcross (Oxford: Oxford Univ. Press, 1907), 2, 9. 142.

15. *Ibid.*, 1, 9. 158.

16. *Notebooks*, 14 April, 1805. *Coleridge: Select Poetry and Prose*, ed. Stephen Potter (London: The Nonesuch Press, n.d.), 175.

17. *Fiction and the Unconscious* (New York: Vintage Books, Random House, 1962), 153–54. Subsequent references to Lesser, parenthetically identified in the text, are to this work.

18. *Symbolism and American Literature* (Chicago: Univ. of Chicago Press, 1966), 15.

19. Leo B. Levy, "Hawthorne's Middle Ground," *Studies in Short Fiction* 2 (Fall 1964): 59–60.

Giving Lustre
to Gray Shadows:
Prospero's Potent Art

I

The life of the flitting moment, existing in the antique shell of an
age gone by, has a fascination which we do not find in either
the past or present, taken by themselves.
—The Marble Faun

It was Hawthorne's basic conviction that "the present shapes of human existence are not cast in iron nor hewn in everlasting adamant, but moulded of the vapors that vanish away while the essence flits upward to the Infinite." (CE 10:446) His works are like those of the poet in "The Great Stone Face"—"living images of things which the poet flung out of his mind." (CE 11:45) His images were given life by bringing them into "the white sunshine of actual life," (CE 10:179) and tallying them with present shapes of reality. Thus the Stone Face resembles the living face of Ernest, an identity discerned by a poet; the Marble Faun resembles Donatello, an identity discerned by an artist.

The living idea must be made to show itself "in that narrow strip of sunlight, which we call Now." (CE 9:179) This narrow

Now is not a moment cut off from time and eternity, an instant absolute. "Hawthorne had only one range of vision: to see the past and the present as they met in a timeless continuum which is the heart of man."[1] More exactly, he saw the past and future as they met in a timeless present in the heart of man: "How wonderful, that this our narrow foothold of the Present should hold its own so constantly, and, while every moment changing, should still be like a rock betwixt the encountering tides of the long Past and the infinite To-come!" (CE 4:411)

This narrow foothold of the Present is timeless in that all time enters the present moment, as in the perception of "a certain remarkable unity" in "the long lapse of mortal life," (CE 2:5) as he remarked in *The House of the Seven Gables*, which instills all time into the Now. Or, paradoxically, it is timeless in that the whole span of the long Past and the infinite To-come starts into life, annihilating the distinct reality of the present moment and of all moments in the whole succession that constitutes time, as when Hawthorne felt, in Rome, "a vague sense of ponderous remembrances; a perception of such weight and density in a bygone life, . . . that the present moment is pressed down or crowded out." (CE 4:6)

In both these modes of experiencing the timelessness of Now, reality is diffused over the entire mindscape, so that distinction of any other moment than one all-comprehending instant, or of any one moment in a succession of moments as living while all others are dead or yet to be born, becomes impossible. Such "timelessness" really amounts to being lost in time, rather than lifted out of time; it is the condition of Hawthorne's "unfortunate friend P.," who "has lost the thread of his life by the interposition of long intervals of partially disordered reason. The past and present are jumbled together in his mind in a manner often productive of curious results." (CE 10:361)

An effect of Hawthorne's sense of "a timeless continuum" was that it erased the distinction between past and present. This accounts for the many *déjà vu* fancies that he had in Europe and especially in England.[2] It explains, too, his frequently uttered conviction that temporal distance is no chasm to like minds, as when he said that Milton "seems quite a man of our own day" (RE 10:93) and that events of Roman history "appear not so distant as the Gothic ages which succeeded them" (CE 4:164)—

a view of history not very different from Spengler's organic or "Copernican" view, which finds epochs remote from each other in time morphologically comparable.

But in gaining this time-machine capability of occupying other moments in history, Hawthorne lost some sense of being fully alive in his own moment, which to his reflective mind was reduced to an abstraction almost as much as the times of the emperor Nero. His consciousness of such loss of the sense of reality of his own moment prompted frequent reminders to himself that "in this world we are things of a moment, and are made to pursue momentary things, with here and there a thought that stretches mistily towards eternity, and perhaps may endure as long. All philosophy that would abstract mankind from the present is no more than words." (CE 11:133)

In the tension between the present and eternity there is a dilemma for the man and the artist. On the one hand, the artist may lose "the thread of life," like the unfortunate P., and thereby lose the sense of his own place and reality in the continuum of time. Or, on the other hand, the man may succumb to his time-bound condition and believe only in "what I can see and touch," like the Virtuoso and Judge Pyncheon, thus becoming a flabby nightmare in a dead world. Hawthorne's dread of this possibility is uttered in many passages such as his complaint, in "The Custom-House," of "the materiality of this daily life pressing so intrusively upon me." (CE 1:37) That the world needed a "busk" such as Thoreau recommended, to get rid of its oppressive accumulation of old things and "mouldy thought," was a theme of "Earth's Holocaust" and other tales in *Mosses From an Old Manse* as well as of *The House of the Seven Gables*. This theme became more insistent in Hawthorne's work when he went from the new world to the old, which he found cluttered with "old shells, out of which human life has long emerged." (EN, 294) In England he wrote,

> I wished that the whole Past might be swept away—and each generation compelled to bury and destroy whatever it had produced, before being permitted to leave the stage. When we quit a house, we are expected to make it clean for the next occupant;—why ought we not to leave a clean world for the coming generation. (EN, 243)

The inner theme of his last romances is that "the present is burthened too much with the past." (EN, 294)

The artist's solution to the dilemma of being either lost in the confused timelessness of time, or being confined in his own moment or crushed under the heaped-up shells of past moments, is to fill the shell of time's moment with the life of eternity's instant. For Hawthorne's "narrow Now" was a coincidence of two Nows: time's moment, "this visionary and impalpable Now, which, if you once look closely at it, is nothing"; (CE 2:149) and eternity's instant, which, if once you are quickened by it, is everything: "I feel that there is a Now—and that Now must be always calm and happy—and that sorrow and evil are but phantoms that seem to flit across it." (LL 1:15)

The Now of time is experienced in a *place* where time's relics are most numerous and visibly accumulated, as in Rome. The Now of eternity is experienced in a *state of feeling* when a person's deepest springs of life have been opened, as in the first season of love. During the early years of his marriage, in the Old Manse, Hawthorne felt that happiness had "opened the gates of Heaven" and given him "glimpses far inward." (CE 8:393) In his fiction, however, his gates of vision opened more often into "the ruined Eden of the present world" than into heaven.

II

A license must be assumed in brightening the materials which time has rusted, and in tracing out half-obliterated inscriptions on the columns of antiquity: Fancy must throw her reviving light on the faded incidents.
—"Sir William Phips"

Hawthorne's continual problem as the kind of writer who tried to see the living Venus through the time-soiled stone was to make his idea material and his material ideal. Since the failure he most dreaded was losing the idea in the stone, he risked the other kind of failure, so that, as he acknowledged, his tales that "purport to be pictures of actual life" are "not always so warmly dressed" in "habiliments of flesh and blood as to be taken into the reader's mind without a shiver." (CE 9:5)

His endeavor was to show not merely the presence of life in forms, but the movement of life through forms, for unless it moves it is not life. In its vocabulary and imagery the conclusion of his sketch "The Toll-Gatherer's Day" epitomizes his fiction:

> Now the old toll-gatherer looks seaward, and discerns the light-house kindling on a far island, and the stars, too, kindling in the sky, as if but a little way beyond; and mingling reveries of heaven with remembrances of earth, the whole procession of mortal travellers, all the dusty pilgrimage which he has witnessed, seems like a flitting show of phantoms for his thoughtful soul to muse upon. (CE 9:211–12)

The toll-gatherer takes his double toll at an intersection of eternity with time. His mind's eye is open to a vision of eternity, as his body's eye is to a vista of time and space; and his two perceptions blend in their "mingling reveries of heaven with remembrances of earth." The mortal travelers on their dusty pilgrimage are immortal pilgrims as well, and the kindling lights and kindling stars fuse the temporal with the eternal. It is the mortal shapes that are phantoms; whatever flits through them is the reality.

This kind of imagery, with this kind of suggestiveness, appears in every fiction that Hawthorne wrote. Sometimes the gist of it can be found in a sentence: "I know these girls to be flesh and blood, yet, glancing at them so briefly, they mingle like kindred creatures with the ideal beings of my mind." (CE 9:457–58) But always it is to be found in a teeming ambiance that circumfuses his story and, in such a tale as "The Wives of the Dead," makes it shimmer with implications of deeper meaning.

Hawthorne envisaged and with varying degrees of success attempted ways of constructing fictions that would move his readers' imaginations to kindle his creations into life. One of these ways, nearest to the usual method of fiction, is to "diffuse thought and imagination through the opaque substance of to-day, and thus to make it a bright transparency." (CE 1:37) That is, he might try to fill the shell of time's present moment with the life of eternity's instant. This was not a congenial method for Hawthorne; his only extended fiction of this kind is *The Blithedale Romance.*

His usual and more characteristic method was to seize "some of the innumerable forms, that wander in nothingness," (CE 9:178) and "start into being" at the "beck" of the artist, giving them a semblance of truth sufficient to procure for these shadows of the imagination that willing suspension of disbelief which constitutes poetic faith.

His type of the artist was Prospero. In "The Seven Vagabonds" he compared "the old magician" with his magic lantern "to Prospero entertaining his guests with a masque of shadows." (CE 9:352) In "The Toll-Gatherer's Day" the toll-gatherer is stationed where he can see "the great globe, as it were, perform its revolutions and shift its thousand scenes before his eyes." (CE 9:205) The title character of "The Village Uncle," after conversing with various imaginary persons, remarks, "I can imagine precisely how a magician would sit down in gloom and terror, after dismissing the shadows that had personated dead or distant people, and stripping his cavern of the unreal splendor which had changed it into a palace." (CE 9:322–23) And one of the choicest items of "The Virtuoso's Collection" is 'Prospero's magic wand, broken into three pieces by the hand of its mighty master." (CE 10:482) The earthy monsters and airy creatures who serve Prospero on his enchanted island (the equivalent of Hawthorne's "fairy precinct")—which is the domain of romance, of free possibility subject to man's power of imagination—are all, as he says, "Spirits, which by mine art I have from their confines called to enact my present fancies."

Although Hawthorne's literary allusions are usually so deeply implicit in his work that it is not easy to detect them, his references to Prospero as the supreme artist are frequent and explicit. The reverie of the painter in "The Prophetic Pictures" is a prose equivalent to Prospero's famous soliloquy on his "rough magic" before he breaks his staff, the wizard wand of his conjuring imagination.

> "O glorious Art!" thus mused the enthusiastic painter as he trod the street; "thou art the image of the Creator's own. The innumerable forms that wander in nothingness, start into being at thy beck. The dead live again. Thou recallest them to their old scenes. . . . O potent Art! As thou bringest the faintly revealed

Past to stand in that narrow strip of sunlight, which we call Now,
canst thou summon the shrouded Future to meet her there?"
(CE 9:179)

This is reminiscent of Prospero's boast that "graves at my command / Have waked their sleepers, oped, and let 'em forth / By
my so potent art."

Hawthorne's fictions never attempted to "summon the
shrouded Future," although his work often glanced toward it as
a "reverberation" of the past, for "it is dangerous to look too
minutely" at the phenomena of yet undetermined possibility:
"it is apt to create a substance, where at first there was a mere
shadow." (LL 1:192)

The remaining way was his usual practice: to bring "the
faintly revealed Past to stand in that narrow strip of sunlight,
which we call Now"; to give the "gray shadows" of things past
"the lustre of a better life, at once earthly and immortal." (CE
9:179) A "better life" in this context does not mean morally
better, but artistically better—an enhancement of vividness, a
fuller realization of idea.

III

*There is hardly a more difficult exercise of fancy than, while
gazing at a figure of melancholy age, to re-create its youth,
and, without entirely obliterating the identity of form and
features, to restore those graces which time has snatched away.*
—"Edward Fane's Rosebud"

Usually Hawthorne's characters are gray shadows recalled
to their old scenes and given the lustre of a better life, but there
is an important exception. Some of his characters are flat abstractions like Spenser's Satyranes and Florimells, because they are
mere personified ideas. Such figures have little more character
than that given by a significant trait—a cold hand, red eyes, false
teeth, a peculiar laugh or sigh. At their thinnest such abstract
characters are mere emblems; sometimes their thinness is acknowledged in their names. But when their ideas are augmented
with realistic circumstance, they may take on enough body to
play credible roles. For example, Pearl, in *The Scarlet Letter,* al-

though she is a personified idea ("the scarlet letter endowed with life"), is augmented successfully with realistic observations of the author's daughter Una (whose Spenserian name betokens Hawthorne's trying to see in his real child an ideal one).

But most of his characters, and all those which have "a better life," are based on observations of actual characters, either his own notices of living persons or written accounts of historic personages."[3] In either case he preferred not to have his imagination inhibited by data so complete that little room was left to him for perfecting the idea presented. Like Henry James he wanted to give his idea of a character the development his imagination required, not the imperfect development that life had supplied.

Such imaginative constructions of character show that Hawthorne, like James, was most interested in "the appearance of waste" in human life—an appearance that results from the inadequacy of actual forms to contain the "essences" lavishly poured into them, so that there is always some spilling away and failure. Any actual definition of life, as James would have said, is "comparatively so limiting;" and the more "abortive" or ruined the person, the more poignant the suggestion of how far realization falls short of ideal possibility.

Such characters are very numerous in Hawthorne's fiction, but one instance will suffice. Clifford Pyncheon was an "example and representative of that great class of people"[4] of whom it may be said that "an inexplicable Providence" is continually "breaking what seems its own promise in their nature." (RE 3:181) Hawthorne acknowledged, "I should not wonder if I had refined upon the principal character [in *The House of the Seven Gables*] a little too much for popular appreciation."[5] The principal character is certainly Clifford, who partly stands for Hawthorne's idea of his own character, and finally for the character of mankind generally, as an abortive "lover of the Beautiful." (CE 2:135) The entire meaning of *The House of the Seven Gables* spreads out from imagination of what Clifford might have been and ought to have been as a personal culmination of a long line of human possibility. Other characters in the story are arranged around him only in order "to make a sufficient ado."

"The lover of the moral picturesque may sometimes find what he seeks in a character which is nevertheless of too negative a description to be seized upon and represented to the imaginative vision by word painting." (CE 10:439) The first manifestation of Clifford in the romance is the faint murmur of his unintelligible and almost inaudible voice in the twilight, and he hardly assumes a more positive character throughout the story. His characteristic posture was "to sit, with a dim veil of decay and ruin betwixt him and the world." (CE 2:106) His aspect is "pale, gray, childish, aged, melancholy." (CE 2:159) The lustre imparted to this gray shadow is given to it by repeated mention of the Malbone miniature, which portrays the bright idea lost in this decay and dimness; by various small devices such as the exhilaration of coffee-drinking which briefly revives animation and vividness; and most of all by the bright liveliness of Phoebe's presence near him.

In Hawthorne's fiction the feminine principle is life-bearing and life-giving. Therefore it is Phoebe who restores life to the gray man dwelling in the decayed house. Hawthorne's most usual and vivid emblem of living beauty is a rose. Consequently, the idea of woman's lustrating and vivifying role is repeatedly figured in his work by roses. John Inglefield's innocent daughter is like "a rose-bud almost blossomed"; (CE 11:179) her twin sister, a blasted rose, "had grown on the same stem." (CE 11:182) In "Main Street," "the lady who leans on the arm of Endicott" is "a rose of beauty from an English garden." (CE 11:56) Pearl, in *The Scarlet Letter,* says that she was "plucked by her mother off the bush of wild roses, that grew by the prison door." (CE 1:112) Zenobia in *The Blithedale Romance* was a "perfectly developed rose." (CE 3:47) Hawthorne called Frederika Bremer "a little withered rose." (RE 10:58) In picturing how "the Rosebud may revive again with all the dewdrops in its bosom," (CE 9:471) the tale "Edward Fane's Rosebud" uses the idea in a parable of the artist's imagination, which revives a whole aborted human past and gives it a more lustrous life than its actual one, just as Dr. Heidegger's potent art revived a dewy rosebud from a pressed and faded flower.

Therefore the Pyncheon females, especially Phoebe, are associated with roses. The "fragrance" of Alice Pyncheon's "rich and delightful character still lingered about the place where she had lived, as a dried rosebud scents the drawer where it has withered and perished" (CE 2:83): Hepzibah is "mildewed" and has wasted "all the bloom" of her life. Phoebe is "a young rosebud of a girl," (CE 2:117) whose

> spirit resembled, in its potency, a minute quantity of attar of rose in one of Hepzibah's huge, iron-bound trunks, diffusing its fragrance through . . . whatever else was treasured there. As every article in the great trunk was the sweeter for the rose-scent, so did all the thoughts and emotions of Hepzibah and Clifford . . . acquire a subtle attribute of happiness from Phoebe's intermixture with them. (CE 2:137)

The presence of "the rosy girl" (CE 2:222) caused the "half-torpid" man's "very heart to tingle." "[T]he fragrance of an earthly rose-bud had come to his nostrils, and, as odors will,[6] had summoned up reminiscences or visions of living beauty amid which he should have had his home." (CE 2:142) When Clifford wishes to assure himself that he is alive, he alternatively asks for a pinch from Phoebe's fingers or a prick from a rose's thorn.

IV

[T]he mosses of ancient growth upon the walls, looked green and fresh, as if they were the newest things and afterthoughts of Time.—"The Old Manse"

The settings of Hawthorne's stories usually remind us that individual existences are not self-subsistent and self-directed, but are only temporary figures of recurrent vital types. Therefore, his characters' actions are not properly *their* actions, but are necessary enactments of primordial roles. As Roger Chillingworth tells Hester Prynne, their sense of self-determination is "a kind of typical illusion." (CE 1:174)

The most evident manifestation of timeless essence quickening an incessant succession of temporal forms is the cyclic process of nature, whose everlasting life consists of endless deaths and rebirths. Hawthorne like Whitman was mindful that life is "the leavings of many deaths."

One of his favorite symbols, to counterpoint events of transient individual existences, is a decaying fallen tree as a sign of natural process. In the early tale "The Hollow of the Three

Hills," an old crone sits on a mass of "decaying wood, formerly
a majestic oak, . . . beside a pool of green and sluggish water"
(CE 9:199–200) [a death symbol] as she whispers a fatal revelation to a young woman who has met her there "at an appointed
hour." (CE 9:199) In a critical scene of *The Scarlet Letter* ("A
Forest Walk"), Hester Prynne and Arthur Dimmesdale, seated
on "a luxuriant heap of moss; which, at some epoch of the
preceeding century, had been a gigantic pine," (CE 1:190) converse like two ghosts in a gray twilight, conscious of themselves
as pale outlines through which some vital essence flits.

The most elaborate use of this symbolic locus is in the
critical chapter of *The Blithedale Romance* called "The
Masqueraders":

> The whole fantastic rabble forthwith streamed off in pursuit of
> me, so that I was like a mad poet hunted by chimaeras. . . . In
> my haste, I stumbled over a heap of logs and sticks that had been
> cut for firewood, a great while ago, by some former possessor of
> the soil, and piled up square, in order to be carted or sledded
> away to the farm-house. But, being forgotten, they had lain there,
> perhaps fifty years, and possibly much longer; until, by the ac-
> cumulation of moss, and the leaves falling around them, and
> decaying there, from autumn to autumn, a green mound was
> formed, in which the softened outline of the wood-pile was still
> perceptible. In the fitful mood that then swayed my mind, I
> found something strangely affecting in this simple circumstance.
> I imagined the long-dead woodman, and his long-dead wife and
> children, coming out of their chill graves, and essaying to make a
> fire with this heap of mossy fuel![7] (CE 3:211–12)

This is a more complex emblem than that of the decaying
tree, for it has added to the basic emblem of nature's process
the imagination of a group of related persons with their wasted
work and defeated plans. It evokes the idea of man's pathetic
hope and useless endeavor working briefly on nature's process
and fading into it. The passage is a revision of one from the
author's notebooks dated September 7, 1850. He found it right
in its suggestions for this critical scene in a romance which,
according to the most persuasive modern reading, is "a Book of
Nature, wherein human endeavors to revise the world are set by
way of ironic contrast against the cycle of the revolving year and
its natural, organic mode of changing the world by periodic de-

struction and rebuilding, by alternations of death and resurrection."[8] The puny and wasted effort of the woodman to provide, provide, and the author's sad fancy of the woodman's ghostly family, every one added to the earth, one lump of mould the more, is a synecdoche of all human endeavor set by way of ironic contrast against the natural, organic mode of changing the world.

V

Two shallow and grass-grown cavities remain, . . . and barberry bushes clustering within them. . . . There I have sometimes sat and tried to rebuild, in my imagination, the stately house.—"Browne's Folly"

Just as Hawthorne's characters and settings are imaginative constructions or reconstructions from gray shadows and mosses, so too are his narrative structures revived by fancy from faded incidents.

For him the most potent datum was some relic of human action and character, now an anachronism, but found in a place where it was once the most significant feature of a full and living scene, so that it retains a metonymic capability of recalling the entire fabric of reality to which it once belonged.

An arrowhead is such a relic, for it conjures up imagination of the vanished redskin world in which it was once a thing of power, and solicits the mind to survey the whole retrospect of successive scenes:

> There is exquisite delight . . . in picking up . . . an arrowhead that was dropped centuries ago and has never been handled since, and which we thus receive directly from the hand of the red hunter, who purposed to shoot it at his game or at an enemy. Such an incident builds up again the Indian village and its encircling forest, and recalls to life the painted chiefs and warriors, the squaws at their household toil, and the children sporting among the wigwams, while the little wind-rocked papoose swings from the branch of a tree. It can hardly be told whether it is a joy or a pain, after such a momentary vision, to gaze around in the broad daylight of reality, and see stone fences, white houses, potato fields, and men doggedly hoeing in their shirtsleeves and homespun pantaloons. (CE 10:11)

Unmistakably, Hawthorne in many of his tales is simply using more elaborately the imaginative capability pointed to in this passage. In such a sketch as "A Rill from the Town Pump" or "Main Street" the potent relic may be something that in modern form belongs to the contemporary scene, so that it requires imagination to recognize and recall its ancient aspect, and connect the town pump with the wilderness spring where Indian sagamores came to drink "from time immemorial" or Main Street in Salem with the "hardly perceptible track" through "the ancient and primitive wood" (CE 11:50) where, "amid the murmur of boughs, go the Indian queen and the Indian priest." (CE 11:51)

Just as certainly, in his more complicated narratives Hawthorne was performing the same kind of recollective feats. *The Scarlet Letter* is a reconstruction of the Boston of Winthrop and Wilson from a tattered piece of scarlet cloth, itself a figment. The House of the Seven Gables in its decayed state prompts imagination of all the phases of life that successively flitted through this shell. And the recognition of the ancient faun in the person of Donatello carries imagination back from the human to the animal, from history to myth.

A most illuminating instance of such an exercise of imagination, instructive because in its scope and complexity it stands between the arrowhead passage and the romances, is "Old Ticonderoga: A Picture of the Past." First the author points out that a prosaic, too circumstantial reconstruction of the past oppresses the imagination:

> In my first view of the ruins, I was favored with the guidance of a young lieutenant of engineers, recently from West Point, where he had gained credit for great military genius. I saw nothing but confusion in what chiefly interested him. . . . His description of Ticonderoga would be as accurate as a geometrical theorem, and as barren of the poetry that has clustered around its decay. (CE 11:187)

But he would have been "glad of a hoary veteran to totter by my side," for the veteran's reminiscences "would harmonize with the scene. A survivor of the long-disbanded garrisons . . . might have mustered his dead chiefs and comrades . . . and bid them march through the ruined gateway, turning their old historic faces on me, as they passed." (CE 11:187–88)

"Next to such a companion, the best is one's own fancy." When he visited Ticonderoga again, it was in circumstances that permitted his reverie. He was alone, and after a ramble over the ramparts he seated himself in one of the roofless barracks to muse upon the scene:

> A most luxuriant crop of weeds had sprung up within the edifice, and hid the scattered fragments of the wall. Grass and weeds grew in the windows, and in all the crevices of the stone, climbing, step by step, till a tuft of yellow flowers was waving on the highest peak of the gable. Some spicy herb diffused pleasant odor through the ruin. (CE 11:188–89)

In this passage there is unusually elaborate development of the motif noted in the description of the mouldering woodpile—what Hawthorne continually remarked as nature's "gradually obiliterating the handiwork of man," and adopting it "as part of her great garden." (EN, 531) Again there appears the familiar emblem of the mouldering log:

> A verdant heap of vegetation had covered the hearth of the second floor, clustering on the very spot where the huge logs had mouldered to glowing coals, and flourished beneath the broad flue, which had so often puffed the smoke over a circle of French or English soldiers. I felt that there was no other token of decay so impressive as that bed of weeds in the place of the backlog. (CE 11:188–89)

When one considers what connotations an open fire had for Hawthorne as a vivifying element,[9] he realizes the emblematic force of having such a fire extinguished in the slow smokeless burning of decay.

With this evocative emblem before him, the author closed his "eyes on Ticonderoga in ruins, and cast a dream-like glance over pictures of the past" (CE 11:189): a procession of scenes that included an "Indian chief . . . armed with a bow of hickory . . . and flintheaded arrows"; a "French chevalier, commandant of the fortress, paying court to a copper-colored lady, the princess of the land"; a "war-party of French and Indians . . . issuing from the gate to lay waste some village of New

England"; a Jesuit preaching "beneath a canopy of forest boughs"; a "series of pictures from the Old French War"; Ethan Allen's conquest of the fortress; and numerous other historic and fanciful scenes. (CE 11:189–90) But roused at last from his reverie by a noise from the present—the bell of a steamer passing on the lake nearby—he muses on the thought that the old fort will never witness such scenes of life again, "or only at some dreamer's summons, gliding from the twilight past to vanish among realities." (CE 11:191)

Many of these emblems so potent for Hawthorne's imagination reappear in the "Custom-House" introduction to *The Scarlet Letter* and infuse their associative potency into his imaginative play with the richest of all his evocative symbols.

He begins with contemplation of a ruined character, the old Collector:

> To observe and define his character . . . was as difficult a task as to trace out and build up anew, in imagination, an old fortress, like Ticonderoga, from a view of its gray and broken ruins. . . .
>
> Nevertheless, looking at the old warrior with affection, . . . I could discern the main points of his portrait. . . . What I saw in him—as evidently as the indestructible ramparts of old Ticonderoga . . . were the features of stubborn and ponderous endurance. . . .
>
> Many characteristics . . . must have vanished, or been obscured, before I met the General. All merely graceful attributes are usually the most evanescent; nor does Nature adorn the human ruin with blossoms of new beauty, that have their roots and proper nutriment only in the chinks and crevices of decay, as she sows wall-flowers over the ruined fortress of Ticonderoga. (CE 1:21–22)

Next the arrowhead emblem occurs, just preliminary to discovery of the scarlet letter, in a passage in which the author deplores the dearth of actual historic documents (which would of course have hindered his imagination, although the idea of them helps it):

> Prior to the Revolution, there is a dearth of records; the earlier documents and archives of the Custom-House having, probably, been carried off to Halifax, when all the King's officials accompanied the British army in its flight from Boston. It has often been a matter of regret with me; for . . . those papers must have

contained many references to forgotten or remembered men, and to antique customs, which would have affected me with the same pleasure as when I used to pick up Indian arrow-heads in the field near the Old Manse. (CE 1:29)

Having thus warmed his imagination to its task, so to speak, by these practice reminiscences of the ruined character, old Ticonderoga, and the arrowhead, the author is ready for his discovery:

> Poking and burrowing into the heaped-up rubbish . . .; glancing at such matters with the saddened, weary, half-reluctant interest which we bestow on the corpse of dead activity,—and exerting my fancy, . . . to raise up from these dry bones an image of the old town's brighter aspect, . . . I chanced to lay my hand on a small package. . . . There was something about it that quickened an instinctive curiosity . . . with the sense that a treasure would here be brought to light. . . . There were traces about it of gold embroidery, . . . greatly frayed and defaced. . . . This rag of scarlet cloth . . . strangely interested me. . . . Certainly, there was some deep meaning in it. (CE 1:29–31)

NOTES

1. Edward Davidson, ed., *Hawthorne's "Doctor Grimshawe's Secret"* (Cambridge, MA: Harvard Univ. Press, 1954), 7.
2. See, e.g., *The English Notebooks of Nathaniel Hawthorne*, ed. Randall Stewart (New York: Russell and Russell, 1962), xxxix, 57, 124.
3. For example, observed persons like those described in his North Adams notebooks.
4. Here I quote the Riverside Edition (3:181), for I regard this phrase as a critical *locus* and am unwilling to accept the obfuscatory reading of the Centenary Edition: "an example and representative of that great chaos of people" (CE 2:149). It is nonsense to speak of an example and representative of a chaos; it is intelligible to speak of an example and representative of a class. The relations of persons in *The House of the Seven Gables* illustrate some of the right and wrong workings of "the sympathy or magnetism among human beings" that "exists, indeed, among different classes of organized life, and vibrates from one to another." (CE 2:174) Clifford is evidently a fully drawn example

of one of the "various classes of people" described in "The Procession of Life." ("The Old Apple Dealer" is an earlier and thinner study of such a character.) Clifford represents the largest class of all, a class so numerous that its "comprehensive principle" brings together "thousands into the ranks where hitherto we have brought one"—namely, "all mortals, who, from whatever cause, have lost, or never found, their proper places in the world." Judge Pyncheon represents that "class" of men whose "field of action lies among the external phenomena of life." Phoebe belongs to "the trim, orderly and limit-loving class." Holgrave, who had been a country schoolmaster, a salesman, political editor of a country newspaper, a peddler, a dentist, a "supernumerary official . . . aboard a packet-ship"—an office that enabled him to see several European countries, a member of a Fourierist community, a lecturer on mesmerism, and now at the age of twenty-two was a daguerreotypist, was in his restless adventurism "the representative of many compeers in his native land."

5. Horatio Bridge, *Personal Recollections of Nathaniel Hawthorne* (New York: Harper, 1893), 139.

6. "Odors, being a sort of element combined of the sensual and spiritual, are apt to deceive us. . . . The recollection of a perfume, the bare idea of it, may easily be taken for a present reality." (CE 10:117)

7. See Norris Yates, "An Instance of Parallel Imagery in Hawthorne, Melville, and Frost," *Philological Quarterly* 36 (April 1957): 276–80.

8. John W. Shroeder, "Miles Coverdale as Actaeon, as Faunus, and as October," *Papers on Language and Literature* 2 (Spring 1966): 138.

9. This should also be noted in connection with the mouldering woodpile. See the tale "Fire-Worship" in *Mosses from an Old Manse*.

Metonymic Symbols: Black Glove and Pink Ribbon

I

[T]here is an influence in the light of morning that tends to rectify whatever errors of fancy, or even of judgment, we may have incurred during the sun's decline, or among the shadows of the night, or in the less wholesome glow of moonshine.
— "Rappaccini's Daughter"

In the mid-chapter of *The Scarlet Letter* the gray-bearded sexton, after an unusually "efficacious" Sabbath sermon preached by the Reverend Arthur Dimmesdale, proffers to "the sainted minister" (CE 1:247) a black glove "found this morning on the scaffold where evil-doers are set up to public shame." The minister accepts it with thanks, acknowledging it to be his own: "Yes, it seems to be my glove, indeed!" (CE 1:158)

This apparently trifling incident is loaded with meaning because of the equivocal symbolism of the black glove, the circumstances of its discovery, the dialogue that accompanies its recognition and restoration, and the crucial point which the incident illuminates in the plot.

The black glove in its proper place on the minister's hand is an unnoticed item in his customary suit of solemn black; but detached from this ensemble of conventional significance, and found in an unhallowed place after a night of supernatural doings, the black glove arouses suspicions that disturb piety. Black suggests evil and concealment, the use of a glove suggests concealment and perhaps gingerliness and caution. The sexton, unable to ignore these sinister indications, alludes to them in some characteristic Puritan wordplay. Satan, he says, "was blind and foolish, as he ever and always is. A pure hand needs no glove to cover it. . . . And, since Satan saw fit to steal it, your reverence must needs handle him without gloves henceforward." (CE 1:158)

The unshakable first premise of the gray-bearded sexton, who is spokesman for all that is experienced and pious and serviceable in the Puritan laity, is that the Puritan community is godly, those in authority are more godly, and the minister who is regarded as "little less than a heaven-ordained apostle" (CE 1:120) is most godly. Therefore, the sexton interprets the situation in an enthymeme as some of Satan's sophistry: "Satan dropped it there, I take it, intending a scurrilous jest against your reverence." (CE 1:158)

The black glove disturbs the sexton not merely by its suggestiveness as a distinct and detached token, but because it is the only tangible retrievement from deeds of night that have astonished God's people, and it seems to indicate the minister's complicity. He asks the minister whether he has heard of the great red letter in the sky last night, a remarkable portent of Providence which may bode some strange eruption to the state: "the letter A, which we interpret to stand for Angel" because "our good governor Winthrop was made an angel this past night." (CE 1:158) Thus the officious graybeard interprets another equivocal sign in a way to quiet any threatful hint that the invisible spheres may be formed in fright. And again the minister concurs. Although he is cognizant of the red *A*, and knows that it might as well stand for Adulterer as Angel, he caps his implicit lie in accepting the sexton's interpretation of the dropped glove with an explicit lie in denying that he knows of the red letter: "No, I had not heard of it." (CE 1:158)

This critical instance of duplicity occurs in the middle of a paradoxical plot in which the good man must publish his badness in order to redeem his goodness, and in which the bad man must uphold the repute of goodness in order to destroy it.

The proffer of the black glove is loaded with these meanings by being made the central symbol, a nonce-symbol, in a structure of meaning extended throughout the narrative.[1] The sexton hands the glove to the minister following the second of three sermons reported in the romance which accompany the three scaffold scenes that structure the plot, at the beginning, the middle, and the end.

The first sermon of *The Scarlet Letter* was an institutional communication preached downward, so to speak, from the head of a body to its members. In it the senior minister of Boston, Mr. John Wilson,

> who had carefully prepared himself for the occasion, addressed to the multitude a discourse on sin, in all its branches, but with continual reference to the ignominious letter. So forcibly did he dwell upon this symbol, for the hour or more during which his periods were rolling over the people's heads, that it assumed new terrors in their imagination, and seemed to derive its scarlet hue from the flame of the infernal pit. Hester Prynne, meanwhile, kept her place upon the pedestal of shame, with glazed eyes, and an air of weary indifference. (CE 1:68–69)

Wilson's sermon was a stock Puritan discourse, officially delivered, on a public occasion. It was a fair instance of official dealing with offenders against the community code. It reduced the offending person to a flagrant example of wrongdoing, ignoring all other aspects of her reality, however obvious and attractive. It seized upon the occasion to admonish the public and reaffirm the validity of the conventions that gave integrity to their corporate life.[2] To an outsider—i.e., to any modern reader—it is a repellently impersonal and inhumane harangue. To Puritan hearers who were inside the community of belief that lived by such doctrine it was a comfortable discourse, in that it found in an apparently disruptive situation an occasion for repeating the formulas that were the life of their life. It was a more extended and public and official affirmation of what the sexton maintained in his dialogue with the minister. It had a binding effect; it reassured and secured the community in their belief that the center still held and mere chaos was not loosed upon the world.

The second sermon, reported in the twelfth chapter of *The Scarlet Letter,* had a different character. It was not formal and categorical, but expressive and personal. It followed the night of penance without penitence during which Dimmesdale stood on the scaffold at midnight with Hester in clandestine acknowledgment of their shared sin, symbolized by the child standing between them holding a hand of each. This served to revive some of the minister's truth, so woefully depleted by the remorseless persecutions of his secret enemy. Holding hands with Hester and Pearl, he felt "a tumultuous rush of new life" bringing "vital warmth to his half-torpid system. The three formed an electric chain." (CE 1:153)

The public consequence of this moral reinvigoration was the sermon that he preached on the following Sabbath day,

> a discourse which was held to be the richest and most powerful, and the most replete with heavenly influences, that had ever proceeded from his lips. Souls, it is said more souls than one, were brought to the truth by the efficacy of that sermon, and vowed within themselves to cherish a holy gratitude towards Mr. Dimmesdale throughout the long hereafter. (CE 1:157)

This sermon was preached, so to speak, on the level of one morally beset soul speaking to other similarly distressed souls. It was the expression of an aroused impulse toward reestablishment of moral truth, which he could transmit to others but could not find strength to declare himself.

In regard to this sermon, the sexton's mistaken supposition that the devil had dropped Dimmesdale's glove is not so severely ironic, after all; that is, it does not altogether belie the essential truth. Dimmesdale is a good man, as the sexton confidently believes, but a weak good man. This mid-chapter is equivocal, as its central symbol of the black glove is equivocal. The first scaffold scene concluded with a kind of ritual rebinding of the godly community in the formulas of its official decency. If, ultimately, official decency itself requires that it be merely the visible manifestation of essential truth, the protagonist lacks the heroism necessary to sacrifice the fine idea of him entertained by his people and cherished by himself. The first scaffold scene represented the situation as officially settled; this mid-scene shows it to be essentially unsettled. It threatens unbinding. The dropped glove is an ambivalent token of the unresolved tension between official appearance and essential truth. The sexton's reading is both wrong and right—literally and temporarily wrong, if essentially and ultimately right.

The third sermon in *The Scarlet Letter* is part of the romance's climactic scene; it is in effect preamble to Arthur Dimmesdale's long-delayed confession and penitence. The burden of its meaning was carried more in plaintive cadences than in intelligible words, "in a tongue native to the human heart."

> The complaint of a human heart, sorrow-laden, perchance guilty, telling its secret, whether of guilt or sorrow, to the great heart of mankind; beseeching its sympathy or forgiveness,—at every moment,—in each accent,—and never in vain! It was this profound and continual undertone that gave the clergyman his most appropriate power. (CE 1:243–44)

This sermon was no categorical application of a formal code to a public occasion, although it ostensibly had this official character as the Election Sermon which dealt, as Hawthorne tells us, with "the relation between the Deity and the communities of mankind, with a special reference to the New England which they were here planting in the wilderness." (CE 1:249) But this prescriptive subject duly noticed, "a spirit as of prophecy had come upon him, constraining him to its purpose as mightily as the old prophets of Israel were constrained."

> According to their united testimony, never had man spoken in so wise, so high, and so holy a spirit, as he that spake this day; nor had inspiration ever breathed through mortal lips more evidently than it did through his. Its influence could be seen, as it were, descending upon him, and . . . continually filling him with ideas that must have been as marvellous to himself as to his audience. (CE 1:248–49)

This was neither a formal and official discourse nor the impulse of one anguished and morally aroused soul imparted to other sinful souls. It was the pentecostal utterance of a soul rapt by descending deity and transporting its hearers with it to a realm of "golden truths" that transcended their official formulas, be-

stowed grace on their ineffectual moral strivings, and revived
the spiritual life of the community. Thus it too was a binding
discourse: not like the first sermon one which bound individuals
into their temporal doctrinal community, but one which bound
their community into the transcendent spiritual one.

II

*[I]t is the snakelike doubt that thrusts out its head, which
gives us a glimpse of reality. Surely such moments are a
hundred times as real as the dull, quiet moments of faith.*
—Septimius Felton

In the midscene of "Young Goodman Brown" the young
goodman, after a succession of dismaying assaults by the Devil
upon his naive belief in human goodness, "fancied" that he
heard the voice of his wife Faith in the midst of a black cloud
filled with a "confused and doubtful sound of voices. (CE 10:82)
He shouted her name "in a voice of agony and desperation";
(CE 10:82) then, as the dark cloud swept away, "something
fluttered lightly down through the air and caught on the branch
of a tree. The young man seized it and beheld a pink ribbon."
(CE 10:83) Recognizing it as belonging to his wife Faith, "after
one stupefied moment," he cried out, "My faith is gone! . . .
There is no good on earth; and sin is but a name. Come, Devil;
for to thee is this world given." (CE 10:83)

This obviously crucial incident is loaded with meaning because of the symbolism of the pink ribbon, the circumstances of
its discovery and the speech that accompanies its recognition,
and the crucial point which the incident illuminates in the
narration.

The pink ribbons that adorn the cap which Faith wears on
her pretty little head are a badge of feminine innocence, which
they inevitably suggest in consequence of the immemorial custom of decking baby girls in pink ribbons.[3] Faith's pink ribbons
worn in the daylight of the Puritan village show her to be an
innocent dwelling in the midst of innocence. But detached from
this ensemble of purity, and found "in the heart of the dark

wilderness" into which Satan beguiles the innocent, the pink ribbon becomes part of "a design of darkness to appall."[4]

It is no longer the unshaken first premise of the young goodman that the Puritan community is godly, or even that the most apparently innocent person is good. The defenses of example, custom, and fear that his Preventing God has set around him do not suffice to keep him from gauging the depths of sin to which human nature may descend. The young man has the vulnerability of youth and, having newly yielded to the persuasions of the Devil, he has been led step by step to mistrust all he had believed in. Therefore, accepting the indications of the pink ribbon which he beheld on the dark forest path, and "maddened with despair," he rushed headlong into the "benighted wilderness."

This crucial incident occurs in the middle one of three scenes including notice of the pink ribbon that structure the tale. The pink ribbon like the black glove has the function of orienting the visible with the invisible world. When Goodman Brown takes leave of Faith at sunset in the street of Salem Village, the pink ribbons give him visual assurance that she is "a blessed angel on earth." (CE 10:75) But the author goes speedily to his business of promoting an insurrection in the moral kingdom of Young Goodman Brown. The mysterious "errand" (CE 10:75) on which the young man "must" (CE 10:74) go is a figure for the fall from innocence to experience; he was impelled to it by "the instinct that guides mortal man to evil." (CE 10:83)

The first half of the tale, from the first glimpse of the pink ribbons to the second, consists of a process which has two symbolic developments that work together to carry the implications of the story. One is the series of conjurations that figure the progress of the goodman's suspicions of evil. The figures are his townsmen; they are also spectres conjured up by the devil in prompt response to the young man's calling them into his mind as figures of certified truth now in effect challenged to witness that their usual appearances are "honest"; the devil himself is a function of the goodman's own haunted mind, ready to furnish the ocular proof that his suspicions call for; the night forest itself is the haunted mind of the goodman, which contains the devil, the goodman's idea of himself, and all the "horrible suspicions that rose, monster-like, out of the caverns of his heart and stared him in the face." (CE 10:116)

Besides the series of conjurations which the diabolic imagination of Brown summons before us, the other figurative work going on is the advance from one mindscape into another. For the characters of reality that appear to the goodman are products of the mindscape which makes just these figures of possibility appear while it obscures and obliterates others. This effect is the technical function of Hawthorne's continual use of light and shade. There is in his work what he considered to be a "Rembrandt" effect,[5] in which appearances—which to Hawthorne are the only knowable reality—are created by changes of light that fall on a "gray medium" which may be taken as the *fond* of reality itself.

III

[Her hearers'] hearts are turning from those whom they had chosen to lead them to heaven; and they feel like children who have been enticed far from home, and see the features of their guides change all at once, assuming a fiendish shape in some frightful solitude.—"Mrs. Hutchinson"

Goodman Brown's Salem Village and Arthur Dimmesdale's Boston are alike in their reality as Puritan communities in which the orthodox dwelt secured by faith against the diabolic terrors that haunted the dark wilderness around them. The one is the necessary antithesis or antiworld of the other, and the citizen of the godly community perforce believed with an equal conviction in the reality of the ungodly wilderness. Further, the citizen of the godly sunlit town believed that he might easily become a denizen of the devilish dark forest, and that denizens of the devilish forest by night might dwell under the seeming of honest citizens in the town by day.

Hawthorne was fascinated by Cotton Mather's *Magnalia*, "a strange, pedantic history, in which true events and real personages move before the reader with the dreamy aspect which they wore in Cotton Mather's singular mind." (CE 6:92) Cotton

Mather's mind was not singular, in Hawthorne's judgment, in its difference from other Puritan minds, but in its typicality—that is, in the morbid intensity with which he projected distinctive features of the Puritan imagination of reality.[6] "He believed that there were evil spirits in the world." "He supposed that these unlovely demons were everywhere, in the sunshine as well as in the darkness, and that they were hidden in men's hearts, and stole into their most secret thoughts." (CE 6:94)

Life in a world imagined in these terms was intensely dramatic. Puritan life was "stern," as Hawthorne so often calls it, but it was not tedious. It was lived more along a scale from despair to ecstasy than within the range of modern satisfactions, which seldom aim at any higher felicity than keeping at bay those three evils, boredom, vice, and need. *The Scarlet Letter* and "Young Goodman Brown," both using the same donnée of historical reality, exhibit the extreme opposite but complementary states of consciousness afforded by Puritanism: the doubtful ecstasy of Dimmesdale's "death of triumphant ignominy," (CE 1:257) and the "distrustful, if not desperate" lifelong shrinking from Faith of Goodman Brown, whose "dying hour was gloom." (CE 10:90)

What Hawthorne saw as dramatic in the life of the Puritans was their living in a state of tension, suspended between possible convictions. He found an objective correlative for his faith-suspicion polarity in the history of New England Puritanism. The action of *The Scarlet Letter* is laid in Boston, the capital of Puritan faith, at the time when, as Wigglesworth wrote, "Our morning stars shone all day long"—that is, when the most venerated civil and religious persons of the first generation of Puritans, such as John Winthrop and John Wilson, were at the culmination of their long sway of authority. In such circumstances men were able to forfend the fiendish shapes that their creed engendered. The action of "Young Goodman Brown," on the other hand, is laid in Salem Village, the center of the witchcraft delusion, in the witching times of 1692, and it shows the populace of Salem Village, those chief in authority as well as obscure young citizens like Brown, enticed by fiendish shapes into the frightful solitude of superstitious fear. The named witches, Goody Cloyse, "that unhanged witch, Goody Cory," and the "rampant hag" Martha Carrier, "who had received the devil's promise to be queen of hell,"[7] are historically identifiable early victims selected by the roulette of suspicion under the impulses of hate and fear deep in human nature.

Hawthorne's brilliant historical imagination is displayed in these stories. His insight is that history's inner meaning is in that complex of ideas which in any given historic scene patterns events to the perception of the actors in the scene. Events do not have their own intrinsic or absolute pattern; they have patterns projected by the persons who move them and are moved by them in a community of thought and action. Hence, it is beside the point to ask what is the "real" meaning of Young Goodman Brown's adventures, or to consider whether he "had only dreamed a wild dream," as the author deprecatingly invites us to do. Every real meaning is real only in the sense that it seems real to persons involved in the world of their imagination; all interpretations of experience are dreams of meaning. Hawthorne's genius was in his ability to dream his way back into the Puritan reality, and to furnish us the means of dreaming their dreams as well.

IV

If a man could pass through Paradise in a dream, and have a flower presented to him as a pledge that his soul had really been there, and if he found that flower in his hand when he awoke—Aye! and what then?—Coleridge, Notebooks

The black glove and pink ribbon are apt to mislead those who like Othello call for "the ocular proof" which will certify some appearance. Such ocular proofs are equivocal, for they are apparent signs of unapparent realities that must be read from them metonymically—a very uncertain mode of inference.

The status of the pink ribbon is more equivocal than that of the black glove because it is found in the wrong mindscape. The black glove is found in the wrong *location*, one in which it is metonymically a piece of a design of darkness to appall, but this location is a fixed and accommodated feature of an unchanged mindscape; the black glove can be readily restored to its *right* location, where "whatever errors of fancy, or even of judgment, we may have incurred during the sun's decline, or

among the shadows of night," are rectified, after only an appall-
ing moment. But the pink ribbon is found, not merely in the
wrong location, but in the wrong mindscape. Young Goodman
Brown finds it while he is actually in his midnight forest; and its
reality is what his fancy and judgment there determine it to be.

I take it that Hawthorne knowingly employs *fancy* and *judgment* in his fiction as seventeenth-century New England Puritans
defined the terms in their psychology, perhaps best distinguished and summarized for modern readers by Perry Miller.
Beginning with the ancient doctrine of a tripartite soul, vegeta-
tive, sensible, and rational,

> they usually took up the three souls in mounting succession; yet
> all treatments center upon a reaction that may be traced through
> the several stages thus: the impression of an object produces in
> the sense an image or replica of the thing, generally called the
> "phantasm" or the "species"; the phantasm is then picked up at
> the eye or ear by the animal spirits and carried posthaste to the
> common sense in the central chamber of the brain; this faculty
> apprehends the phantasms, distinguishes one species from an-
> other, and relays them to the imagination, fancy or "phantasy,"
> which, located in the front part of the brain, judges and compares
> one phantasm with another, retains them when the objects are
> absent, and sways the sensual inclination by holding and vivify-
> ing the objects of desire; after meaning and intelligibility have
> been attached to phantasms, they are stored in the memory,
> which is situated in the posterior lobe of the brain, where they
> may be "committed to it to keep as to their secretarie"; the
> reason or the understanding, which dwells somewhere above the
> middle, summons phantasms before its judgment seat from
> either the imagination or the storehouse of memory, determines
> which are right and true, and sends the image representing its
> decision, by the agency of the animal spirits, along the nerves to
> the will, which lives in the heart; the will then embraces true
> images as the good to be pursued, and commands the "sensitive
> appetite," which consists of affections and passions; the proper
> emotions, being thus aroused, transmit the impulse to the mus-
> cles. So the bear, encountered in the wilderness, causes in the
> eye a phantasm of the bear, recognized as dangerous in the imag-
> ination, associated with remembered dangers in memory, de-
> clared an object to be fled in reason, made the signal of command
> to the will, which then excites the affection of fear, which finally
> prompts the muscles of the legs to run.[8]

So, too, the phantasm of the pink ribbon found in the midnight forest is compared by the judgment with that supplied by "the imagination, fancy, or phantasy" of Young Goodman Brown. He is unable, however, to "determine which is right and true." The mindscape in which he finds the ribbon contradicts that in which he last beheld it; to accept the ocular proof of the ribbon in the midnight forest is to deny the truth of the Puritan village in the morning light in which he next sees it.

The agonizing dilemma of doubt of which Young Goodman Brown's dark forest adventure is an objective correlative would have been recognized by Puritans as a figure for mistrust of their own corrupt faculties. The pink ribbon seen in the forest may be merely a lustful projection of the goodman's depraved fancy, which wills wickedness (obeys "the instinct which guides mortal man to evil") even as it reluctantly departs from its forfeited innocence.[9] The imagination, as Miller says,

> had never been bound to the senses and could form images beyond and in excess of nature; once it is depraved it becomes utterly lawless, and will throw up phantasms of unnatural lusts to seduce the will and affections; it can lead enfeebled reason in its train, or if the reason objects, cut short the arc of the reflex and present its perverted images directly to the will or immediately to the passions. Furthermore, it is dangerous because Satan, retaining his angelic incorporeality, can insert images into it without the agency of the senses, thus tempting the will with imaginations of such vices as could never have been conceived merely from experience. The Devil has no need "of speaking with an audible voice, or representing things to our bodily eyes, &c, but hath a closer and more secret way of access to our imaginations, in which he can represent the Images of things, and hold them before us."

Miller goes on to cite Richard Hibbes's *The Soul's Conflict*, "which was widely read in New England," who declares that in consequence of the imagination's thus "forging matter out of itself without any external sensation," "The life of many men . . . is almost nothing else but a fancy." (257–58)

Hawthorne does not merely admit the epistemological uncertainty arising from confusions of the subjective self and the world; he deliberately exposes and artfully exploits it in his tales. If there is such a thing as "certainty," it is in subjective conviction, not in objective certification. How anyone reads the signs of reality depends upon the condition of his "fancy" and "judgment." Either the gray-bearded sexton or the young goodman must use the ideas that possess him to explain the apparent facts; the facts cannot propound and certify their own meanings. Goodman Brown's advance into the dark forest from the daylight village is like Ishmael's or the Ancient Mariner's advance into strange seas—a gradual departure from limited "land-truths" into shoreless immensities. His return to the village is the apparent reversal of his departure; he left at sunset and returned at sunrise; his return was marked as significantly by his "turning the corner by the meeting-house" as his departure had been by his turning the same corner; his wife Faith greeted him with the same anxious affection she had shown at his departure. But although he returned to the same facts as those he had left, he could not return to the same certainties. His was the anxious agony that led some Puritans to cut their own throats or throw their babies down the well or to hang their neighbors if their cows fell sick. Forever thereafter Brown "shrank from the bosom of his Faith," and never recovered his trust that he "might cling to her skirts and follow her to Heaven." (CE 10:75)

V

In a sense, all explanation must end in an ultimate
arbitrariness. My demand is, that the ultimate arbitrariness
of matter of fact from which our formulation starts should
disclose the same general principles of reality, which we
dimly discern stretching away into regions beyond our
ultimate discernment.—A. N. Whitehead, Science and
the Modern World

Whether the pink ribbon is real in the sense in which the black glove is real—that is, in having a putative physical existence rather than being a cheat of fancy—is not only unascertainable but is finally beside the point. For what matters is that it is of the same order of reality as everything else in the forest adventure, no more and no less real than any other phenomenon in that realm of consciousness: e.g., it is just as tangible and visible as the maple-stick which the Devil gives to Brown to speed him on his way. Unmistakably the maple-stick is a magic stick, like the staff that Quick-silver lends to Perseus in Hawthorne's tale of the Gorgon's Head in *Grandfather's Chair*. Whether the maple-stick and the pink ribbon exist naturalistically, so that if cast aside they might be found by some other wayfarer passing that way in daylight on some other day, is a question that diverts attention from their significant reality—that is, their moral-psychological significance.

In this as in other basic points of interpretation, I agree with the positions taken by David Levin in his cogent discussion of "Young Goodman Brown": that "it is the perception of Goodman Brown through which Hawthorne asks us to see almost all the action"; and that "the Devil is consistently presenting evidence to a prospective convert who is only too willing to be convinced."[10]

Perhaps the most frequently and persistently reiterated theme of Hawthorne's work is that every reading of facts, every version of "truth," is an arbitrary determination. His eye was "discerning," as his friend Horatio Bridge said, in that it could find different truths in different combinations and perspectives. "There is much to be learnt, always, by getting a glimpse at rears." (CE 8:239) "The prospect from the top of Wachuset is the finest that I have seen—the elevation being not so great as to snatch the beholder from all sympathy with the earth. [There are many separate things], each with their little knot of peculiar interests, but all gathered into one category by the observer above them." (CE 8:259–60) "A man's individual affairs look not so very important, when we can climb high enough to get the idea of a complicated neighborhood." (RE 12:132) "We who stood so elevated above mortal things, and saw so wide and far, could see the sunshine of prosperity departing from one spot and rolling towards another; so that we could not think it much matter which spot were sunny or gloomy at any one moment." (CE 8:129) "I think we are very happy—a truth which is not always so evident to me, until I step aside from our daily life." (LL 2:173) "The scaffold of the pillory was a point of view that revealed to Hester the entire track along which she had been treading since her early infancy." (CE 1:58) "You do not know what a mixture of good there may be in things evil; and how the greatest criminal, if you look at his conduct from his own point of view, or from any sidepoint, may not seem so unquestionably guilty, after all." (CE 4:383) "It is a good lesson for a man who has dreamed of literary fame . . . to step aside out of the narrow circle in which his claims are recognized, and to find how utterly void of significance, beyond that circle, is all that he achieves, and all that he aims at." (CE 1:26–27) "My position was lofty enough to serve as an observatory, not for starry investigations, but for those sublunary matters in which lay a lore as infinite as that of the planets." (CE 3:99) "A large portion of [the roses] had blight or mildew at their hearts; but, viewed at a fair distance, the whole rose-bush looked as if it had been brought from Eden that very summer." (CE 2:71) "The mountains look much larger and more majestic sometimes than at others—partly because the mind may be variously situated so as to comprehend them, and partly that an imperceptible (or almost so) haze adds a gret deal to the effect." (CE 8:125) "Sit farther back, . . . and take my word for it, the slips of pasteboard shall assume spiritual life; and the bedaubed canvas become an airy and changeable reflex of what it purports to represent." (CE 11:63) "Take them in precisely the proper point of view, [and these tales] may amuse a leisure hour as well as those of a brighter man; if otherwise, they can hardly fail to look excessively like nonsense." (CE 10:92)

This clutch of quotations, which could be expanded to fill a volume, reveals Hawthorne's almost Berkeleyan conviction of the subjective relativism of any version of facts or "truth." (I do not mean to say, of course, that he thought truth itself was relative, but only that any version of it is.) "The ultimate arbitrariness of matter of fact" consists in the unavoidability of the condition that every pattern of phenomena is composed or imposed by point of view, by accidents of revealing light or obscuring shade, by atmosphere, by displacement of a conventional or arranged view of life.

What composes the scene is not only the objective set of facts visible in any given perspective and in given circumstances of light and revealed feature, but just as much as these *who* has "authority" in the scene, in the Jamesian sense. In "Young Goodman Brown" the young goodman has the only available

"window," as James might again have said, through which to
view and make report of reality. His situation is precisely that of
the governess in James's "The Turn of the Screw," as the sole
reporter of "intense anomalies and obscurities," and as an authority whose testimony cannot be questioned for veracity of
intention, but can be questioned for competence to interpret
and judge, and is verifiable by no other observer or "control."
Therefore, Hawthorne's tale like James's is essentially an "amu-
sette," an "excursion into chaos"—but with this significant difference, that Hawthorne's tale has an historic correlative,
whereas James's is altogether fictive.

NOTES

1. Corresponding to the minister's dropping his glove and resuming it, with all the symbolism this implies, is Hester's throwing
away and afterwards taking up again her scarlet letter. For detailed
discussion of this parallelism see my article on "Hawthorne's *The Scarlet Letter*" Item 62, *Explicator* 29 (April 1971).

2. "As Mr. Wilson delivers his 'discourse' . . . the minds of the
populace are confirmed in the mold of Puritan thought."—Charles
Feidelson, Jr., *Symbolism and American Literature* (Chicago: Univ. of
Chicago Press, 1953), 10. "Puritanism in the early seventeenth century
. . . was more properly symbolized, not by the secluded individual,
but by the social tableau of the covenanted church and the public
discourse. . . . Puritan life, in the New England theory, was centered
upon a corporate and communal ceremony, upon the oral delivery of a
lecture."—Perry Miller, *The New England Mind: The Seventeenth Century*
(Boston: Beacon Press, 1965), 297–98.

3. Thomas Hardy made use of the same connotations of pink
ribbons in *Tess of the D'Urbervilles*. Mrs. Derbyfield, dressing Tess before she set out to live with the D'Urbervilles, put her in a white frock,
washed her abundant brown hair, and "tied it with a broader pink
ribbon than usual."

4. For discussion of a similar use of equivocal metonymies in
Robert Frost's poem "Design," see Randall Jarrell's essay "To the
Laodiceans" in *Poetry and the Age* (New York: Vintage Books, 1955),
42–45.

5. "Towards the dimness of evening, a half-length figure appearing at a window:—the blackness of the background and the light upon the face cause it to appear like a Rembrandt picture." (CE 8:259)

6. "Cotton Mather, . . . the representative of all the hateful features of his time; the one bloodthirsty man, in whom were concentrated those vices of spirit and errors of opinion that sufficed to madden the whole surrounding multitude."—"Alice Doane's Appeal" (CE 11:279)

7. These are among the witches whose trials are reported in Robert Calef's *More Wonders of the Invisible World*. The characterization of Martha Carrier is quoted almost verbatim from Cotton Mather.

8. Miller, 240–41. Subsequent references to Miller, parenthetically identified in the text, are to this work.

9. "The greatest narrative works deal with what might be called sacred crimes, transgressions of the tabus on which human society is founded."—Simon O. Lesser, *Fiction and the Unconscious* (New York: Random House, 1962), 107.

10. See David Levin, "Shadows of Doubt: Specter Evidence in Hawthorne's 'Young Goodman Brown,' " *American Literature* 34 (November 1962):344–52.

THIRTEEN

"A Vast Deal of Human Sympathy"

Hawthorne's fiction, as Roy R. Male has remarked, consistently distinguished between man's role of "speculation" and woman's role of "investment." "Hawthorne customarily symbolized the humane qualities of investment in the unobtrusive feminine task of sewing."[1] This chapter will examine how Hawthorne combined the symbolism of needlework as actualizing power (investment) with his favorite symbolism for imaginative power ("snow-images") to give visible figure to ideal imaginations in the tale "The Snow-Image: A Childish Miracle."

I

SILKEN THREADS

The feminine craft or mystery denoted by needlework is often indicated in Hawthorne's fiction by other signs. The tale "The New Adam and Eve," written during the author's honeymoon in the Old Manse and published in 1843 in *The Democratic Review*, provides a convenient and fairly early key to his notation of feminine (and masculine) traits. The unsophisticated responses of the New Adam and Eve to things encountered in a depopulated modern city (Boston) are noted in order to discern "how much is merely the interpolation of the perverted mind and heart of man." (This sentence characteristically blends a romantic assumption of man's natural goodness with a Calvinistic conviction of man's inherited depravity.) "Such a pair would at once distinguish between art and nature." Adam "appears to have the stronger tendency toward the material world"; (CE 10:249) but Eve, whose character "comprises the whole nature of womanhood," (CE 10:258) shows slight interest in public buildings and civic life. Her "instincts and intuitions" are domestic and maternal. The signs of this are detailed in a series of incidents in which she shows a natural disposition to needlework, music, housewifery, tending flowers, and maternity.

Of several signs of womanhood, the one most usually and prominently displayed by Hawthorne's female characters is needlework, perhaps because of its analogical or allegorical versatility. Needlework is, in fact, to be taken as a synecdochic sign of traits which comprise "the whole nature of womanhood." It is, for example, used in the tale "The Artist of the Beautiful" (written and published at the same time as "The New Adam and Eve") to distinguish woman's sensitive perceptions from masculine materialism on the one hand and artistic idealism on the other hand. The four adult characters of the tale represent grades of humanity between the material and the ideal, ranging from the temporal or mundane-abstract (Hovenden the watchmaker) and the material or mundane-concrete (Danforth the blacksmith), through the more sensitive and delicate feminine type of the mundane (Annie Hovenden Danforth, who as daughter, sweetheart, wife, and mother combines all phases of her sex), to the altogether "spiritual" person (Warland the Artist). The man who cannot transcend time, the man who cannot transcend material, and the woman whose senses are refined almost to spirituality are all alike incapable of comprehending the Artist's ideal. All in different degrees threaten and oppress his imagination, although the woman approaches his ideas, and her needle and thimble are signs both of her refined perception and delicate manipulation of life and of her inescapable involvement in the same temporal-material world as her watchmaker father and her blacksmith husband.

Woman's "delicate and imaginative skill" (CE 1:81) in needlework is used symbolically or mentioned synecdochically in all four of Hawthorne's romances.

Hester Prynne, in *The Scarlet Letter*, used her "art" of needlework to earn a livelihood for herself and Pearl by "investment" of the most literal kind: making garments for life-and-death events such as swaddling babies and shrouding corpses, and making vestments for ceremonial occasions "such as ordinations, the installation of magistrates, and all that could give majesty to the forms in which a new government manifested itself to the people." (CE 1:82) She used her needlework also to clothe the needy, thereby acknowledging "her sisterhood with the race of man." (CE 1:160–61) Thus she wrought with her woman's art to make actual a fabric of human life and to weave her own life and little Pearl's into that fabric, from which they would otherwise have been cut off. She used her needlework not only to maintain a social connection, but also to sustain a personal expression. "She had in her nature a rich, voluptuous, Oriental characteristic," (CE 1:83) which she indulged, not in embroidering her own attire, but in emblazoning "the scarlet letter endowed with life," (CE 1:102) little Pearl, who was herself the most vivid product of Hester's voluptuousness. These two uses of Hester's needlework, the social and the personal, are a figure for her paradoxical relation to society, which was one of both affiliation and opposition; her needlework both performed sisterly and ceremonial service to society, and expressed a "taste for the gorgeously beautiful" (CE 1:83) which was scarcely permissible in that society.

Needlework symbolism is not prominent in *The House of the Seven Gables*. It is referred to only metonymically and allusively, although Phoebe, the Eve installed in the ancient house of Pyncheon, and Holgrave her Adam exactly fit Male's distinction of sexual roles in Hawthorne's fiction. Phoebe, who fears to be led out of "her own quiet path," (CE 2:306) is one of what Hawthorne calls "the limit-loving class"; (CE 2:131) and Holgrave is a young man with a rage to rend the fabric of society, to "speculate." Although the visible activity of needlework which is Hawthorne's usual sign of woman's function of "conserving and clothing in time"[2] is only slightly indicated, the womanhood which it signifies is manifested by Phoebe in other signs: a love of flowers, a "gift of song," (CE 2:138) an adeptness in the ordinary little toils of housewifery. Hawthorne's characterization of Phoebe and all such simple Eves combines reminiscences both literary and personal: of Milton's Eve entertaining the Angel Raphael with "savoury fruits" and "pleasant liquors"; of Wordsworth's Phantom of Delight, who was "a spirit, yet a woman too"; and of Hawthorne's own Sophia.

One explicit mention of needlework occurs in an early passage of *The House of the Seven Gables*. In this scene Phoebe barters for some yarn with "a very ancient woman" who "was probably the very last person in town who kept the time-honored spinning-wheel in constant revolution." During the exchange, the voices of Phoebe and the ancient woman mingle "in one twisted thread of talk." (CE 2:78–79) The ancient woman resembles one of the Parcae, and in this there is a hint of mythic significance.

Needlework symbolism is important in *The Blithedale Romance*. The curious specialty of the pale little seamstress Priscilla is knitting little silk purses of which "the peculiar excellency, besides their great delicacy and beauty of manufacture, lay in the almost impossibility that any uninitiated person should discover the aperture." (CE 3:35) In this emblem there are unmistakable suggestions of sex and money, the means (real but enhanced into quasi-symbolism in Hawthorne, as later in Henry James) by which persons bargain for what they want, and influence or control the lives of other persons. Priscilla, a pale virgin shrouded in snow, merely displays the signs of these resources which are her birthright, while her sister Zenobia flaunts a double share of them. Nevertheless, because pale Priscilla has not spent these resources, it is she who retains management of what Hawthorne called the "web" of life, as is suggested by an elaborate thread analogy which he first developed explicitly in *The Blithedale Romance*. It occurs in a passage in which Coverdale, hidden high in his leafy "hermitage," has indulged his voyeuristic habit so far that he supposes he has seized intimate secrets of Zenobia's sexual experience with Westervelt, and gives a fanciful message to a bird flitting by, to be carried to Priscilla: "Tell her . . . that her fragile thread of life has inextricably knotted itself with other and tougher threads, and most likely it will be broken." (CE 3:100) But eventually Priscilla's thread proves the

tougher, and it is the other life-threads knotted with hers that
are broken.

This symbolism of the thread of life which women spin,
Clotho-like, and weave into a web of human relations, becomes
a more definite figure and acquires mythic significance in Hawthorne's retelling of the tale of the Minotaur in *Tanglewood Tales*,
published the year after *The Blithedale Romance*. "The value of
investment may be summed up," as Male says, "in the myth
of Ariadne, whose thread leads Theseus out of the labyrinth
of speculation."[3]

The thread or "clue" and the labyrinth are complementary
symbols in Hawthorne's fiction, which frequently refers to the
world and its microcosm, the heart of man, as a labyrinth, maze,
hieroglyphic, riddle, puzzle, or mystery. Thus, in "The Toll-
Gatherer's Day," he wrote of "the mysterious confusion, the
apparently unsolvable riddle, in which individuals, or the great
world itself, seem often to be involved." (CE 9:211) In "Footprints on the Sea-Shore" a huge rock "in monumental shape"
bears veins that "resemble inscriptions" (a detail used again in
"Roger Malvin's Burial") which the author fancies to be "characters of an antediluvian race" or a mystery recorded by "Nature's own hand" (CE 9:455)—a suggestive symbolism like that
in Poe's *Narrative of Arthur Gordon Pym*. Dimmesdale in *The
Scarlet Letter* suggests that not until the Judgment Day can men
expect to "see the dark problem of this life made plain." (CE
1:131–32) Pearl is a "living hieroglyphic" (CE 1:207) of her
parents' sin—one whose secret, however, the profane scientist
Chillingworth surmises to be not "beyond a philosopher's research." (CE 1:116) Holgrave, in *The House of the Seven Gables*,
says that "this is such an odd and incomprehensible world" that
"the more I look at it the more it puzzles me, and I begin to
suspect that a man's bewilderment is the measure of his wisdom." (CE 2:178)

It is not man's rational understanding but woman's intuitive
wisdom which can guide man through this maze. The passage
in *Tanglewood Tales* to which Male evidently refers in his mention
of the myth of Ariadne elaborates the figure:

> [Theseus] would have felt quite lost and utterly hopeless of again
> walking in a straight path, if, every little while, he had not been

> conscious of a gentle twitch at the silken cord. . . . [T]here was
> a vast deal of human sympathy running along that slender thread
> of silk. (CE 7:206–7)

This literal manipulation of the silken thread in the myth of Ariadne became a complex figure for Hawthorne later, in *The Marble Faun*.[4] In an early scene in which the artist Miriam is "busied with the feminine task of mending a pair of gloves," Hawthorne introduced a significant excursus on "this peculiarity of needlework, distinguishing men from women":

> The slender thread of silk or cotton keeps them united with the
> small, familiar, gentle interests of life, the continually operating
> influences of which do so much for the health and the character,
> and carry off what would otherwise be a dangerous accumulation
> of morbid sensibility. A vast deal of human sympathy runs along
> this electric line, . . . keeping high and low in a species of
> communion with their kindred beings. (CE 4:39–40)

The "electric line" as analogy or emblem of woman's subtle conductive energy was almost a cliché in mid-nineteenth-century American writing. Margaret Fuller, in *Woman in the Nineteenth Century*, opined that "the especial genius of Woman" is "electrical," whereas "you will often see men of high intellect absolutely stupid in regard to . . . the fine invisible links which connect the forms of life around them."[5] In such passages, as in much of Hawthorne's writing, the author borrows terms and concepts on a frontier of science, not from any interest in science *per se*, but in order to give a modern rendering to a banal thought.

The Ariadne figure of the silken thread as an electric line of connection which runs throughout "organized life" is employed in *The Marble Faun* as if the "subtle and universal" "sympathy" (CE 2:174) it carries were an actual force, something like the phenomenon of "direct action at a distance" which was a puzzle even to Isaac Newton. Kenyon, at Monte Beni, sees in the clouds (another frequent medium of imaginative perception and projection in Hawthorne, as in Shakespeare) "a reclining figure, . . . feminine, and with a despondent air"; (CE 4:265) and his heart is moved, as Theseus's was when Ariadne twitched her silken thread. This, as the author explains in a later passage, is a result of "Hilda's hand pulling at the silken cord that was connected with his heartstrings," while she stood in Rome yearning toward him "as he stood looking towards Rome from the battlements of Monte Beni." (CE 4:343) The author violates his symbol in making it so crudely explicit as it is in this instance.

The symbolism of thread and needlework of which I have thus traced the evolution occurs throughout Hawthorne's fiction. In his last "abortive" romances it still appears. Thus little Elsie of *Doctor Grimshawe's Secret* has the "truly feminine" "idiosyncrasy" of twisting a kind of "emblematic embroidery"[6] full of strange, fanciful, and graceful devices" which "grew beneath her fingers as naturally as the variegated hues grow on a flower as it opens." (CE 12:410) She thus enacts woman's role of giving life and lustre to patterns of reality designed by men. Woman weaves and embroiders the fabric of life, but man invents its forms.

II

SNOW-IMAGES

Hawthorne's fiction abounds in images of human beings: stone images ("The Great Stone Face"), wooden images ("Drowne's Wooden Image"), painted images ("Edward Randolph's Portrait"), flesh-and-blood images, mirror images ("Monsieur du Miroir"), and snow-images. All such images, even flesh-and-blood images which are actual persons, are alike in being material embodiments or presentments of ideas of persons. The differences between these several kinds of images are differences in the substantiality with which the ideas are embodied: that is, in the degree to which idea has been hypostasized into material. The more tenuous the material embodiment, the larger the proportion of idea, or the nearer the beholder approaches to viewing pure idea. Conversely, the more perdurable the material, the less the proportion of idea, or the more completely it has been reduced to material. Tenuousness, then, is an indication of the continuous tendency of idea to escape material envisagement; and durability is the condition of an idea subdued to its material. Thus Elinor, in "The Prophetic Pictures," responds to Walter's rapture over a portrait that has preserved the beauty of a woman's pictured countenance for more than two hundred years with the comment: "But where all things fade, how miserable to be one that could not fade!" (CE 9:170) In *The Marble Faun* Hawthorne called Roman portrait-busts "the concretions and petrifactions of a vain self-estimate." (CE 4:118)

The supposition of an ideal-material ratio pervades all of Hawthorne's work; he habitually applied it to his observation of the corporeality of human beings. Several of his characters are blacksmiths whose massive bodies indicate that to them the world of mass and force is the "real" world. Among such characters are John Inglefield, whose features looked as if they had been "rudely fashioned at his own anvil"; (CE 11:179) the "man of iron" (CE 10:468) Robert Danforth; and Hollingsworth in *The Blithedale Romance*, who "seemed to have been hammered out of iron." (CE 3:28) All of these unmalleable persons destroy ideal values of other characters, not through malice but through insensitiveness.

Even if not associated with iron hardness, Hawthorne's bulky characters[7] have a very slight infusion of ideal or spiritual existence. Examples of this are the Old Inspector in "The Custom-House" and two gross Pyncheons, the old Colonel and the modern Judge. One of Hawthorne's *American Notebook* entries humorously suggests: "Supposing a man to weigh 140 lbs. when married, and after marrige to increase to 280 lbs.—then, surely, he is half a bachelor, especially if the union be not a spiritual one." (CE 8:314) The narrator in "P's Correspondence" speaks for his author when he says, "A prodigious fat man always impresses me as a kind of hobgoblin." (CE 10:366)

Characters who represent the other extreme of this spiritual-material equation are persons whose physical make is so slight that they are in perpetual danger of slipping their hold on mortal existence. Examples of this are Georgiana in "The Birthmark," Sylph Etherege, and Priscilla in *The Blithedale Romance*.

This supposition of an ideal-material ratio was not merely a literary device for Hawthorne; he employed it in his conceptions of actual persons. Thus, of Samuel Johnson he wrote that "his awful dread of death showed how much of muddy imperfection was to be cleansed out of him before he could be capable of a spiritual existence." (CE 5:122) He opined that in a few more centuries John Bull "will be the earthliest creature that the earth ever saw," (CE 5:64) taking such corpulency as a sign of spiritual deficiency.

Conversely, such slight persons as Elizabeth Barrett Browning and the Brownings' son Robert prompted Hawthorne's speculation that they were spiritual in proportion to their physical frailty: "Really, I do not see how Mr. Browning can suppose that he has an earthly wife any more than an earthly child; both are of elfin race, and will flit away some day when he least thinks of it." (RE 10:244)

In Hawthorne's fiction the embodiment or "image" is not the person himself, but merely an artifice of eternity by which an idea is made sensible, or given temporary envisagement. The ideal person exists in himself and to himself, and perhaps in some realm of absolute being, but his image exists only to those who can discern it and only so long as the physical circumstances which define it maintain their organization within the beholder's field of perception. Such an envisagement is always an imaginative action of the beholder, who sees only as much of a person's reality as his faculties and the conditions of the medium enable him to recognize.

Consequently, in Hawthorne's stories the ontological question of what or who a person is resolves into the epistemological question of to whom a person exists and in what circumstances. An "image" invariably tells as much about the person who imagines or sees it as it does about the person seen in the image. Feathertop is a witch's conjuration, a mere spectre whose lack of any original connection with an ideal world is exposed by his scarecrow reflection in a mirror. (Mirrors function in Hawthorne's fiction as magical devices which reveal idea by divesting it of body.) The wooden images of Drowne the woodcarver are merely dead sticks until the inspiration of love enables him to see spirit in an image in which he had previously seen only matter.

In view of such assumptions, we see the significance to Hawthorne of "snow-images" as ideas envisaged with the least possible investment of material, the perceptions of persons of refined imagination rather than strong sense. In his work falling snow, because of its ghostly, shifting, and transitory appearances, is a medium of imagination. "There is an influence," he wrote, "favorable to imaginative thought, in the atmosphere of a snowy day." (CE 9:344) Then, while logs blaze in an open fireplace and coals glow on the hearth, comes the author's "hour of inspiration," (CE 9:344) when the wind

> shall seem like an articulate voice, and dictate wild and airy matters for the pen. Would it might inspire me to sketch out the personification of a New England winter! And that idea, if I can seize the snow-wreathed figures that flit before my fancy, shall be the theme of the next page. (CE 9:346)

It proved to be the theme not only of the next page but also of his story of a "childish miracle," "The Snow-Image."

"The Snow-Image" was first published in the same year as *The Scarlet Letter* (in October 1850, in *The International Magazine*). Although the narrative substance of the tale was probably furnished by Hawthorne's observation of his own children making a snow-image on a winter afternoon, while his wife fondly regarded them through the window in the intervals of her sewing, the elements of myth and miracle which enhance the story may be traceable to the same reverie as the famous passage in "The Custom-House" which describes how the warm light of a dim coal-fire "mingles itself with the cold spirituality of the moonbeams, and communicates, as it were, a heart and sensibilities of human tenderness to the forms which fancy summons up. It converts them from snow-images into men and women." (CE 1:36)

III

A CHILDISH MIRACLE

In the tale "The Snow-Image" the girl Violet and the boy Peony, making a snow-child in a winter garden, are an innocent Adam and Eve. The garden is so pure and so chilling to sense that it has congealed all that it contains into mere paradigms of natural forms. Besides the children, the only animate creatures in the garden are snow-birds, "old Winter's grandchildren," (CE 11:17) which "take delight only in the tempest." (CE 11:8) The only vividness in the garden (vivid color suggests sexuality in Hawthorne) is the gold of Violet's hair and the red of Peony's cheeks, colors assimilated to the sunset and rosy clouds.

The making of the snow-image is an example of organic creation. It "seemed, in fact, not so much to be made by the children, as to grow up under their hands." (CE 11:10) They do not originate the idea which the image makes visible; they merely procreate a form for it. They get the idea after they have "frosted one another all over with handfuls of snow," so that their appearance prompts Violet to tell Peony that he looks "'exactly like a snow-image.'" (CE 11:8–9)

The procreative conception and impulse are thus the girl's, and the boy is her willing collaborator, but both are passive agents of Nature. This process resembles that suggested in "The New Adam and Eve." In this tale, when the innocent pair "discover the marble statue of a child . . . so exquisitely idealized that it is almost worthy to be the prophetic likeness of their first born," Eve archly whispers to Adam, "[S]omething tells me that we shall not always be alone. And how sweet if other beings were to visit us in the shape of this fair image!" (CE 10:257) Ultimately, such passages appear to be private references to the connubial joys of the Hawthornes during their honeymoon years when "The New Adam and Eve" was written, and may hint something of their sexual roles. The making of Pearl by Hester Prynne and Arthur Dimmesdale is an adult erotic version of such image-making as that carried on by Violet and Peony—with Hester, like Violet, presumably initiating it, and Arthur acting as her willing collaborator. Hester maintained that what they did "had a consecration of its own" (CE 1:195)—that is, Nature approved, although it was a sin by social definition. Pearl was an infant "worthy to have been brought forth in Eden," (CE 1:90) though an unworthy outcast in Puritan Boston. Hawthorne apparently wrote "The Snow-Image" and *The Scarlet Letter* at about the same time; so such parallels are both legitimate and suggestive.

While the children make the snow-child in the winter garden, their mother sits sewing in a room overlooking the scene and watches their procreative play with love and sympathy. Her character had "a strain of poetry," "a trait of unworldly beauty" "that had survived out of her imaginative youth, and still kept itself alive amid the dusty realities of matrimony and motherhood." (CE 11:7) She shares the children's thought as they begin their work, "that the new snow, just fallen from heaven, would be excellent material to make new beings of, if it were not so very cold." (CE 11:9) And while they make the child, she carries on her work of investment, "either trimming a silken bonnet for Violet, or darning a pair of stockings" for Peony's "short and sturdy legs." (CE 11:9–10) Again, . . . and again, and yet other agains, she could not help turning her head to the window to see how the children got on with their snow-image." (CE 11:10)

Meanwhile, as the children make the image, they are in telepathic accord with their mother, soliciting and expecting her sympathy. Peony says that "mamma shall see it," (CE 11:9) and Violet agrees that "mamma shall see the new little girl." (CE 11:9) Violet, "graceful and agile, and so delicately colored that she looked like a cheerful Thought more than a physical reality," (CE 11:9) is "the guiding spirit" (CE 11:12) and shapes out "all the nicer parts." (CE 11:10) Peony, "as substantial as an elephant," (CE 11:9) acts "rather as a laborer," (CE 11:12) bringing her "snow from far and near."

While the children and their mother share this imagination and carry on their work of creation and investment, a magical change of light is occurring. Just as the last direct ray of sunlight on this "one of the shortest days of the whole year" (CE 11:12) dazzles through falling snow on the image, a miraculous moment arrives, when the image-making instinct of the children and the force of love of the mother collect and organize the suffused life of nature and quicken the image into life.

In this instant the children notice that the snow-image has assumed the vivid colors of the sunset sky. Golden-haired Violet calls to Peony that "A light has been shining on her cheek out of that rose-colored cloud! and the color does not go away!" And rosy-cheeked Peony answers, "O Violet, only look at her hair! It is all like gold!" Violet explains, "That color, you know, comes from the golden clouds, that we see up there in the sky." (CE 11:14)

Thus light is used as a transforming medium which makes the winter garden "a neutral territory, somewhere between the real world and fairy-land, where the Actual and the Imaginary may meet, and each imbue itself with the nature of the other"

(CE 1:36) (to quote again from the famous "Custom-House" passage on imagination). Hawthorne regularly uses a certain slant of light coinciding with a transitory state of heightened consciousness in persons to mark such miraculous moments. An important instance is the climactic scene in *The House of the Seven Gables*, at the conclusion of Holgrave's mesmeric reading to Phoebe just at the instant of sunset's merging into moonrise. (Other stories in which mingled effects of light are a magical medium of envisagement are "Alice Doane's Appeal," "The Wives of the Dead," "My Kinsman, Major Molineux," "An Old Woman's Tale," and "The Hollow of the Three Hills.")

To bring their snow-child into the communion of living things, by giving her the consummating touch of vivid affectional life, the children then give her a "life-giving kiss." Violet remarks, "She is almost finished now. But her lips must be made very red,—redder than her cheeks. Perhaps, Peony, it will make them red if we both kiss them!" (CE 11:14) "But, as this did not seem to make the lips quite red enough, Violet next proposed that the snow-child should be invited to kiss Peony's scarlet cheek." (CE 11:14) When this was done, Violet noted with satisfaction that "now her lips are very red. And she blushed a little, too!" (CE 11:42) In this exchange of kisses there are delicate suggestions that the snow-child's sexual feelings as well as her human affections have been quickened.

The life-giving kiss (sometimes the symbolic gesture is a life-giving touch, as in "Drowne's Wooden Image") is a frequently recurring figure in Hawthorne, who felt that he had himself been rescued from a torpid, merely formal existence by Sophia's life-giving kiss. In the *American Notebooks* he wrote that "Caresses, expressions of one sort or another, are necessary to the life of the affections, as leaves are to the life of a tree." (CE 8:551) He used the same simile later in the *English Notebooks*, where he called caresses "the foliage of affection." (EN, 112) One needs, therefore, to heed the symbolism of caresses in Hawthorne's fiction, as significant of two things: the offer and acceptance of membership in a living communion, and the specific act and moment in which contact is made and the circuit of life is completed. It has such significance no matter whether the creature brought to life is a pond-lily or a person. In "The Old

Manse" he described the pond-lily as "that delicious flower, which, as Thoreau tells me, opens its virgin bosom to the first sunlight and perfects its being through the magic of the genial kiss." (CE 10:23) One of the best examples of the symbolic significance of human kisses is the series of kisses offered to Pearl by various characters, and refused, submitted to, or returned by her, according to the ways and degrees in which she instinctively recognizes that they are life-giving or otherwise; the climax of these is Pearl's voluntarily kissing Dimmesdale on the lips after his dying public confession. Hawthorne's symbolic kisses relate to an underlying romantic assumption of a loving-living communion of all creatures like that expressed in Wordsworth's conviction that every flower enjoys the air it breathes, and in Coleridge's figure of the spring of love that gushed forth from the Ancient Mariner's heart when he beheld the watersnakes, "happy living things."

The breath of life is breathed into the snow-child by the benign principle in Nature, the West Wind. Just as Peony is exclaiming that his snow-sister has given him a cold kiss, "there came a breeze of the pure west-wind, sweeping through the garden and rattling the parlor-windows. It sounded so wintry cold, that the mother was about to tap on the window-pane with her thimbled finger, to summon the two children in, when they both cried out to her with one voice." (CE 11:14) What they announced was: "We have finished our little snow-sister, and she is running about the garden with us." (CE 11:15) The west-wind which has breathed animation into the snow-figure is necessary to sustain her continued sensible life. The mother, watching through the window, suspected the child might be "only a light wreath of the new-fallen snow, blown hither and thither about the garden by the intensely cold west-wind." (CE 11:16) Violet is aware that the little snow girl "cannot live any longer than while she breathes the cold west-wind." (CE 11:19)

The East-Wind West-Wind symbolic opposition often used in Hawthorne's work is made explicit in one of his love letters to Sophia (April 18, 1839; the terms are very frequently used in the love letters):

> As to the east wind, if ever the imaginative portion of my brain recover from its torpor, I mean to personify it as a wicked, spite-

ful, blustering, treacherous—in short, altogether devilish sort of body, whose principle of life is to make as much mischief as he can. The west wind . . . shall assume your aspect, and be humanized and angelicized with your traits of character, and the sweet West shall finally triumph over the fiendlike East, and rescue the world from his miserable tyranny. (LL 1, 16–17)

Hawthorne saw his own history as that of a person involved in such a contention of influences. Perhaps his most striking fictional use of this mythology is in the climaxing chapters of *The House of the Seven Gables*, in which the east-wind influences which drove Hepzibah and Clifford from the house give way, during a stormy night of death and resurrection, to "humanizing and angelicizing" west-wind influences, which assert their mastery when the "wind has veered about" and "comes now boisterously from the north-west." (CE 2:277) After the wind has "swept the sky clear," (CE 2:278) the new day that dawns finds the Pyncheon elm "all alive, and full of the morning sun and a sweetly tempered little breeze," (CE 2:284) so that the aged tree dangles a golden branch "before the main-entrance of the seven gables," "like the golden branch, that gained Aeneas and the Sybil admittance into Hades." (CE 2:285) Everything about the house contributed to "a mystic expression that something within the house was consummated." (CE 2:286)

As the mother's sympathetic action of sewing has continued during the making of the snow-girl, so also is it finished just as the children announce to her that they have finished the snow-child and entreat her acceptance of their child. She hears their call just as she is "putting the last few stitches into Peony's frock." (CE 11:15) She thinks "what imaginative little beings" (CE 11:15) her children are, reflects that "they make me almost as much a child as they themselves are!" (CE 11:15), and acknowledges, "I can hardly help believing, now, that the snow-image has really come to life!" (CE 11:15) Looking forth from the window, she sees that the sun "has now gone out of the sky, leaving, however, a rich inheritance of his brightness among those purple and golden clouds which make the sunsets of winter so magnificent." But "there was not the slightest gleam or dazzle." (CE 11:15) That is, the world of garden and heaven were still charged with the colors of life, but the transitory moment of miracle had passed; the ideal had become the actual.

As the tenuous existence of the snow-girl is sustained by faith, it is dissolved by unfaith. "Faith is the soul's eyesight," (CE 6:229) as one of Hawthorne's story-tellers remarks; so when it is lacking, existences which are mainly spiritual become imperceptible. Masculine intelligence is likely to regard only coarse material realities; and the father of Violet and Peony "was an excellent but exceedingly matter-of-fact sort of man, a dealer in hardware, and was sturdily accustomed to take what is called the common-sense view of all matters that came under his consideration." (CE 11:7) The children agree that "Mamma will see how very beautiful" the snow-girl is; but "papa will say, 'Tush! nonsense!—come in out of the cold!' " (CE 11:12) And so it falls out: the father, returning at nightfall, exclaims against permitting the strange little girl outdoors in flimsy clothing "in such bitter weather." (CE 11:18) He is himself heavily wrapped against the cold, "in a pilot-cloth sack, with a fur cap drawn down over his ears, and the thickest of gloves upon his hands." His face is "wind-flushed and frost-pinched," (CE 11:18) and he unhesitatingly rejects the mother's diffident suggestion that the girl "is nothing but a snow-image" (CE 11:18–19) which the children have made. "Do not tell me of making live figures out of snow." (CE 11:19) Despite Violet's insistence that she "cannot live any longer than while she breathes the cold west-wind," (CE 11:19) and Peony's warning that she "will not love the hot fire," this "honest and very kind-hearted man" (CE 11:19) compels the snow-girl to enter the house, and chides his wife's remonstrance with the remark that "you are as much a child as Violet and Peony." (CE 11:20)

The very approach and presence of kind Mr. Lindsey are baneful to such an ideal creature. "As he approached, the snow-birds took to flight. The little white damsel, also, fled backward," (CE 11:20) until he caught her and seized her by the hand. As the snow-girl's form moved hither and thither about the garden blown by gusts of the west-wind, she "gleamed and sparkled, . . . and seemed to shed a glow all round about her; and when driven into the corner, she positively glistened like a star!" (CE 11:21) But when she was led into the house in the grip of Mr. Lindsey, "whereas just before she had resembled a bright, frosty, star-gemmed evening, with a crimson gleam on the cold horizon, she now looked as dull and languid as a thaw." (CE 11:21)

This device of waxing and waning vividness, according to the creature's nearness to ideas which affirm or deny its life, is a common one in Hawthorne's fiction. One such instance is in the tale "Feathertop." The lifeless scarecrow fashioned by the witch Mother Rigby, although "merely a spectral illusion, and a cunning effect of light and shade so colored and contrived as to delude the eyes of most men," (CE 10:228–29) has hell-fire as the diabolical principle of its sham life, breathed into the witch's puppet from her pipe, lit by a coal fetched from hell; "the life of the illusion seemed identical with the vapor of the pipe" (CE 10:234) thrust into its mouth by the witch. So long as Feathertop believes in his own possible reality, and puffs his pipe with energy, he glistens "with illusory magnificence"; (CE 10:234) but when he has seen himself for what he is, he puffs his pipe more languidly, and becomes dim, faded, and lustreless.

A more congruent figure for the destruction of the ideal by skeptical materialism occurs in "The Artist of the Beautiful," when the Artist's butterfly, which "glistened apparently by its own radiance," (CE 10:470) "dropped its wings" and "grew dim" (CE 10:473) when it alit for a moment on the finger of the sneering watchmaker Hovenden, who doubted "in everything but a material existence," and believed that he would "understand it better when once I have touched it." (CE 10:473) If Hawthorne supposed that there is a life-giving touch of faith, he also supposed a death-giving touch of doubt. One of his child characters remarks that "some people have what we may call 'The Leaden Touch,' and make everything dull and heavy that they lay their fingers upon." (CE 7:58) The same idea appears in *The House of the Seven Gables*, in the scene in which the Judge and other fat and greasy citizens on the dusty pathway destroy with contemptuous touch the "airy spheres" (CE 2:171) which Clifford from his arched window is scattering abroad from his soap-bubble pipe.

Noting the phenomenon of the snow-girl's alternately waxing and waning brightness, "The wife thought it strange that good Mr. Lindsey should see nothing remarkable in the snow-child's appearance." (CE 11:21) Further, she fancied "that she saw the delicate print of Violet's fingers (a "birthmark") on the child's neck." (CE 11:22) Again she admonished the husband, "I do believe she is made of snow!" (CE 11:22) "A puff of the west-wind blew against the snow-child, and again she sparkled like a star." (CE 11:22) But still the common-sensible man insisted on standing her beside the stove, muffling her in thick garments, and giving her boiled milk to drink. When, presently, the father departs, he is recalled to the parlor "by the screams of Violet and Peony, and the rapping of a thimbled finger against the parlor window." (CE 11:24) There remains "no trace of the little white maiden, unless it were the remains of a heap of snow." (CE 11:24) Mr. Lindsey thereupon remarks "What a quantity of snow the children have brought in on their feet. It has made quite a puddle here before the stove." (CE 11:25)

This account of a childish miracle is of course not intended by the author to be taken as a literally possible occurrence, but as an allegory expressing the difference between the realities seen by idealist and materialist. The snow-image obviously does not and cannot become a creature in the only world that is real to "wise men of good Mr. Lindsey's stamp." "And, should some phenomenon of nature or providence transcend their system, they will not recognize it, even if it come to pass under their very noses." (CE 11:25) Hawthorne makes his point that common-sensible men *cannot enter the ideal world*, by fashioning an elaborate trope which turns the merely negative assertion of their incapacity into a positive demonstration that amounts to the same thing: that they *cannot recognize how the ideal enters into their material world*. His fable has the same point that Coleridge made in one of the aphorisms in *Aids of Reflection:* "Faith elevates the soul not only above sense and sensible things, but above reason itself. As reason corrects the errors which sense might occasion, so supernatural faith corrects the errors of natural reason judging according to sense."[8]

Among Hawthorne's tales, "The Snow-Image" is remarkable as that one of his shorter fables which brings together most of his major themes and figures. As an epitome of his fiction, it illuminates in one way or another almost every one of his more often admired works.

NOTES

1. *Hawthorne's Tragic Vision* (New York: Norton Library, 1964), 74.

2. *Ibid.*, 8.

3. *Ibid.*, 73.

4. The use of the Ariadne myth in *The Marble Faun* is reinforced by allusion to the myth of the Parcae (hinted also, as I have noted above, in *The House of the Seven Gables*). Kenyon sees old Italian countrywomen herding sheep or pigs, meanwhile "spinning yarn with that else forgotten contrivance, the distaff," and thinks that they might be taken for "the Parcae, spinning the thread of human destiny." (CE 4:290)

5. *Woman in the Nineteenth Century* (Boston: Roberts Brothers, 1893), 115, 103.

6. The quasi-art of embroidery is, in Hawthorne's view, woman's most proper artistic creation, although as mere ornamentation it is inferior to masculine designs. His women characters who are graphic artists are either copyists of men's works or painters who project their own distempered natures into the subjects that they paint. "Woman's light and fanciful embroidery," he wrote in "Mrs. Hutchinson," "should sparkle upon the garment without enfeebling the web." (RE 12:217)

7. See James F. Ragan, "Hawthorne's Bulky Puritans," *PMLA* 75 (September 1960):420–23.

8. (London: "Bohn's Popular Library," George Bell & Sons, 1913), 137.

PART THREE

The Scarlet Letter: "A Drama of Guilt and Sorrow"

CHAPTER

FOURTEEN

"The Strong Division-Lines of Nature"

Mason Wade has remarked that "the relations between the Hawthornes and Margaret [Fuller] were both close and intimate" in the early 1840s during Hawthorne's stay at Brook Farm and the early years of his marriage while he and Sophia were living in the Old Manse in Concord. He rightly says that although Hawthorne "consciously disliked intellectual women and judged them unfit for authorship," "the evidence that Hawthorne and Margaret felt friendship for each other, once he, like all her friends, had passed through the avenue of sphinxes, is far more weighty than can be mustered in support" of the view that he had "an early and steadily increasing dislike for her."[1] In fact, from the beginning of their acquaintanceship until the end of his life Hawthorne had ambivalent feelings toward Fuller which sometimes showed themselves in mingled expressions of liking and disapproval, and at other times in distinct phases of friendliness and hostility. Further, it is evident that this actual experience of ambivalent feelings toward a passionate intellectual woman entered into and colored his representations of such women in his romances—notably, Hester Prynne, Zenobia, and Miriam Schaefer.

The mentions in Hawthorne's letters to Sophia from Brook Farm of "the transcendental heifer belonging to Miss Margaret

Fuller" are essentially good-natured. His attribution of ownership of the heifer to Fuller is poetic license, a whimsical
recognition of temperamental affinity between two females:
"She is very fractious, I believe, and apt to kick over the milk
pail. Thou knowest best, whether in these traits of character,
she resembles her mistress." (LL 2:47) His comments are in-
dulgent, even appreciative: "She is not an amiable cow; but she
has a very intelligent face, and seems to be of a reflective cast of
character." (LL 2:10) But, at the same time, the transcendental
heifer's arrogance is reprehended: "Belovedst, Miss Fuller's cow
hooks the other cows, and has made herself ruler of the herd,
and behaves in a very tyrannical manner." Finally, "the herd
have rebelled against the usurpation of Miss Fuller's cow; but I
doubt not that she will soon perceive the expediency of being
on good terms with the rest of the sisterhood." (LL 2:7) When
Sophia inserted these sentences in *Passages from the American
Notebooks*, she excised portions explicitly attributing the heifer's
traits to Fuller, but the cluster of comments nevertheless was
obviously a metonymic characterization of Fuller. It is needless
to labor the obvious point that Hawthorne might at one and the
same time appreciate Fuller's intellectuality and disapprove of
her forwardness in exhibiting it and in trying to take the lead
among her associates; but I think there is, nevertheless, something to be learned from examining Hawthorne's and Fuller's
disagreements about sexual roles. The purpose of such investigation is to use the comparison and contrast to define
Hawthorne's idea of the role (*i.e.*, of what he would have
called the "propriety") of woman; and to examine the artistic
result of his idea of woman's proper role in some of his characteristic fiction.

In order to expose differences in Hawthorne's and Fuller's
ideas of propriety, the following dialogue is pieced together from
passages abridged and rearranged from Fuller's *Woman in the
Nineteenth Century* and from Hawthorne's early sketch, "Mrs.
Hutchinson."[2]

> *H:* "There are portentous indications, changes gradually
> taking place in the habits and feelings of the gentle sex, which
> seem to threaten our posterity with many of those public women,
> whereof one [Mrs. Anne Hutchinson] was a burden too grievous
> for our fathers." (RE 12:217)

F: "Women who share the nature of Mrs. Hutchinson [give] example and instruction to the rest. Many women are considering within themselves what they need that they have not, and what they can have if they find they need it. Many men are considering whether women are capable of being and having more than they are and have, *and* whether, if so, it will be best to consent to improvement in their condition." (MW, 120) "We would have every arbitrary barrier thrown down. We would have every path laid open to Woman as freely as to Man." (MW, 124)

H: "But, allowing that such forebodings are slightly exaggerated, is it good for woman's self that the path of feverish hope, of bitter and ignominious disappointment, should be left wide open to her? Is the prize worth the having if she win it? Fame does not increase the peculiar respect which men pay to female excellence." (RE 12:218)

F: "Though there has been a growing liberality on this subject," (MW, 119) "not one man in the million shall I say? no, not one in the hundred million can rise above the belief that Woman was made *for Man*." (MW, 124) "If there is a misfortune in Woman's lot, it is in obstacles being interposed by men which do *not* mark her state." (MW, 132)

H: "Woman's intellect should never give the tone to that of a man; and even her morality is not exactly the material for masculine virtue. A false liberality, which mistakes the strong division-lines of Nature for arbitrary distinctions, and a courtesy, which might polish criticism, but should never soften it, have done their best to add a girlish feebleness to the tottering infancy of our literature. The evil is likely to be a growing one. As yet, the great body of American women are a domestic race; but when a continuance of ill-judged inducements shall have turned their hearts away from the fireside, there are obvious circumstances which will render female pens more numerous and more prolific than those of men, and the ink-stained Amazons will expel their rivals by actual pressure, and petticoats wave triumphant over all the field." (RE 12:217–18)

F: "Woman the heart, Man the Head! Such divisions are only important when they are never to be transcended. If nature is never bound down nor the voice of inspiration stifled, that is enough." (MW, 152–53) [A] "sign of the times is furnished by the triumphs of Female Authorship. These have been great and are constantly increasing. Women have taken possession of so many provinces for which men had pronounced them unfit, that though these still declare there are some inaccessible to them, it is difficult to say just *where* they must stop." (MW, 162) "Male and female represent the two sides of the great radical dualism, but in fact they are perpetually passing into one another. There is no wholly masculine man, no purely feminine woman. History jeers at the attempts of physiologists to bind great original laws by the forms which flow from them. They make a rule; they say from observation what man can and cannot be. In vain! Nature provides exceptions to every rule. She sends women to battle, and sets Hercules spinning." (MW, 176–77) "As to the use of the pen, there was quite as much opposition to Woman's possessing herself of that help to free agency as there is now to her seizing the rostrum or the desk."[3] (MW, 123)

H: "The press is now the medium through which feminine ambition manifests itself; and we will not anticipate the period (trusting to be gone hence ere it arrive) when fair orators shall be as numerous as the fair authors of our own day." (RE 12:217) "[T]here is a delicacy . . . that perceives, or fancies, a sort of impropriety in the display of woman's natal mind to the world, with indications by which its inmost secrets may be searched out . . . [W]oman, when she feels the impulse of genius like a command of Heaven within her, should be aware that she is relinquishing a part of the loveliness of her sex."[4] (RE 12:218)

F: "Ye cannot believe it, men, but the only reason why women ever assume what is more appropriate to you, is because you prevent them from finding out what is fit for themselves. Were they free, were they wise fully to develop the strength and beauty of woman; they would never wish to be men, or manlike. The well-instructed moon flies not from her orbit to seize on the glories of her partner." (MW, 142) "The numerous party, whose opinions are already adjusted and labeled too much to their mind to admit of any new light, strive by lectures on some model woman of bridelike beauty and gentleness to mark out with precision the limits of Woman's sphere and Woman's mission." (MW, 120) "Whether much or little has been done, or will be done—whether women will add to the talent of narration the power of systematizing—whether they will carve marble as well as draw or paint—is not important. But that it should be acknowledged that they have intellect which needs developing—that they should not be considered complete if beings of affection and habit alone—is important." (MW, 163)

H: (aside, *sotto voce*) "We will not look for a living resemblance of Mrs. Hutchinson, though the search might not be altogether fruitless." (RE 12:217)

II

The preceding juxtapositions were arranged to show basic disagreements between Hawthorne and Fuller, but there were agreements as well. Hawthorne accepted Fuller's proposition that "male and female represent the two sides of the great radical dualism," and he was as much convinced as she that sexual characters are not to be absolutely distinguished from each other but are "perpetually passing into one another." His works continually expose the monstrousness of "wholly masculine" men who have so little of "the spiritual element" in them that they are unfit for immortality, such as Judge Pyncheon, who understood only those "solid unrealities" which "we call real estate"; (CE 2:263) or old Peter Hovenden in "The Artist of the Beautiful," too cognizant of time to be aware of eternity; or Mr. Lindsey the common-sensible hardware-merchant of "The Snow-Image."

Likewise, his works as consistently show the incompetence for worldly life of "purely feminine" women, such as Georgiana of "The Birthmark," the "now perfect woman" who "passed into the atmosphere" (CE 10:56) as a result of her husband's "eager aspiration towards the infinite" through science; or Sylph Etherege, who might at last "fade into the moonlight" and "flit away upon the breeze, like a wreath of mist." (CE 11:119) Sylph is a parody by Hawthorne of his over-etherealized heroines. She is a *reductio ad absurdum* of the too "purely feminine" woman; and Mrs. Bullfrog, in the tale by that name, is a *reductio* in the opposite direction, or rather a complementary and hyperbolical example of practical and material (that is, masculine) attributes which ought to accompany essential femininity. Laura Bullfrog, espoused by an "accomplished graduate of dry-goods store," (CE 10:130) who was resolved "to wed nothing short of perfection," (CE 10:129) is evidently developed from a note in Hawthorne's *American Notebooks* in 1835: "To represent the process by which sober truth gradually strips off all the draperies with which imagination has enveloped a beloved object, till from an angel she turns out to be a merely ordinary woman." (CE 8:11) "So painfully acute was my sense of female imperfection . . . that there was an awful risk of my getting no wife at all." (CE 10:130) Mrs. Bullfrog, despite the author's notebook reminder to himself that the sketch is to be "done without caricature," (CE 8:11) turns out to be all cosmetics and millinery, with no spirit in her other than that imbibed from a brandy-bottle. Nevertheless, the fastidious Mr. Bullfrog heeds the admonition of his experienced wife: "Women are not angels. If they were, they would go to heaven for husbands" (CE 10:136) (as, apparently, Sylph Etherege did). Since the five thousand dollars Mrs. Bullfrog has won in a breach-of-promise suit against a former lover are secure, Bullfrog accepts such solid assets as a "basis for matrimonial bliss." (CE 10:137)

Although, as these examples show, Hawthorne agreed that either sex must be tempered with some of the "predominating" traits of the other, Hawthorne did not endorse the opinion asserted by Fuller that there were no "provinces" that should be "inaccessible" to women, or that there were no provinces belonging to women upon which men should not intrude. He could hardly have tolerated Hercules spinning, for he held that the manipulation of a "slender thread of silk or cotton" is a "peculiarity" "distinguishing women from men. Our own sex is incapable of any such by-play aside from the main business of life." (CE 4:39) Certainly he could not have endured sending women to battle. Mrs. Hannah Duston, who avenged the outrages of an Indian captivity by slaying and scalping ten Indians, he pronounced an "awful woman," "a bloody old hag" whose memory should be "accursed"; while her "tender-hearted, yet valiant" husband deserved to be "held in affectionate remembrance."[5]

In short, Hawthorne had no liking for the monstrous regiment of women. His ideal of womanhood was "the sweet, chaste, faithful, and courageous Imogen, the tenderest and womanliest woman that Shakespeare ever made immortal in the world." (CE 5:80) In portraying such an ideal woman, he begins with the idea of an angel-woman who is to be made humanly real by fulfilling a double role to man: the role of Venus, which unites woman to man physically; and the role of mediatrix between the spiritual world and man, which makes man spiritually real by awakening his soul just as man makes woman physically real by arousing her sense.[6] Each gives the other a "life-giving touch."

Hawthorne's only fully drawn portrait of a heroine complete in both carnal capability and spiritual vitality is Phoebe Pyncheon. She is Hawthorne's version of Wordsworth's "lovely Apparition" of Woman, an "example of feminine grace and availability combined." (CE 2:80) (Sylph Etherege was all grace; Mrs. Bullfrog was all availability.) Phoebe fitted and discharged "woman's office to move in the midst of practical affairs, and to gild them all . . . with an atmosphere of loveliness and joy." (CE 2:80) And, withal, she belonged to "the trim, orderly, and limit-loving class" (CE 2:131)—that is, she stayed within her propriety and province, and refused to be led out of "her own quiet path." (CE 2:306)

There is an obvious difficulty in combining the roles of Venus and angel. The angelic principle may inhibit the venereal principle, resulting in such blank figures as Priscilla and Hilda, whose purity would be stained by carnal experience; or the Venus in woman may be developed so early and strongly that a woman's spiritual nature becomes recessive rather than dominant, and persists only as a guilty conscience rather than as an effective monitor, as in such dark ladies as Hester, Zenobia, and Miriam.

The perplexities of these dark ladies are increased by the fact that, having lost their spiritual orientation or "clue" through carnal license or abuse—that is, having forfeited the birthright of their sex—they attempt to compensate by orienting themselves to mundane realities and directing "practical" affairs. It is, in Hawthorne's view, the function of women to give life to forms, but of men to give forms to life; so such interferences of women in practical affairs are improper. For all the prominence of women in Hawthorne's fictions, and the fact that they are his warmer and more vivid characters (when they are not his coolest and palest), his plots make them auxiliaries to men.

Some women characters in his works are simply examples of such usurped masculinity, but these are no more numerous than his "perfect woman" types, and are even less important. They appear in early sketches such as "The Duston Family" and "Queen Christina" as pre-studies of one element of tragic womanhood; but in their simple manifestations they did not interest him enough to earn prominent roles in his stories, for he regarded them as being so entirely unwomaned that they are not sympathetic persons but monsters.

Hawthorne's sketch of Queen Christina was intended to be "chiefly profitable as showing the evil effects of a wrong education, which caused this daughter of a king to be both useless and unhappy." (CE 6:275) "Gustavus should have remembered that Providence had created her to be a woman, and that it was not for him to make a man of her." (CE 6:277) (Hawthorne no doubt thought the same thing of Margaret Fuller's having been given a masculine education by her father, who had wanted her to be a boy.) "There was nobody to teach her the delicate graces and gentle virtues of a woman. She was surrounded almost entirely by men, and had learned to despise the society of her own sex." (CE 6:281) He concluded: "Happy are the little girls of America, who are brought up quietly and tenderly at the domestic hearth, and thus become gentle and delicate women! May none of them ever lose the loveliness of their sex by receiving such an education as that of Queen Christina!" (CE 6:283) It was not Christina's intellectuality, but her forfeiture of womanliness, that made her a monster; for "it is very possible for a woman to have a strong mind, and to be fitted for the active business of life, without losing any of her natural delicacy." (CE 6:283–84)

Such a character as Hester Prynne remained sympathetic and womanly for her author, and was not a Christina; for, although her "heart had lost its regular and healthy throb," so that she "wandered without a clew in the dark labyrinth of mind," (CE 1:66) obsessed with problems that a woman "never overcomes" "by any exercise of thought"; (CE 1:166) and although she risked the danger that thereby, "perhaps, the ethereal essence, wherein she has her truest life, will be found to have evaporated" (CE 1:165–66)—nevertheless she never lost the attribute "essential to keep her a woman," (CE 1:163) the capability of response to "the magic touch to effect the transfiguration." (CE 1:164) Despite her "studied austerity" (CE 1:163) and "the marble coldness of Hester's impression," (CE 1:164) when such a life-giving touch was given her, "her sex, her youth, and the whole richness of her beauty, came back from what men call the irrevocable past." (CE 1:202)

The wavering sympathy of Hawthorne for Fuller resulted from his doubt as to whether she was in fact a Queen Christina rather than a Hester, and his apparently harsh final judgment of her as one who "had not the charm of womanhood," but was a "great humbug" who "had stuck herself full of borrowed qualities," is more pitying and sympathizing than Fuller's biographers suppose, for it permits his conclusion that "she proved herself a very woman after all, and fell as the weakest of her sisters might."[7] Hawthorne could give pity and sympathy to a "very woman" who had fallen, but not to a woman who had succeeded in the role of a man.

That Hawthorne retained until the end of his life such sentiments about women is made evident by traits of the heroines of his "abortive" romances, most of them varied reincarnations of his wraithlike Alices who expressed womanhood to him; as well as by his travesty of women who are "desirous of being ranked among men" in his portrait of modern woman as Bloomer Girl drawn by Alice in *The Ancestral Footstep:* "I think I see one of these paragons now, in a Bloomer . . . swaggering along with a Bowie knife at her girdle, smoking a cigar, no doubt, and tippling sherry-cobblers and mint juleps." (RE 11:504)

III

The opposite extremes of the Queen Christina type and of "perfect womanhood" are not numerous or important characters in Hawthorne's work. Neither monsters nor paragons are capable of interesting literary treatment, because they lack the instability and variability which permits dramatic responses to changing circumstances, and because it is equally impossible to sympathize with perfect virtue or total perversity. Hawthorne was most interested in what Henry James later called "the appearance of waste" in human life—the same thing that Hawthorne meant in designating some of his characters as "abortive." Perfect persons in a state of absolute felicity may be fit subjects for poetic con-

templation, but they are impossible subjects for dramatic or
tragic action; and perverse persons in a hell of miserable alienation do not solicit pity enough to evoke a purgative terror. "Even
a woman may be good," as Aristotle said, and Hawthorne's heroines meet within the terms of his own ontology the Aristotelian
conditions for tragic character. They are "persons above the
common level," neither entirely virtuous nor utterly bad, but
more good than bad, "whose misfortune is brought about not by
vice or depravity, but by some error or frailty."[8] Hawthorne's
principal women characters are persons who in one way or another deviate from the pattern of female excellence and "go
astray" in life, usually in consequence of some early wrong done
them by men and thereafter through the recoil of their baffled
sexuality and spirituality into aberration from woman's "own
quiet path."

The prototypical Hawthorne heroine is Mrs. Anne Hutchinson, who, to use terms he often employed to mark the modes
of his thinking about characters, stood as an "example" of the
"class" of wronged and spoiled womanhood. He saw her fate as
initially and partly a tragedy of circumstances, but finally a consequence of her passionate perversity and disorientation. Anne
Hutchinson's character and situation were the "germ" of Hester
Prynne's. The differences between their stories are all ac-
counted for by Hawthorne's heightening of the literary and dramatic values. These differences are specifically two, both
permitted by the fact that a romance gave the author more "latitude" than an historical sketch: (1) he augmented the wayward
woman's personality and personal history in various ways to
make her more appealing—by giving her youth and beauty, by
making her an image of motherhood, by adding pathetic circumstances about a marriage that "wronged" her by betraying her
"budding youth into a false and unnatural relationship" (CE
1:75) with an old man's decay; and (2) he protracted the development of his effects, and especially reserved moral commentary and judgment until later passages of the story, instead of
making them an accompaniment to the woman's public trial and
disgrace. Thus he was enabled to establish the pathos of Hester's situation and make her a sympathetic character before he
intimated the appropriate moral judgments, which might have

had a confusing or dampening effect if they had accompanied the trial scene.

Hawthorne's two allusions to Anne Hutchinson in *The Scarlet Letter* identify Hester with her; Hester is a more deeply imagined, a more dramatically circumstanced example of the same class. In the first chapter, following description of the emblematic wild rose-bush by the prison-door, which offered its blossoms "to the condemned criminal as he came forth to his doom, in token that the deep heart of Nature could pity and be kind to him," the suggestion is made that "there is fair authority for believing, it had sprung up under the footsteps of the sainted Anne Hutchinson, as she entered the prison-door." (CE 1:48) In chapter 8, "The Elf-Child and the Minister," Pearl's wayward assertion to the Reverend John Wilson that "she had not been made at all, but had been plucked by her mother off the bush of wild roses that grew by the prison-door" (CE 1:112) links Mistress Prynne as well as Mistress Hutchinson to a Nature not subjected to civil and religious restraints. The sympathy Nature has for their behavior is a sympathy of "that wild, heathen Nature of the forest, never subjugated by human law, nor illumined by higher truth." (CE 1:203)

The second mention of Mrs. Hutchinson in *The Scarlet Letter* occurs in the middle of the book in the chapter "Another View of Hester," which comments on the effect upon Hester of her ostracism and moral alienation from society. Especially, it discussed her "freedom of speculation," which "our forefathers, had they known it, would have held to be a deadlier crime than that stigmatized by the scarlet letter." (CE 1:164) The author says that despite Hester's bold speculation, she conformed "with the utmost quietude to the external regulations of society," (CE 1:164) because her having little Pearl gave her a sufficient human relation; otherwise, "she might have come down to us in history, hand in hand with Anne Hutchinson, as the foundress of a religious sect. . . . She might . . . have suffered death from the stern tribunals of the period, for attempting to undermine the foundations of the Puritan establishment." (CE 1:165) This subject is taken up again at the end of the story. We are assured that Hester retains "her firm belief, that at some brighter period, when the world shall have grown ripe for it, in

Heaven's own time, a new truth would be revealed, in order to establish the whole relation between man and woman on a surer ground of mutual happiness." (CE 1:263) But Hester no longer thought, stained and sorrowful as she was, that she "might be the destined prophetess." (CE 1:263) Thus Hester Prynne is significantly identified with Anne Hutchinson in two respects: her estrangement from civil and religious regulation and escape into wild Nature, and her imagination of a better moral and social order of which she might be the prophetess. What Hawthorne intended by this identification I will defer to state until I have investigated parallels more thoroughly.

First, it is to be noted that the author not only identifies the characters with each other, but, in fact, he has his earlier sketch of Anne's character and situation in view throughout his telling of Hester's story.[9] The opening scene of "Mrs. Hutchinson" is similar in both matter and style to the opening scene of *The Scarlet Letter:* "A crowd of hooded women, and of men in steeple-hats and close-cropped hair, are assembled at the door and open windows of a house newly built." (RE 12:220) "A throng of bearded men, in sad-colored garments, and gray, steeple-crowned hats, intermixed with women, some wearing hoods and others bareheaded, was assembled in front of a wooden edifice, the door of which was heavily timbered with oak, and studded with iron spikes." (CE 1:47)

Intellectually, the two heroines are similar. "Mrs. Hutchinson was a woman of extraordinary talent and imagination," who had early "shown symptoms of irregular and daring thought," which, given encouragement and opportunity by "the enthusiasm of the times" and the less rigorous restraints of society in the American wilderness, "prompted her to stand forth as a reformer in religion." (RE 12:219) "Hester Prynne, with a mind of native courage and activity, and for so long a period not merely estranged, but outlawed, from society, had habituated herself" to a wild "latitude of speculation." (CE 1:199) "It was an age in which the human intellect, newly emancipated, had taken a wider range than for many centuries before. . . . Hester Prynne imbibed this spirit." (CE 1:164) "Her intellect and heart had their home, as it were, in desert places, where she roamed as freely as the wild Indian in his woods." (CE 1:199)

These two intrepid women confront their inquisitors in public scenes of trial and humiliation in similar attitudes of defiance and self-justification. Mrs. Hutchinson "stands loftily before her judges with a determined brow; and, unknown to herself, there is a flash of carnal pride half hidden in her eye, as she surveys the many learned and famous men whom her doctrines have put in fear." (RE 12:224) Hester's demeanor is similar. She displayed "natural dignity and force of character" (CE 1:52) in her actions as she came from the prison; her face had "the impressiveness belonging to a marked brow and deep black eyes"; (CE 1:53) on the scaffold she bore "the heavy weight of a thousand unrelenting eyes" with such fortitude that, had the crowd jeered at her, "she might have repaid them all with a bitter and disdainful smile." (CE 1:57) The author invites sympathy for Anne as she faces her fierce inquisitors, stern and self-righteous members of the "priesthood" who "stand full in front of the woman, striving to beat her down with brows of wrinkled iron, and whispering sternly and significantly among themselves." (RE 12:221) Hester likewise faced "sages of rigid aspect," incapable of "sitting in judgment on an erring woman's heart, and disentangling its mesh of good and evil." (CE 1:64)

The result of their outcast state is that both women, instead of becoming more amenable to orthodoxy, turn more decidedly away from it. Anne Hutchinson, exiled from Massachusetts, migrated at last to "the Dutch jurisdiction," where "she became herself the virtual head, civil and ecclesiastical, of a little colony," "[s]ecluded from all whose faith she could not govern." (RE 12:225) Hester "assumed a freedom of speculation . . . which our forefathers, had they known it, would have held to be a deadlier crime than that stigmatized by the scarlet letter"; (CE 1:264) and, if she had not had Pearl to keep her in tenuous relation to society, "she might have come down to us, hand in hand with Anne Hutchinson, as the foundress of a religious sect." (CE 1:265)

It is likely that the maternal relationship so significant in *The Scarlet Letter* is an imaginative development of something in the sketch of Anne Hutchinson. Hawthorne concludes Anne's story with a pathetic notice of the likelihood that Anne's daughter relapsed into the physical and moral savagery which is kept in the foreground as a distinct possibility also for Pearl in *The Scarlet Letter*, if her parents do not restore her connection with civil and religious community: "It was a circumstance not to be unnoticed by our stern ancestors, in considering the fate of her who had so troubled their religion, that an infant daughter, the sole survivor of the terrible destruction of her mother's household, was bred in a barbarous faith, and never learned the way to the Christian's heaven. Yet we will hope that there the mother and child have met." (RE 12:226)

Nevertheless, the author's sympathy with these strong-minded, passionate women beaten down by authority does not amount to extenuation of their waywardness. He is explicit in his justification of the severity of Anne Hutchinson's judges, in view of her "strange and dangerous opinions, tending, in the peculiar situation of the colony, and from the principles which were its basis and indispensable for its temporary support, to eat into its very existence": (RE 12:219)

> The present was a most remarkable case, in which religious freedom was wholly inconsistent with public safety, and where the principles of an illiberal age indicated the very course which must have been pursued by worldly policy and enlightened wisdom. Unity of faith was the star that had guided these people over the deep; and a diversity of sects would either have scattered them from the land to which as yet they had so few attachments, or, perhaps, have excited a diminutive civil war among those who had come so far to worship together. (RE 12:222)

Thus Hawthorne not only reprehends Mrs. Hutchinson for departing from Woman's propriety, but also excuses her expulsion from society on grounds of necessary public policy. He is just as explicit in his discommendation of Hester's "tendency to speculation." Even were she to succeed in instituting such reforms as she imagines, "the ethereal essence, wherein she has her truest life, will be found to have evaporated. A woman never overcomes these problems by any exercise of thought." (CE 1:165–66)

The author's feelings toward Anne and Hester are finally and inextricably mixed. The usual either/or presentation of Hester's case is beside the point.[10] Does Hawthorne sympathize with Hester? He does. Does he consider her in error? He does.

Does he deplore the severity and inhumanity of the system which tries and punishes her and estranges her from society and inhibits fulfillment of her womanhood? He does. Does he justify the system and its dealings with Hester? He does. Such dark dilemmas of heart and head are, his stories intimate, finally insoluble. Essentially, Hawthorne defines Anne's and Hester's cases as being (so Melville says of Billy Budd's) among those "involving considerations both practical and moral" in which "natural justice" must yield to practical "duty and the law."

Critics commonly fail to distinguish between an author's imaginative capability and his conventional opinions. Every writer is probably sometimes conscious of the doubleness of which Thoreau and Whitman have written: the transcendence of their citizen selves by their artist imaginations. One William Faulkner may acknowledge a readiness to man the southern barricades in the event of a racial war, but another writes *Intruder in the Dust*. Hawthorne the descendant of Puritans may acknowledge the justice of suppression of dissent and rebuke woman's intrusions into a masculine sphere, while his "other I am" sympathizes deeply with a woman's wrongs and frustrations, and with her impulse toward liberation from the bondage of her sex.

NOTES

1. References in this paragraph are to Mason Wade's *Margaret Fuller: Whetstone of Genius* (New York: Viking Press, 1941), 112, 108, 109.

2. I have quoted from Mason Wade's edition of *Woman in the Nineteenth Century,* included in *Writings of Margaret Fuller* (New York: Viking Press, 1941). The original version of this work was published in *The Dial* under the title "The Great Lawsuit—Man *versus* Men; Woman *versus* Women." Hawthorne's sketch "Mrs. Hutchinson" was first published in the *Salem Gazette,* December 7, 1830.

3. In regard to woman's seizing the rostrum as a sequel to using the pen, see Zenobia's remarks in *The Blithedale Romance:* "You let us write a little, it is true, on a limited range of subjects. But the pen is not for woman. Her power is too natural and immediate. It is with the living voice alone that she can compel the world to recognize the light

of her intellect and the depth of her heart!" (CE 3:120) This statement of course echoes Margaret Fuller's well-known preference for speaking to writing, and is the rationale of her "Conversations." Coverdale's judgment of Zenobia's writings, which is doubtless Hawthorne's judgment of Fuller's, was that her "poor little stories and tracts never half did justice to her intellect. It was only the lack of a fitter avenue that drove her to seek development in literature." (CE 3:44) Coverdale's diagnosis of what ails women authors is Hawthorne's—that is, an unsuitable sublimation of frustrated sexuality.

4. Sophia Hawthorne, in a letter to her mother shortly after the publication of *Woman in the Nineteenth Century*, comically echoed her husband's Miltonic sentiments on the subject of woman's rights:

> What do you think of the speech which Queen Margaret Fuller has made from the throne? It seems to me that if she were married truly, she would no longer be puzzled about the rights of woman. This is the revelation of woman's true destiny and place. . . . Even before I was married, however, I could never feel the slightest interest in this movement. It then seemed to me that each woman could make her own sphere quietly, and also it was always a shock to me to have women mount the rostrum. Home, I think, is the great arena for women.—Julian Hawthorne, *Nathaniel Hawthorne and His Wife* (Boston: Houghton Mifflin, 1884), 1:257.

Sophia's sister, Elizabeth Palmer Peabody, was of a different opinion (perhaps, the Hawthornes supposed, because she never married)—having mounted the rostrum and advocated woman's rights even before Margaret Fuller did. The subject of "woman's true destiny and place," which preoccupied Hawthorne in all four of his major romances, was a major theme of American fiction throughout the nineteenth century, being central to the novels of Howells and James, among others.

5. "The Duston Family," *Hawthorne as Editor*, ed. Arlin Turner (Baton Rouge, LA: Louisiana State Univ. Press, 1941), 136–37.

6. See Hawthorne's comments on the Venus di Medici, quoted in chapter 7 above. On woman as mediatrix, the comment of Coverdale in *The Blithedale Romance* is characteristic: "Heaven grant that the ministry of souls be left in charge of woman! . . . God meant her for it. . . . I have always envied the Catholics their faith in that sweet, sacred Virgin Mother who stands between them and the Deity, intercepting somewhat of his awful splendor, but permitting his love to stream upon the worshipper more intelligibly to human comprehension through the medium of a woman's tenderness." (CE 3:121–22)

7. *Nathaniel Hawthorne and His Wife*, 1:260–62.

8. *Aristotle's Theory of Poetry and Fine Art*, trans. S. H. Butcher, 4th ed. (New York: Dover Books, 1951), 53, 45.

9. Hawthorne had earlier sketched a similar character in "Endicott and the Red Cross," first published in the *Salem Gazette*, November 14, 1837.

10. See, e.g., Seymour L. Gross, " 'Solitude, and Love and Anguish': The Tragic Design of *The Scarlet Letter*," *College Language Association Journal* 3 (March 1960):154–65.

FIFTEEN

Hester:
"In the Dark Labyrinth
of Mind"

Hester Prynne, the heroine of *The Scarlet Letter*, typifies romantic individualism, and in her story Hawthorne endeavored to exhibit the inadequacy of such a philosophy. The romantic individualist repudiates the doctrine of a supernatural ethical absolute. He rejects both the authority of God, which sanctions a pietistic ethic, and the authority of society, which sanctions a utilitarian ethic, to affirm the sole authority of Nature. Hester, violating piety and decorum, lived a life of nature and attempted to rationalize her romantic self-indulgence; but, although she broke the laws of God and man, she failed to secure even the natural satisfactions she sought.

Many modern critics, however, who see her as a heroine *à la* George Sand, accept her philosophy and regard her as the central figure of the romance—the spokesman of Hawthorne's views favoring "a larger liberty." Hawthorne's women are usually more sympathetic and impressive than his men; because Hester is more appealing than either her husband or her lover, it is easy to disregard their more central roles in the story.[1] Furthermore, the title of the romance is commonly taken to refer mainly to the letter on Hester's dress and thus somehow to designate her as the central figure; but, in fact, the ideal letter, not any particular material manifestation of it, is referred to in the title. Actually its most emphatic particular manifestation is the stigma revealed on Dimmesdale's breast in the climaxing chapter of the book, "The Revelation of the Scarlet Letter."

Hester's apologists unduly emphasize circumstances which seem to make her the engaging central figure of the romance, and they ignore or even decry the larger tendency of the book, which subordinates her and exposes her moral inadequacy. "She is a free spirit liberated in a moral wilderness."[2]

> She has sinned, but the sin leads her straightway to a larger life. . . . Hawthorne . . . lets the sin elaborate itself, so far as Hester's nature is concerned, into nothing but beauty. . . . Since her love for Dimmesdale was the one sincere passion of her life, she obeyed it utterly, though a conventional judgment would have said that she was stepping out of the moral order. There is nothing in the story to suggest condemnation of her or of the minister in their sin. . . . The passion itself, as the two lovers still agree at the close of their hard experience, was sacred and never caused them repentance.[3]

This opinion disregards Hawthorne's elaborate exposition of the progressive moral dereliction of Hester, during which "all the light and graceful foliage of her character [was] withered up by this red-hot brand" of sinful passion. It even more remarkably ignores her paramour's seven-year-long travail of conscience for (in his own dying words) "the sin here so awfully revealed."

Another advocate of Hester as the prepossessing exponent of a wider freedom in sexual relations is Frederic I. Carpenter:

> In the last analysis, the greatness of *The Scarlet Letter* lies in the character of Hester Prynne. Because she dared to trust herself to believe in the possibility of a new morality in the new world, she achieved spiritual greatness in spite of her own human weakness, in spite of the prejudices of her Puritan society, . . . in spite of the prejudices of her creator himself.[4]

It is a tribute to Hawthorne's art that Hester's champion believes in her so strongly that he rebukes her creator for abusing her and rejoices in his conviction that she triumphs over the author's "denigrations."

In fact, Hawthorne does feel moral compassion for Hester, but her role in the story is to demonstrate that persons who engage our moral compassion may nevertheless merit moral censure. We sympathize with Hester at first because of her personal attraction, and our sympathy deepens throughout the story because we see that she is more sinned against than sinning.

The prime offender against her is Roger Chillingworth, who married her before she was mature enough to know the needs of her nature. There is a tincture of Godwinism—even of Fourierism—in Hawthorne's treatment of Hester's breach of her marriage obligations. Godwin held that marriage was "the most odious of all monopolies" and that it was everyone's duty to love the worthiest. After her lapse, Hester told her husband, "Thou knowest I was frank with thee. I felt no love, nor feigned any." (CE 1:74) According to Godwinian principles, then, her duty to him was slight, especially if a man came along whom she could love. Chillingworth freely acknowledged that he had wronged her in marrying her before she was aware of the needs of her nature: "Mine was the first wrong, when I betrayed thy budding youth into a false and unnatural relation with my decay." (CE 1:74–75) His second, less heinous, offense was his neglectfully absenting himself from her after their marriage. His experience understood what her innocence could not foresee, that the awakening passion in her might take a forbidden way: "If sages were ever wise in their own behoof, I might have foreseen all this." (CE 1:74) His third and culminating offense was his lack of charity toward her after her disgrace. Although he admitted his initial culpability in betraying her into "a false and unnatural relation," (CE 1:75) he refused to share the odium brought upon her in consequence of the situation he had created. True, he plotted no revenge against her, but cold forbearance was not enough. He was motivated not by love but by self-love; in his marriage and in his vengeance he cherished and pursued his private objects, to the exclusion of the claims of others, whose lives were involved with his own. He regarded his wife jealously, as a chattel,[5] not as a person with needs and rights of her own. Her error touched his compassion only perfunctorily, but it gave a mortal wound to his *amour-propre*. Hester's adulterous passion was nobler, for she wished that she might bear her paramour's shame and anguish as well as her own. Thus Chillingworth triply offended against her: he drew her into a relationship which made her liable to sin, did not duly defend her from the peril in which he had placed her, and cast her off when she succumbed.

The nature of Dimmesdale's offense against Hester is too obvious to require specification, but both Hester's conduct and his own deserve whatever extenuation may be due to the passionate and impulsive errors of inexperience: "This had been a sin of passion, not of principle, nor even purpose." (CE 1:200) The minister's conduct toward Hester, then, is less blameworthy than her husband's, who had knowingly and deliberately jeopardized her happiness and moral security; Dimmesdale tells Hester: "We are not, Hester, the worst sinners in the world. There is one worse than even the polluted priest!" (CE 1:195) A distinction must be made, however, between Dimmesdale's moral responsibility and Hester's; her sin was contingent upon his, and her conduct is therefore more deserving of palliation than his. Besides, he had moral defenses and moral duties which she did not have. He had a pastoral duty toward her and a professional duty to lead an exemplary life. Also, according to Hawthorne's view of the distinctive endowments of the sexes, Hester depended upon her womanly feeling, but he had the guidance of masculine intellect and moral erudition. Above all, he was free to marry to satisfy "the strong animal nature" in him, but Hester met her happiest choice too late, when she was "already linked and wedlock bound to a fell adversary." But the minister's really abominable fault was not his fornication; it was his unwillingness to confess his error, his hypocrisy. Hester wished she might bear his shame as well as her own, but he shrank from assuming his place beside her because his perilous pride in his reputation for sanctity was dearer to him than truth. Like Chillingworth, he wronged Hester and left her to bear the punishment alone.

Society wronged Hester as grievously as, though less invidiously than, particular persons wronged her. Hawthorne distinguished between society under its instinctively human aspect and society under its institutional aspect. Society as collective humanity sympathized and was charitable: "It is to the credit of human nature, that, except where its selfishness is brought into play, it loves more readily than it hates." (CE 1:160) But society under its institutional aspect pursued an abstraction, conceived as the general good, which disposed it vindictively toward errant individuals. Hawthorne remarked in "The New Adam and Eve": "The Judgment Seat [is] the very symbol of man's perverted state." (CE 10:253) A scheme of social justice supplants the essential law of love which is grounded in human hearts; any system of expedient regulations tends to become sacrosanct eventually, so that instead of serving humanity it becomes a tyrannical instrument for coercing nonconformists.

Harsh legalism has been remarked as a characteristic of the Puritan theocracy by social historians: "The effect of inhumane punishments on officials and the popular mind generally . . . [was apparently] a brutalizing effect . . . , rendering them more callous to human sufferings."[6] "To make the people good became the supreme task of the churches, and legalism followed as a matter of course."[7] "The theory was that Jehovah was the primary law-giver, the Bible a statute-book, the ministers and magistrates stewards of the divine will."[8] Hester, then, Hawthorne tells us, suffered "the whole dismal severity of the Puritanic code of law" (CE 1:52) in "a period when the forms of authority were felt to possess the sacredness of Divine institutions." (CE 1:64) Her punishment shows how society had set aside the humane injunction that men should love one another, to make a religion of the office of vengeance, which in the Scriptures is exclusively appropriated to God. The wild-rose bush, with "its delicate gems," which stood by the prison door, and "the burdock, pigweed, apple-peru, and other such unsightly vegetation" (CE 1:48) which grew with such appropriate luxuriance in the prison yard symbolize the mingled moral elements in "the dim, awful, mysterious, grotesque, intricate nature of man."[9] (EN, 240) Puritan society, unfortunately, had cultivated the weeds and neglected the flowers of human nature and attached more significance to "the black flower of civilized life, a prison," (CE 1:48) than to the rose bush, "which, by a strange chance, has been kept alive in history" "to symbolize some sweet moral blossom." (CE 1:48) There is powerful irony in Hawthorne's picture of the harsh matrons who crowded around the pillory to demand that Hester be put to death: "Is there not law for it? Truly, there is, both in Scripture and the statute-book." (CE 1:51–52) Surely Hawthorne was here mindful of the question which the scribes and Pharisees put to Jesus concerning the woman taken in adultery: "Now Moses in the law commanded us that such should be stoned: but what sayest thou?" The harshness of the matrons' tirade reflects the perversion of womanliness which has been wrought among this "people amongst whom religion and law were almost identical." (CE 1:50) A man in the crowd offered timely reproof to the chider: "Is there no virtue in woman, save what springs from a wholesome fear of the gallows?" (CE 1:52)—a reminder that virtue must be voluntary, an expression of character, and that there is little worth in a virtue that is compulsory, an imposition of society.

The ostracism called too lenient a punishment by the perhaps envious matrons of the town was almost fatal to Hester's sanity and moral sense, for it almost severed "the many ties, that, so long as we breathe the common air . . . , unite us to our kind." "Man had marked this woman's sin by a scarlet letter, which had such potent and disastrous efficacy that no human sympathy could reach her, save it were sinful like herself." (CE 1:89) Even children "too young to comprehend wherefore this woman should be shut out from the sphere of human charities" (CE 1:81) learned to abhor the woman upon whom society had set the stigma of the moral outcast. The universal duty of "acknowledging brotherhood even with the guiltiest" (CE 9:226) was abrogated in the treatment of Hester:

> In all her intercourse with society, . . . there was nothing which made her feel as if she belonged to it. . . . She was banished, and as much alone as if she inhabited another sphere, or communicated with the common nature by other organs and senses than the rest of human kind. She stood apart from moral interests, yet close beside them, like a ghost that revisits the familiar fireside, and can no longer make itself seen or felt. (CE 1:84)

The peculiar moral danger to Hester in her isolation was that it gave her too little opportunity for affectionate intercourse with other persons. Hawthorne regarded a woman's essential life as consisting in the right exercise of her emotions. His attitude toward women is that of Victorian liberalism; he looked upon them as equal to men, but differently endowed. To him, the distinctive feminine virtues were those characteristic of ideal wifehood and motherhood: instinctive purity and passionate devotion. His prescription for the happiest regulation of society was "Man's intellect, moderated by Woman's tenderness and moral sense."[10] (CE 10:253) Dimmesdale's history shows the corruption of the masculine virtues of reason and authority in a sinner who has cut himself off from the divine source of those virtues; Hester's history shows the corruption of the feminine virtues of passion and submission in a sinner who has been thrust out from the human community on which those virtues depend for their reality and function. In this essential feminine attribute, the workings of her moral sensibility through her feelings rather than her thought, she bears a strong general resemblance to Milton's Eve (who is, however, more delicately conceived). She is a pure (as Hardy used the term) or very (as Shakespeare would have said) woman: that is, a charmingly real woman whose abundant sexuality, "whatever hypocrites austerely talk," was the characteristic and valuable endowment of her sex.

In consequence of her ostracism, Hester's life turned, "in a great measure, from passion and feeling, to thought"; she "wandered without a clew in the dark labyrinth of mind." (CE 1:166) Reflecting bitterly upon her own experience, she was convinced equally of the injustice and the hopelessness of a woman's position in society:

> Was existence worth accepting, even to the happiest among them? As concerned her own individual existence, she had long ago decided in the negative. . . . [A woman who considers what reforms are desirable discerns] a hopeless task before her. As a first step, the whole system of society is to be torn down, and built up anew. Then, the very nature of the opposite sex, or its long hereditary habit, which has become like nature, is to be essentially modified, before woman can be allowed to assume what seems a fair and suitable position. Finally, all other difficulties being obviated, woman cannot take advantage of these preliminary reforms, until she herself shall have undergone a still mightier change; in which, perhaps, the ethereal essence, wherein she has her truest life, will be found to have evaporated. (CE 1:165–66)

Although Hawthorne sympathized with Hester's rebellious mood, he did not, as Stuart P. Sherman averred, represent her as "a free spirit liberated in a moral wilderness," but as one who "wandered, without rule or guidance, in a moral wilderness." (CE 1:199) "A woman never overcomes these problems by any

exercise of thought," (CE 1:166) and Hester's teachers—
"Shame, Despair, Solitude!"—had "taught her much amiss."
(CE 1:199–200) Thus, unfitted by her intense femininity for
intellectual speculations, as well as by her isolation from the
common experience of mankind, which rectifies aberrant
thought, she unwomaned herself and deluded herself with mistaken notions.

The pathetic moral interdependence of persons is strikingly
illustrated in the relations of Hester, Dimmesdale, and little
Pearl. Dimmesdale acceded to Hester's plan of elopement because his will was enfeebled and he needed her resolution and
affection to support him, but he was well aware that her propos-
als would be spiritually fatal to them. He evaded this death of
the soul by the grace of God, who granted him in his death hour
the strength to confess and deliver himself from the untruth
which threatened his spiritual extinction. His dramatic escape
fortuitously prevented Hester from surrendering her soul to
mere nature in flight from her unhappiness. The rescue of her
soul is as much a matter of accident as the shipwreck of her
happiness had been. It is one of the truest touches of Hawthorne's art that Hester was not reclaimed to piety by the edifying spectacle of Dimmesdale's death in the Lord but that
persistent in error, even as he expired in her arms breathing
hosannas, she frantically insisted that her sole hope of happiness
lay in personal reunion with him—in heaven, if not on earth.

One channel of moral affection in her life, however, had
never been clogged—her love for little Pearl. This had sustained
her in her long solitude by affording a partial outlet for her
emotions, and Hawthorne's rather perfunctory and improbable
"Conclusion" informs us that, when she had abated her resentment at being frustrated of worldly happiness, the affection between her and little Pearl drew her into a state of pious
resignation and thus served as a means of positive redemption.

In the last analysis, the error for which Hester suffered was
her too-obstinate supposition that human beings had a right to
happiness. "Hester's tragedy came upon her in consequence of
excessive yielding to her own heart."[11] Hawthorne remarked in
his notebooks that "happiness in this world, if it comes at all,
comes incidentally. Make it the object of pursuit, and it leads us
a wild-goose chase, and is never attained." (CE 8:313) The

proper pursuit of man, he thought, was not happiness but a virtuous life; he inherited the Puritan conviction that

> the good which God seeks and accomplishes is the display of infinite being, a good which transcends the good of finite existence. If the misery of the sinner is conducive to such a display, which it must be because sinners are in fact miserable, then it is just and good that sinners should be punished with misery.[12]

Although we are expected to love and pity Hester, we are not invited to condone her fault or to construe it as a virtue.[13] More of a victim of circumstances than a wilful wrongdoer, she is nevertheless to be held morally responsible. In her story Hawthorne intimates that, tangled as human relationships are and must be, no sin ever issues solely from the intent and deed of the individual sinner, but that it issues instead from a complicated interplay of motives of which he is the more or less willing instrument. Even so, however strong, insidious, and unforeseeable the influences and compulsions which prompted his sin, in any practicable system of ethics the sinner must be held individually accountable for it. This is harsh doctrine, but there is no escape from it short of unflinching repudiation of the moral ideas which give man his tragic and lonely dignity in a world in which all things except himself seem insensate and all actions except his own seem mechanical. The Puritans were no more illogical in coupling the assumption of moral determinism with the doctrine of individual responsibility to God than is our own age in conjoining theories of biological and economic determinism with the doctrine of individual responsibility to society. The Puritan escaped from his inconsistency by remarking that God moves in a mysterious way; we justify ours by the plea of expediency. Hawthorne, however, was content merely to pose the problem forcibly in the history of Hester Prynne.

NOTES

1. "Hester Prynne . . . becomes, really, after the first scene, an accessory figure; it is not upon her the denouement depends" (Henry James, *Hawthorne* (New York: Harper and Brothers, 1879), 109. James

had a virtue excellent and rare among readers: he attended to his author's *total* intention and exposition. Apparently Hester's modern champions are misled by their prepossessions; they share the general tendency of our time to believe more strongly in the reality and value of natural instincts than in the truth and accessibility of supernatural absolutes.

2. Stuart P. Sherman, "Hawthorne: A Puritan Critic of Puritans," in *Americans* (New York: Scribner, 1922), 148.

3. John Erskine, *CHAL* (New York: Macmillan, 1945), 2:26–27.

4. "Scarlet A Minus," *College English* 5 (January 1944):179.

5. "Woman is born for love, and it is impossible to turn her from seeking it. Men should deserve her love as an inheritance, rather than seize and guard it like a prey"—Margaret Fuller, *Woman in the Nineteenth Century* (Boston: Roberts Brothers, 1893), 337.

6. L. T. Merrill, "The Puritan Policeman," *American Sociological Review* 10 (December 1945):768.

7. Joseph Haroutunian, *Piety Versus Moralism: The Passing of the New England Theology* (New York: Henry Holt & Co., 1932), 90.

8. Merrill, 766.

9. Hawthorne remarked in the *American Notebooks*, that "there is an unmistakeable analogy between the wicked weeds and the bad habits and sinful propensities which have overrun the moral world." (CE 8:389) There is an excellent explication of the symbolism of *The Scarlet Letter* in H. H. Waggoner's "Nathaniel Hawthorne: The Cemetery, the Prison, and the Rose," *University of Kansas City Review* 14 (Spring 1948):175–90.

10. Tennyson wrote in "The Princess" that "woman is not undeveloped man, but diverse," and looked for a happier state of society when there should be "everywhere / Two heads in council, two beside the hearth, / Two in the tangled business of the world." Then, man would "gain in sweetness and in moral height," and woman in "mental breadth."

11. F. O. Matthiessen, *American Renaissance* (New York: Oxford Univ. Press, 1941), 348.

12. Haroutunian, 144.

13. Hester's fault is, of course, only a "sin" by definition, a definition that Hawthorne and his Calvinist ancestors accepted. Some modern critics err in their judgment of his work by imposing their own moral criteria on Hawthorne's fiction, but every author needs to have his work interpreted according to the author's "givens"; which does not mean that the interpreter endorses them. For Hawthorne's obsession with chastity, see, e.g., in *American Notebooks*, CE 8:58–59, 145–46.

SIXTEEN

Pearl:
"The Scarlet Letter
Endowed with Life"

Τhe role of Pearl in *The Scarlet Letter* is important for what she represents, for what she senses and imagines, and for what she does. She represents childhood with its undeveloped human and moral potentiality. She senses and imagines the moral and psychological realities of other persons and their possibilities of realization as Hawthorne supposed that artists do. By her actions and symbolic gestures she points out and urges right moral determinations of other characters.

I

THE ROMANTIC CHILD OF NATURE

Fundamentally, Pearl is a Child of Nature, significantly comparable to the Romantic Child of Nature described in Wordsworth's Lucy poems—especially, in its ideal form, in "Three Years She Grew." It is helpful in considering the role of Pearl, a much more complex conception, to note the main features of the pure Child of Nature as Wordsworth pictured her in Lucy.

Lucy is significantly cut off from human relationships. She is not even acknowledged to be engendered from human stock:

> Three years she grew in sun and shower,
> Then Nature said, "A lovelier flower
> On earth was never sown."

The avoidance of mention of her human origin and the elaboration of the flower metaphor to characterize her earliest years imply that Lucy's human antecedents were of no importance, that her natural character alone was significant. More specifically, they imply that what Lucy was to become was not dependent upon, or determined or limited by, her inheritance of human possibility.

In her upbringing she was utterly removed from human influence, without parent or companion. The pure Child of Nature, then, is totally under the influence of nature, with whom alone she enjoys immediate and entire intimacy.[1] Nature said,

> This Child I to myself will take;
> She shall be mine, and I will make
> A Lady of my own.

In effect, Wordsworth shows Nature undertaking a controlled experiment, with a selected specimen of humanity, to demonstrate what can be achieved in the way of producing a perfect person. Nature assumes a more nearly entire control over her Child than a human parent could assume. Not only will Nature be "law" to her darling and "restrain" her; she will also be "impulse" and "kindle" her. Nature's elaborate program is designed both to shape the Child's innate and burgeoning tendencies and to impart and incorporate into her being certain extrinsic qualities of the natural world: the sportiveness of young animals, "the silence and the calm of mute insensate things," the moving grace of cloud-forms and the linear grace of bending willows, the visible beauty of midnight stars and the audible beauty of sounds in nature—and finally the more ambiguous "vital feelings of delight" which presumably will give her an inner grace and beauty correspondent to her physical perfection.

Nature's powers were adequate to her purposes. With apparently as little strain as was imposed upon God's powers by the creation of the world, she succeeded in making a Lady of her own: "Thus Nature spake—The work was done." The total

intimation of "Three Years She Grew" is that the Child of Nature, in pure realization, is an ideal and perfect creature. Recognition of this perfection, and satisfaction in contemplation of
it ("the memory of what has been, and never more will be")
account for the calmness of the poet's acceptance of Lucy's early
death. Not length of life matters, but fulfilment. For a Lucy,
not death at the consummating moment, but longer life—the
gradual decay of her perfection—would be tragic.

In this perfect Child of Nature Wordsworth pictured a par-
agon that could not be produced by human upbringing.

Hawthorne partly agreed with Wordsworth about the influence of nature on the growing child. Like Wordsworth he
thought that intimacy with nature exercised "the essential passions of the heart" and prepared the child for human and spiritual affections, so that moral truths might be received. Many of
his comments on the value of nature to the developing child
echo Wordsworth. "Is not Nature better than a book?" he asked
in "Earth's Holocaust" (CE 10:398), adopting the theme of
"Expostulation and Reply" and "The Tables Turned." He created a company of fictional children (among them the dream-
children in "The Village Uncle," the mountain children in
"The Ambitious Guest," and Ernest in "The Great Stone
Face") who like Lucy were moulded by "silent sympathy" with
nature. Hawthorne's children of nature discover conscious and
valuable affinities with the natural world and enjoy an active and
formative relationship with it.

Again like Wordsworth, he thought that a child was the
"best Philosopher" . . . "Eye among the blind." "Often, in a
young child's ideas and fancies, there is something which it
requires the thought of a lifetime to comprehend"—a prosaic
rephrasing of Wordsworth's lines:

> Mighty Prophet! Seer blest!
> On whom those truths do rest
> Which we are toiling all our lives to find.[2]

Whether or not the adult can recall these fresh visions of
childhood, their influence is not lost, for they have "peopled the
mind with forms sublime and fair," so that mature life is made
better "by force of obscure feelings representative of things forgotten."[3] Hawthorne talked of this with Margaret Fuller one
languid August afternoon in Sleepy Hollow. "We talked . . .

about the experiences of early childhood, whose influence remains upon the character after the recollection of them has passed away." (CE 8:343). Thus, while the infant Pearl stood at the threshold of spiritual life, she was gathering impressions that would influence her conscious thoughts and acts when in the time to come she should have acquired a moral character.

In an essential point, however, Hawthorne did not agree with the early Wordsworthian view of the influence of nature on the growing child. He did not think that nature could teach "more of moral evil and of good than all the sages can."[4] Wordsworth conceived of Lucy as a perfect creature fashioned by nature, but Hawthorne supposed that a pure Child of Nature would lack the most essential human quality, that of moral awareness. He held views nearer to those Wordsworth expressed more than forty-five years after writing the Lucy poems in "The Westmoreland Girl":

> This brave child
> Left among her native mountains
> With wild nature to run wild

is imperfect. The poet acknowledges her "unruly fire" and "froward impulse" (phrases that describe Pearl before the climaxing scene of *The Scarlet Letter*), and says that she needs human cultivation:

> Easily a pious training
> And a steadfast outward power
> Would supplant each weed and cherish
> In their stead each opening flower.

Pearl, unlike Lucy, is shown to be from the beginning of her development influenced by her human inheritance of traits and by the human relationships she has.

II

THE PURITAN CHILD OF NATURE

According to the Calvinist creed of the Puritans, infants were corrupt from birth. They looked upon an infant as a young person with a moral character already formed—and that charac-

ter was the sinful one settled upon all mankind in the decree of
damnation consequent to Adam's fall. In their ABC's Puritan
children were taught that "In Adam's fall we sinned all," and
their parents were exhorted to

> Consider them as creatures, whom you (as instruments) have
> brought into being, tainted with innate corruption. . . .
> Your children are born with a corrupted nature, perverted by
> sinful examples, ignorant of God, in a state of growing enmity to
> him, and in consequence of all, exposed to his wrath and curse,
> and in the way of everlasting ruin.[5]

This doctrine was consistent with Calvinist theory of the
constitution of nature:

> The processes of nature are not mere successions of events,
> but sequences in which one event "springs" from another and
> partakes of a common nature. Flowers and fruits are not sponta-
> neous, external appendages of branches, but grow out of them
> and possess characters peculiar to themselves. A man born of a
> given pair of parents "inherits" their traits. Such continuities in
> nature are evidences of a "constitution or established order."[6]

Hawthorne, like his Puritan ancestors, believed in the
grand scheme of existence that they called God's Sovereign
Constitution. He also agreed that a child inherits the moral as
well as the physical potentialities of its parents. In Pearl's case
this inheritance threatened moral disaster:

> The child could not be made amenable to rules. In giving her
> existence, a great law had been broken; and the result was a
> being whose elements were perhaps beautiful and brilliant, but
> all in disorder. . . .
> The mother's impassioned state had been the medium through
> which were transmitted to the unborn infant the rays of its moral
> life, and, however white and clear originally, they had taken the
> deep stains of crimson and gold, the fiery lustre, the black
> shadow, and the untempered light of the intervening substance.
> (CE 1:91)

Pearl's brilliant attire, as "the scarlet letter endowed with
life" (CE 1:102), was an illustration of her mother's passionate temperament. Also, as Roger Chillingworth shrewdly con-
jectured, the father's traits were not beyond discerning in
the child.

In his conception of the child's inheritance of moral as well as physical traits of resemblance, Hawthorne agreed with Calvinist thought. But he significantly disagreed that she was born with a corrupted nature. She was not one of those "infants flagitious" the justice of whose damnation Wigglesworth vindicated in "The Day of Doom."

III

PEARL: THE "WILD INFANT"

As Pearl was a "natural child" in the euphemistic sense of the term, she stood in a less sufficient relationship with the moral community than regularly conceived children. The nature that she associated with was "that wild heathen Nature . . . never subjugated by human law, nor illumined by higher truth" (CE 1:203) that assumed a brighter aspect for her adulterous parents when they decided to turn their backs on moral truth to satisfy carnal desires.[7] Her relationship with nature was intensified by her ostracism. Her dwelling with Hester on the verge of the forest, at the outskirts of the town, symbolized her more intimate association with nature than with the human community.

There is in Hawthorne's work no opposition between mankind and nature. Throughout his writings he stressed the refreshing influence of nature and the human being's sympathies with nature's creatures. Little Pearl had such sympathies with nature. "The Mother-forest, and these wild things which it nourished, all recognized a kindred wildness in the human child." (CE 1:204–5) This wildness, however, is not the wildness of savagery but the wildness of innocence, like the prelapsarian innocence in which Adam and Eve, as well as "all Beasts of th' Earth since wild,"[8] were innately gentle and sportive.

So Hawthorne said of Pearl, "The infant was worthy to have been brought forth in Eden," (CE 1:90) and recorded (with characteristic deprecation) a rumor that even a wolf in the forest, responsive to her primitive innocence, "came up and smelt of Pearl's robe, and offered his savage head to be petted by her hand." (CE 1:204)

It was Pearl's conscious kinship with nature that prompted her to respond perversely, when the Reverend Mr. Wilson asked

who had made her, "that she had not been made at all, but had
been plucked by her mother off the bush of wild roses that grew
by the prison door"[9] (CE 1:112)—an answer which, like other
parts of her speech and conduct, expresses her symbolic character. To stand for Pearl's naturalness Hawthorne as inevitably
chose a flower metaphor as Wordsworth did to indicate Lucy's.

IV

PEARL: "THE GERM AND BLOSSOM OF WOMANHOOD"

When Nature took Lucy in order to make a Lady of her
own, Lucy was three years old—an age fixed upon, apparently,
as approximately marking the beginning of a child's conscious
development. We first see Pearl when she emerged from prison
in her mother's arms,

> a baby of some three months old, who winked and turned aside
> its little face from the too vivid light of day; because its existence,
> heretofore, had brought it acquainted only with the gray twilight
> of a dungeon. (CE 1:52)

At this stage of her existence, when her responses were not
volitional but sensory, she was not yet a person.[10] Her reflexive
turning away from the light of the sun, which, like the love of
God and unlike the charity of His debased images, shines alike
on the just and the unjust, is a symbolic, not a characteristic,
act. Hawthorne, like Wordsworth, first introduced his natural
child at an age when her character was still undetermined.

As the conditions of Pearl's birth were unfavorable, her
upbringing would be effectual in the degree to which it realized
the best possibilities latent in those conditions. In "the constitution or established order," children play the same part that
new growth does in the natural world. Hawthorne remarked, "It
is a marvel whence [the white pond lily] derives its loveliness
and perfume, springing, as it does, from the black mud over
which the river sleeps." (CE 10:7) Analogously, he wrote of
Pearl that "her innocent life had sprung, by the inscrutable decree of Providence, out of the rank luxuriance of a guilty pas-

sion." (CE 1:89) Pearl thus stands as a regenerative possibility, a phenomenal resurgence among the sullied adult members of society of the power of goodness that mankind can obscure but not extinguish in its nature.

Pearl is a reincarnation of the best human possibilities of her progenitors—of potentialities that, imperfectly realized in past generations, are once more offered opportunity for better realization in this "germ and blossom of womanhood." (CE 1:165) Given Hawthorne's conviction that an individual is real and significant only insofar as he or she incarnates a type of humanity, Pearl's role as germ and blossom is more significant than her personal character and fate.

Although she enjoyed an unusually rich natural life, to compensate for the insufficiency of human associations, Pearl as Child of Nature was infrahuman, in a pre-moral phase of development. She was neither an animal nor an infant damned from birth, but an Undine, a beautiful incipiently human being who instinctively aspired to spiritual existence. Coleridge, who thought that "Undine's character, before she receives a soul, is marvellously beautiful,"[11] remarked that "all lower natures find their highest good in semblances and seekings of that which is higher and better. All things strive to ascend, and ascend in their striving."[12] The variability of Pearl's temper resulted from her insistent yearning toward connection with moral community. If her restricted human associations were with unregenerate persons, her yearning toward moral life would be defeated; but if those to whom she was related affirmed moral truth, her moral nature would be realized. Her apparently capricious disposition could be regularized only when her parents recovered integrity. "Before the establishment of principles, what is character but the series and succession of moods?" (CE 8:413) It was Hawthorne's belief, expressed in "The Christmas Banquet" and other tales, that intimate sympathy with another human being was necessary to attach a person to the great chain of being, and thus to quicken sensibilities into spiritual life.

Nature could arouse the child's sensibilities, so that she might be receptive to moral awareness, but nature alone could not do more. The instinct toward goodness, as spontaneous as a seedling's leaning toward the sun, had to be met by a shower of benign influence. The pathos of Pearl's situation results from

our awareness that her humanization depended upon her parents' resumption of their lapsed powers. Through it we are made
aware that, as Hawthorne wrote, "Every crime destroys more
Edens than our own." (CE 4:212) Not only Pearl's personal
fulfillment, but all the upward yearning and striving generations
behind her that were awaiting better realization in her life, might
be defeated.

Pearl did, however, have a sufficient though defective opportunity for humanization. The most indispensable influence
on a child is the maternal one, and this was strengthened even
to morbidity by the ostracism of Hester and Pearl, who "stood
together in the same circle of seclusion from human society."
(CE 1:94) To effect her transformation from a wild infant, however, a critical event was required, as so often in Hawthorne's
fiction. She needed a "deep distress" to "humanize" her
soul."[13] Hawthorne wrote, "She wanted—what some people
want throughout life—a grief that should deeply touch her, and
thus humanize and make her capable of sympathy." (CE 1:184)
Her father's dying confession, which announced his resumption
of moral truth, supplied her with a connection with the moral
order of the world, and simultaneously touched her sympathies
deeply, so that an enduring moral impression was made on her:
"The great scene of grief, in which the wild infant bore a part,
had developed all her sympathies; and as her tears fell upon her
father's cheek, they were a pledge that she would grow up amid
human joy and sorrow, not forever do battle with the world, but
be a woman in it." (CE 1:256)

V

PEARL: "THE MESSENGER OF ANGUISH"

Although Pearl's reincarnative and regenerative role is in-
trinsically significant, it is less important dramatically and less
central to the situation in *The Scarlet Letter* than her agency as a
"messenger of anguish" (CE 1:256) to her parents.

Hawthorne's characterization of Pearl endowed her with
traits suited to this role. The most essential of these is that, like
many of his sensitive fictional children, she had an instinctive
perception of the moral states of adults associated with her and

an innate impulse toward good. "As the pure breath of children revives the life of aged men, so is our moral nature revived by their pure and simple thoughts." (CE 9:129) But she also had in her nature an imp of the perverse, which made possible a bad development; so the author often called her an "elf-child," "demon offspring," or "witch-baby." Sometimes "a freakish, elfish cast came into the child's eyes." "It was as if an evil spirit possessed the child, and had just then peeped forth in mockery." (CE 1:97)

These opposed tendencies in her nature were expressed in apparently capricious behavior and mercurial changes of mood. "Pearl's aspect was imbued with a spell of infinite variety; in this one child there were many children." (CE 1:97)

> Above all, the warfare of Hester's spirit, at that epoch [while Pearl was imbibing her soul from the spiritual world, and her bodily frame from its material of earth], was perpetuated in Pearl. She could recognize her wild, desperate, defiant mood, the flightiness of her temper, and even some of the very cloud-shapes of gloom and despondency that had brooded in her heart. They were now illuminated by the morning radiance of a young child's disposition, but, later in the day of earthly existence, might be prolific of the storm and whirlwind. (CE 1:91)

Hawthorne copied these traits of Pearl from his observations of his daughter Una as recorded in his American notebooks. Una's aspect, like Pearl's, was imbued with a spell of infinite variety: "Some evanescent and intangible cause may, at any moment, make her look lovely; for such changes come and go, as unaccountably as the changes of aspect caused by the atmosphere in mountain scenery." (CE 8:425)

The opposed tendencies in Pearl's nature were also modeled on Una's. Sometimes "Una is in her sweetest mood." (CE 8:408) "It is but fair to conclude, that, on these occasions, we see her real soul; when she seems less lovely, we merely see something external." (CE 8:413) At other times, when she is mischievous, "there seems to me a little spice of ill-nature in it." (CE 8:407) Such behavior is

> the physical manifestation of the evil spirit that struggles for mastery of her: he is not a spirit at all, but an earthly monster, who lays his grasp on . . . parts of her body that lie in closest contiguity to her soul. (CE 8:420–21)

> There is something that almost frightens me about the child—I
> know not whether elfish or angelic, but, at all events, superna-
> tural. . . . I now and then catch an aspect of her, in which I
> cannot believe her to be my own human child, but a spirit
> strangely mingled with good and evil . . . (CE 8:430–31)

As in Pearl, the opposed tendencies in Una appeared to be
struggling for mastery. "The sentiment of picture, tale, poem,
or action is seldom lost upon her," but "she has, often, a rhinoc-
eros-armor against sentiment or tenderness; you would think she
were marble or adamant." (CE 8:414–15) She "has a very strong
craving for sympathy, and yet, a hundred times a day, she seems
to defy sympathy, and puts herself in a position where she knows
she cannot receive it." (CE 8:411)

Another trait of Pearl's was her violent display of temper
when she was angered, as in the brook-side scene in chapter 19
of *The Scarlet Letter*: She

> now suddenly burst into a fit of passion, gesticulating violently,
> and throwing her small figure into the most extravagant contor-
> tions. She accompanied this wild outbreak with piercing shrieks,
> which the woods reverberated on all sides; so that, alone as she
> was in her childish and unreasonable wrath, it seemed as if a
> hidden multitude were lending her their sympathy and encour-
> agement. (CE 1:209–10)

Una, too, was subject to strange fits of passion. "Violence—
exhibitions of passion—strong expression of any kind—destroy
her beauty." (CE 8:420)

Pearl's lively imagination was, Hawthorne thought, a trait
generally belonging to children, until deadened by the restraints
of conventional teaching and the literal-mindedness of adults.
Hawthorne regarded such freedom of imagination as an essential
trait of artists, and in this respect, as well as in her insight into
characters, Pearl was a child artist.

> At home, within and around her mother's cottage, Pearl wanted
> not a wide and various circle of acquaintance. The spell of life
> went forth from her ever-creative spirit, and communicated itself
> to a thousand objects, as a torch kindles flame wherever it may
> be applied. The unlikeliest materials—a stick, a bunch of rags, a
> flower—were the puppets of Pearl's witchcraft, and, without
> undergoing any outward change, became adapted to whatever

drama occupied the stage of her inner world. . . . It was wonderful, the vast variety of forms into which she threw her intellect. . . . Pearl, in the dearth of human playmates, was thrown more upon the visionary throng which she created." (CE 1:95)

This trait again was copied from Hawthorne's observation of the imaginative play of his children:

Children always seem to like a very wide scope for imagination, as respects their babies, or indeed any playthings; this cushion, or a rolling-pin, or a nine-pin, or any casual thing, seems to answer the purpose of a doll, better than the nicest little wax figure that the art of man can contrive. (CE 1:410)

Pearl's childish trait of imitativeness, most strikingly and significantly exhibited in her contrivance of a green A on her bosom in imitation of Hester's scarlet letter, was also like Una's:

Una passes from one character to another, male and female, youth, age, or infancy—a mother, a baby, a pedler, a market-man—subsiding in one, and starting up in another, like the little flames that quiver and dance at the top of a coal-grate. (CE 8:411)

Pearl's insatiable curiosity, her persistent questioning, is a trait every parent has sometimes been wearily aware of in children. Hawthorne wrote of Una, "She is certainly a most pertinacious teaser." (CE 8:412)

All of these traits are usual and observable aspects of child behavior, carefully observed by Hawthorne and used to give psychological realism to his characterization of Pearl; but he invested all of them with deeper meaning to a degree that obscured the intended realism. The deeper meaning of these characteristics was developed in Pearl's role as a messenger of anguish to her parents. Her sensitiveness to good and evil dispositions in other persons, her apparent capriciousness, the seemingly opposed elfish and angelic tendencies at war in her nature, her imagination of possibilities, her violent displays of temper alternating with amiability, her imitativeness, and her persistent questioning, are all seen to be, considering her deeper meaning, harmonized into consistency with her role as messenger of anguish.

Pearl's agency as "a spirit messenger no less than an earthly child" (CE 1:180) is steadily developed throughout the romance, but is most explicit and insistent in five crucial scenes: the Governor's Hall, in chapter 7; the scaffold at midnight, in chapter 12; the green A scene in the forest, in chapter 15; the brook-side scene, in chapter 19; and the revelation scene, in chapter 23.

In the Governor's Hall scene, Hester declared that Pearl was a messenger of anguish to her. In the midnight scaffold scene, Pearl addressed her message chiefly to Dimmesdale. In the green A scene, she addressed it to Hester. In the brook-side scene, she addressed both Hester and Dimmesdale. In the final scene, she addressed neither, but by her actions showed that she comprehended that her errand as messenger of anguish had been accomplished.

In all of these scenes, appropriate setting and atmosphere reinforced the significance of the action; in all of them, Pearl's message is emphasized by characteristic expressions: ambiguously significant laughs, finger-pointing, kisses given or refused, hands held or withheld, affectionate or hostile behavior, facial expressions, persistent questioning, and verbal chidings or endearments. And in all of them old Mistress Hibbins appeared or was mentioned, to invite adherence to the Black Man who haunts the forest.

In the inquisition scene in the Governor's Hall, where Pearl was catechised and responded perversely, Hester declared that Pearl was a messenger of anguish to her. "See ye not, she is the scarlet letter, only capable of being loved, and so endowed with a million-fold the power of retribution for my sin?" Her plea was supported by Dimmesdale, after her "wild and singular appeal" that was a veiled threat of exposure: "Thou wast my pastor, and hadst charge of my soul, and knowest me better than these men can. I will not lose the child! . . . Speak for me!" (CE 1:113) Thus endorsed by the minister, her entreaty was successful; and "Pearl, that wild and flighty little elf," took the minister's hand "in both her own, and laid her cheek against it" in a tender caress. He kissed her brow, and she did not resist his kiss. Since Dimmesdale in this incident spoke under compulsion, it is not clear that he yet recognized Pearl as a messenger of anguish to himself.

In the midnight scaffold scene, however, Pearl unmistakably and urgently addressed her message to him. On his refusal of her demand that he stand hand in hand with her and Hester on the scaffold at noontide before all the people, she withdrew her hand from his grasp. Her pointing a finger at Chillingworth simultaneously with the meteoric appearance of the great red A in the sky was a double admonition to Dimmesdale, of the need for open revelation and of the perdition that otherwise awaited him.

In the green A scene, after Pearl had fashioned a letter of eel-grass on her bosom in imitation of Hester's scarlet letter, she "contemplated this device with strange interest; even as if the only thing for which she had been sent into the world was to make out its hidden import." What it signified is the possibility that green innocence may develop into scarlet sin. In this scene "the thought occurred to Hester, that the child might really be seeking to approach her with childlike confidence, and doing what she could, and as intelligently as she knew how, to establish a meeting-point of sympathy." (CE 1:179)

This supposition went beyond Hester's perception in the Governor's Hall of Pearl, the scarlet letter endowed with life, as a mere unconscious but perpetual reminder of her sin. She now suspected that Pearl had an instinctive sense of her spiritual mission and an impulsion to execute it. "Pearl's inevitable tendency to hover about the enigma of the scarlet letter seemed an innate quality of her being. From the earliest epoch of her life, she had entered upon this as her appointed mission." (CE 1:180) But Hester turned aside the child's overtures, and denied the suggestion that the scarlet letter was worn for the same reason that the minister obsessively held his hand over his heart. "What know I of the minister's heart? And as for the scarlet letter, I wear it for the sake of its gold thread." "In all the seven bygone years, Hester had never been false to the symbol on her bosom. . . . As for the little Pearl, the earnestness soon passed out of her face." (CE 1:181) At this point Pearl's mission had not succeeded with either parent.

In the forest scene Hester recovered some of the moral truth she had lost by lying about the meaning of the scarlet letter. She sadly demurred against Pearl's suggestion that, when she became a woman, she too might wear a scarlet letter. And she answered Pearl's query, "Didst thou ever meet the Black Man, mother?" "Once in my life I met the Black Man! This letter is his mark!" Thus she retracted her previous lie. (CE 1:185)

In the brook-side scene Pearl explicitly and emphatically admonished both parents. Until Hester picked up and replaced on her bosom the scarlet letter that she had thrown away, Pearl refused to cross the running stream, a traditional barrier against evil spirits, to join them. Dimmesdale apprehended that she would not favor him, for "children are not readily won to be familiar with me." Pearl refused to hold his hand, and washed off his unwelcome kiss in the brook.

In the final scene of Dimmesdale's confession and revelation of his scarlet letter, Pearl made no appeal to either parent, for the initiative had passed to the minister. When he called to her, "she flew to him, and clasped her arms about his knees." When he asked for her kiss, she kissed his lips. But Hester, "slowly, as if impelled by inevitable fate, and against her strongest will—likewise drew near, but paused" before she joined the two on the scaffold. (CE 1:252) She reluctantly but ultimately acquiesced in this providential dispensation. "Towards her mother, too, Pearl's errand as a messenger of anguish was all fulfilled." (CE 1:256)

Pearl is the most complex figure in the romance, with a character compounded of Romantic and Calvinist conceptions of childhood blended with Hawthorne's observations of his daughter Una, and enacting a triple role as representative of childhood, as artist presence, and as spiritual messenger. By burdening her characterization with multiple meaning, the author sacrificed her individuality and with it realism and credibility; but his sacrifice was necessitated by his plot.

NOTES

1. Wordsworth's other children of Nature of the same period as Lucy have human associations, although the poet minimizes their importance. "Ruth," for instance, is conceived more realistically; Ruth's

growing-up in Nature is recognized to be extraordinary, the consequence of orphanhood and human neglect.

> When Ruth was left half desolate,
> Her Father took another Mate;
> And Ruth, not seven years old,
> A *slighted child*, at her own will (my italics)
> Went wandering over dale and hill,
> In thoughtless freedom bold.

Therefore she grew up

> As if she from her birth had been
> An infant of the woods.

Although her "father's roof" is mentioned, the poet asserts that she lived as much "alone" in thought and activity as if other human beings were not near.

Likewise, Wordsworth's other Lucy, Lucy Gray, although she apparently had regular and affectionate relations with her parents, was "a solitary child":

> No mate, no comrade Lucy knew;
> She dwelt on a wide moor,
> —The sweetest thing that ever grew
> Beside a human door!

"*Beside* a human door" suggests only accidental connection with human life, and the end of the poem indicates that the Child's disappearance is to be regarded as an abandonment of human ties to resume a more intimate life in nature.

2. "Ode: Intimations of Immortality from Recollections of Early Childhood," 11.115–17.

3. *Prelude*, 1, 11.546, 605–7.

4. Wordsworth, "The Tables Turned."

5. Quoted from a sermon (author not identified) in Sandford Fleming, *Children and Puritanism* (New Haven: Yale Univ. Press, 1933), 118.

6. Joseph Haroutunian, *Piety versus Moralism: The Passing of the New England Theology* (New York: Henry Holt & Co., 1932), 16–17.

7. Nature, though amoral, is in Hawthorne's view an index to a person's moral condition, for whenever a person errs from spiritual law through absorption in sense, his link with nature, she assumes in sympathy with his nearer approach a brighter and friendlier aspect. This is subjectively explicable: the ascendancy of sense in man makes natural life a more central element in his consciousness than it normally is or

ought to be, thus rendering more vivid his perception of sensual experience while it beclouds his spiritual sensitiveness.

8. *Paradise Lost*, 4.341.

9. Pearl's answer is psychologically plausible. A child, when pressed to answer a question, will often snatch a response from the nearest or most recent observation. For a similar incident, see Wordsworth's poem "An Anecdote for Fathers."

10. There has never been an established legal or scientific definition of a person, as the current controversy about the legality of abortion shows. "A person is a unity of a spiritual nature endowed with freedom of choice and so forming a whole which is independent of the world, for neither nature nor the state may invade this unity without permission."—Jacques Maritain, *The True Humanism*, trans. M. R. Adamson, 2d ed. (New York: Scribner, 1939), 2. To this Catholic humanist definition Hawthorne would have added that other individuals might not invade this unity.

11. *Table Talk*, entry for May 31, 1830. (*Table Talk and Omniana* (London: George Bell and Sons, 1884), 88. Hawthorne read *Table Talk* in 1836. He mentioned the incident of Undine's receiving a soul in one of his love letters to Sophia. (LL 1:97)

12. *Aids to Reflection* (London: "Bohn's Popular Library," George Bell & Sons, 1913), 75. Hawthorne read *Aids to Reflection* in 1833.

13. See Wordsworth's "Elegiac Stanzas, Suggested by a Picture of Peele Castle."

CHAPTER
SEVENTEEN

Chillingworth: The Devil in Boston

Roger Chillingworth, the dia-
bolized physician in Hawthorne's *The Scarlet Letter*, embodies
concepts of human nature and its moral possibilities which more
resemble the Calvinist humanism of the seventeenth century in
England than the transcendentalist optimism of nineteenth-
century New England. Puritan humanism, like all humanisms,
was preoccupied with the problems of a person's progress in his
earthly career. It differed from the secular, scientific humanism
of post-Newtonian times, which is oriented primarily towards a
supposed world of moral absolutes.[1] To Puritan humanists, a
good man was a man who had in his earthly career realized his
moral potentialities; whereas to modern humanists (except such
"humanists" as Maritain), a good man is a man who has refined
his own nature and erected it above mere naturalism. This emphasis upon the self-amelioration of the individual, without
the supposition of "leadings from above," accounts for the fact
that, although the older humanism was always preoccupied with
ethical fulfillment of the individual in his temporal existence,
modern humanism is equally concerned with his esthetic refinement, and indeed often makes no clear distinction between the
ethical and the esthetic.

Hereinafter I shall discuss Chillingworth's role in *The Scarlet
Letter* as an embodiment of certain Calvinist conceptions of the
development of moral personality. My quotations from other

authors are not intended to show "influence,"[2] but merely to
establish a correspondence of ideas.[3] My thesis about Chillingworth's role in the novel is that he is a Miltonic Satan given the
meaner, more realistic embodiment appropriate to the villain of
an historical romance. My discussion of his role in the novel and
of his embodiment of seventeenth-century conceptions will not
be separated, but concurrent.

Chillingworth was an aborted spirit—not in the sense of the
modern humanist, to whom human failure is failure to rise above
the brute, but in the sense of the Puritan humanist, to whom
human failure is a lapsing from excellence or from the possibility
of excellence.

I

CHILLINGWORTH'S ANIMUS TOWARD HIS VICTIMS

The psychology of Chillingworth's covert vengefulness
toward his wife's paramour, the minister Dimmesdale, is ambiguous, but its essential traits are distinguishable. His vindictive
obsession was not a fatal and inevitable opposition of the kind
which Melville illustrated in the malignancy shown by John
Claggart toward Billy Budd—a natural antipathy which seems to
imply in the author some Zoroastrian conviction of two absolutely sundered orders of being, good and evil, implacably pit-
ted against each other. Chillingworth and the "Black Man"
whom he served stand for goodness perverted.

Chillingworth was capable of love, and we sympathize with
and approve of his desire for a life cheered by domestic
affections:

> My heart was a habitation large enough for many guests, but
> lonely and chill, and without a household fire. I longed to kindle
> one. It seemed not so wild a dream,—old as I was, and sombre
> as I was, and misshapen as I was,—that the simple bliss, which
> is scattered far and wide, for all mankind to gather up, might yet
> be mine. And so, Hester, I drew thee to my heart, into its inner-
> most chamber, and sought to warm thee by the warmth which
> thy presence made there! (CE 1:74)

Nevertheless, Chillingworth was at fault in marrying a girl a generation younger than himself, who declared moreover that she did not love him. In Bishop Fuller's *Holy State* (which Hawthorne read in 1834) the expectations proper to a Christian entering into holy matrimony are discussed.[4] Much happiness is not to be expected in marriage. One's spouse should be loved for grace (presumably spiritual rather than physical) and goodness. A wife should not be chosen for her beauty. There should be no great disproportion in age. Chillingworth's marriage to Hester violated all these prudent admonitions of the good Bishop. From the husband's point of view, it was folly, since it promised ill for his future; from the wife's point of view, it was injustice, since it would prevent her legitimate union with someone she could love. (Love, of course, to Hawthorne, although hardly to Bishop Fuller, was a more indispensable bond of marriage than any legal or sacramental tie.)

Chillingworth, disappointed in his hope of gaining his wife's affection, hated the man who had gained it unsought and even unwished. In a sense, his malice was less a personal resentment against Dimmesdale than an expression of anger at the scheme of things which had cheated his hopes. Like envious Satan, observing the love of Adam and Eve in the Garden, "Imparadised in one another's arms,"[5] he was "stirred up with envy and revenge."

Although his anger was natural and forgivable, it became a fatal sin when he nourished it, like Blake's Poison Tree, and made it the settled disposition of his existence. Bishop Fuller, in "Of Anger," describes his case well: "Anger is one of the sinews of the soul; he that wants it, hath a maimed mind. . . . Nor is it good to converse with such as cannot be angry." Anger is heavenly, or hellish, or earthly. One should not be angry without cause, nor mortally angry for a venial fault, nor driven by anger to an irrevocable act, nor uncontrollably and violently angry, nor implacably angry. *"He that keeps anger long in his bosome giveth place to the devil."* The anger of such a person shows itself in fits of diabolical violence.[6]

Chillingworth, implacably angry, violent even to frenzy, suffered this diabolical possession. Never very benevolent, he easily converted his injured self-love into hatred of his supplan-

ter. He and Hester agreed that his earlier life had been
blameless:

> "All my life had been made up of earnest, studious, thoughtful,
> quiet years, bestowed faithfully for the increase of mine own
> knowledge, and faithfully, too, though this latter object was but
> casual to the other,—faithfully for the advancement of human
> welfare." (CE 1:172)

But Hawthorne emphasizes that the physician's benevolence
had never been so innate and habitual that a lapse into malevolence would be implausible. He had been "kindly, though not
of warm affections"; (CE 1:129) his efforts to advance human
welfare had been admittedly "casual to" (CE 1:172) the increase
of his own knowledge. His goodness had been rather a matter
of deliberate choice and policy, so long as he had no motive to
do ill, than of strong inclination; knowledge rather than beneficence had always been clearly his chief object; and his character
had thus always retained the possibility of maleficence.

> Consequently, when angry resentment gave him a motive, he
> chose to withdraw his name from the roll of mankind, and, as
> regarded his former ties and interests, to vanish out of life as
> completely as if he indeed lay at the bottom of the ocean, whither
> rumor had long ago consigned him. This purpose once effected,
> new interests would immediately spring up, and likewise a new
> purpose; dark, it is true, if not guilty, but of force enough to
> engage the full strength of his faculties. (CE 1:118–19)

The expression *chose to* in this passage is significant: to Chillingworth, righteousness had never been more than expedient conduct. Although his acts had been conformable to the "external
covenant" of Calvinism, his good works had been the cool, detached, deliberated good works which are dictated more by
judgment than by affection for virtue. Jonathan Edwards taught
that true virtue "has its roots in an emotional rather than intellectual state of mind."[7] Of this virtue, Chillingworth had never
evinced any sign. Therefore, he could say, "Evil, be thou my
good," and with perfect self-possession bend his energies stren-
uously toward malign as he had hitherto directed them incidentally toward benign ends. He was too fatally his own master.

That Hawthorne looked upon the power of good and the power of evil as different expressions of identical capacities, rather than as expressions of different capacities in man, is perfectly explicit, especially in the "Conclusion" to the romance:

> Nothing was more remarkable than the change which took place, almost immediately after Mr. Dimmesdale's death, in the appearance and demeanor of the old man known as Roger Chillingworth. All his strength and energy—all his vital and intellectual force—seemed at once to desert him. . . . This unhappy man had made the very principle of his life to consist in the pursuit and systematic exercise of revenge; and when . . . there was no more Devil's work on earth for him to do, it only remained for the unhumanized mortal to betake himself whither his Master would find him tasks enough, and pay him his wages duly. . . . It is a curious subject of observation and inquiry, whether hatred and love be not the same thing at bottom. Each, in its utmost development, supposes a high degree of intimacy and heart-knowledge; each renders one individual dependent for the food of his affections and spiritual life upon another; each leaves the passionate lover, or the no less passionate hater, forlorn and desolate by the withdrawal of his object. Philosophically considered, therefore, the two passions seem essentially the same.[8] (CE 1:260)

Chillingworth, then, was not badness incarnate, but goodness perverted. Like Milton's Satan, he could pity his victims; although himself "dehumanized" by his malice, he left his property to the "demon offspring" (CE 1:261) of those whom he had injured and who had injured him, "a wild infant" (CE 1:256) whose progress in humanization had paralleled his regress: and Hawthorne even suggested at the conclusion of the passage quoted above, that Chillingworth himself was perhaps not irredeemably lost: "In the spiritual world, the old physician and the minister—mutual victims as they may have been—may, unawares, have found their earthly stock of hatred and antipathy transmuted into golden love." (CE 1:260–61) "Neither do the spirits damned lose all their virtue." (*PL* 2:482–83.) In fine, we are to understand Chillingworth's sin as a tragic perversion of a force which sought its right expression in love, and, thwarted in that, turned to hate.

II

FORBIDDEN KNOWLEDGE

The physician was enabled to effectuate his malice by his adeptness in a science which Hawthorne looked upon as dangerous if applied outside its proper sphere. The notion of a forbidden knowledge is as old as recorded thought, although it is very nearly an exploded notion in Western civilization. It can be a potent concept only in a framework of thought which rests upon the assumption of two orders of existence, natural and supernatural. During the Middle Ages it was held that Revelation supplied all the knowledge needful of spiritual things, if duly interpreted by the reason of inspired apostolic ministers. Knowledge of natural things, beyond that to be collected by everyday experience and observation, was not so much forbidden as impertinent, liable to divert the mind from transcendent concerns of prime importance to all men sojourning for a time on this dark isthmus of a middle state. There was, of course, a strong and abiding tincture of real mistrust of natural science, expressed in the legends which grew up about Paracelsus and Roger Bacon and Faustus, because of the theological doctrine that Satan worked through Nature, and that the man who learned the mysteries of natural science and employed the agencies of nature was thereby lending himself to Satanic purposes. Descartes and Francis Bacon effected a revolution in thought when they rationalized investigations of the natural world:

> Bacon's argument is of great importance, because it furnished the scientists of the following two centuries with a technique for reconciling science with religion, and gave a first impulse to the movement towards scientific deism. Bacon's purpose requires that Nature should be established as divine instead of Satanic, and this he secures by arguing that God has revealed himself to man by means of *two* scriptures: first, of course, through the written word, but also, secondly, through his handiwork, the created universe. To study nature, therefore, cannot be contrary to religion; indeed, it is part of the duty we owe to the great Artificer of the world.[9]

Bacon, however, did not discard the theory of forbidden knowledge; instead, he practically inverted its application, by calling it presumptuous of man to endeavor by his mundane reason to penetrate the secrets of spiritual existence; while he sanctioned experimental investigations of the material world, he deplored logical speculations about the spiritual world:

> To Bacon the logic-spinning of the schoolmen was a kind of forbidden knowledge; it was a presumptuous attempt to read the secret purposes of God, and to force his works into conformity with the laws of the human mind. This was for him the real hubris, this metaphysical arrogance, which "disdains to dwell upon particulars," and confidently explains all things by syllogism. The true humility is the attribute of the Baconian scientist, who is content to come forth into the light of things, and let nature be his teacher.[10]

Hawthorne's theory of forbidden knowledge was a characteristic variety of the Baconian.[11] In the lapse of more than two centuries since *The Advancement of Learning* and the *Novum Organum*, the battle for natural science had been too thoroughly won; men had become so preoccupied with the supposition that they could make a heaven on earth through physical science that they had practically discarded the belief in a supernatural realm of values inaccessible to their techniques of materialistic investigation. But to Hawthorne, the distinction between matter and spirit, and the ascendancy of the latter over the former, were still undoubted truths, and he regarded the scientist's willingness to probe spiritual nature with his mundane investigations as an impious trespass. His theory of forbidden knowledge was not that of Milton, which recommended the circumscription of knowledge on essentially the old grounds that Revelation has supplied as much knowledge of the mysteries as Man is fitted to comprehend, and which points out the pragmatic wisdom of being content with "useful" knowledge:

> Not to know at large of things remote
> From use, obscure and subtle, but to know
> That which before us lies in daily life,
> Is the prime wisdom. (*PL* 8.191–94.)

Pope, in the *Essay on Man* reduced the same idea to a platitude in pointing out that man's knowledge is "measured to his state and place," and in unfavorably contrasting "proud Science" with the ignorant humility of the poor Indian.

But Hawthorne was less concerned to draw a line about the knowledge which man might explore than to reassert the old, but by the generality of men in his time almost forgotten, supposition that matter and spirit were not the same, and that it was profanation to subdue spiritual things to material. To cite a contemporaneous view that agreed with his own:

> Go, demand
> Of mighty Nature, if 'twas ever meant
> That we should pry far off yet be unraised;
> That we should pore, and dwindle as we pore,
> Viewing all objects unremittingly
> In disconnection dead and spiritless;
> And still dividing, and dividing still,
> Break down all grandeur, still unsatisfied
> With the perverse attempt, while littleness
> May yet become more little; waging thus
> An impious warfare with the very life
> Of our own souls!
>   And if indeed there be
> An all-pervading Spirit, upon whom
> Our dark foundations rest, could he design
> That this magnificent effect of power,
> The earth we tread, the sky we behold
> By day, and all the pomp which night reveals;
> That these—and that superior mystery
> Our vital frame, so fearfully devised,
> And the dread soul within it—should exist
> Only to be examined, pondered, searched,
> Probed, vexed, and criticised?[12]

The old distinction between the ideal and real worlds had broken down so far that ideas had been lost in phenomena; Man had joined the things which God had put asunder, and it was Hawthorne's endeavor to reaffirm their distinctness. What was forbidden, in his view, was not a *knowledge* actually, but the employment of a mundane *technique* in a spiritual realm. The materialistic investigator's murderous dissection would not yield him any forbidden knowledge, but it would disregard and destroy a spiritual existence incidentally to its pursuit of gross understanding.

The physician was peculiarly liable to trespass upon "the dread soul" within the "superior mystery," because it was specifically his business to examine, ponder, search, and probe the "vital frame" of man, and he might easily violate the soul by carrying his profane researches too far:

> It has been said, that Physicians were more inclined to infidelity and skepticism, than men of other professions. And it has been attributed to their peculiar studies and pursuits. They perceive the subjection of the animal frame to the laws of chemistry.[13]

In Chillingworth's characterization Hawthorne further developed the conception of the impious physician which he had earlier represented in Dr. Rappaccini.[14] Rappaccini had perverted Nature in order to concoct his poisons. A man of "intellect and cultivation," (CE 10:95) he had not much "warmth of heart." (CE 10:95) He had "a look as deep as Nature herself, but without Nature's warmth of love."[15] (CE 10:107) The flowers his art had "created"

> would have shocked a delicate instinct by an appearance of artificialness indicating that there had been such a commixture, and, as it were, adultery, of various vegetable species, that the production was no longer of God's making, but the monstrous offspring of man's depraved fancy, glowing with only an evil mockery of beauty. (CE 10:110)

His worst profanation, however, was in his tampering with the constitution of his lovely daughter, who was a spiritual as well as a material creature. The poisons which he substituted for the healthy principle in her were baneful to her natural life but could not touch her soul: "Though my body be nourished with poison, my spirit is God's creature and craves love as its daily food." (CE 10:125) Rappaccini had used his science to turn his garden into a paradise of evil: "Was this garden, then, the Eden of the present world?" The death of his daughter's body, so perverted by his tamperings that the most salubrious medicines were fatal to it, made her a "victim of man's ingenuity, and of the fatality that attends all such efforts of perverted wisdom." (CE 10:128)

Chillingworth's "guilty purpose" was even more damnable than Rappaccini's. Rappaccini had perverted Nature and tampered with spiritual things from a disinterested, though fanatical, love of science; he was "as true a man of science as ever distilled his own heart in an alembic." (CE 10:119) But Chillingworth sought to pervert best things to worst abuse:

> Calm, gentle, passionless, as he appeared, there was yet, we fear, a quiet depth of malice, hitherto latent, but active now, in this unfortunate old man, which led him to imagine a more intimate revenge than any mortal had ever wreaked upon an enemy. To make himself the one trusted friend, to whom should be confided all the fear, the remorse, the agony, the ineffectual repentance, the backward rush of sinful thoughts, expelled in vain! All that guilty sorrow, hidden from the world, whose great heart would have pitied and forgiven, to be revealed to him, the Pitiless, the Unforgiving! (CE 1:139)

Even in those years which he later looked back upon as beneficent, he had scarcely been behind Rappaccini in his "insane zeal for science." (CE 10:119) "The increase of [his] own knowledge" (CE 1:172) had been a deeper motive in his life than the conferring of benefits on humanity. He had the physician's too exclusive regard for "magik naturel":

> In their researches into the human frame, it may be that the higher and more subtle faculties of such men were materialized, and that they lost the spiritual view of existence amid the intricacies of that wondrous mechanism, which seemed to involve art enough to comprise all of life within itself. (CE 1:119)

Nevertheless, he lacked even the poor justification that he had "lost the spiritual view." (CE 1:119) He was fully aware of the spiritual implications of his conduct, and did not shrink from employing his materialistic arts in investigation of spiritual mysteries. During his "long search into the minister's dim interior," (CE 1:130) he turned over

> many precious materials, in the shape of high aspirations for the welfare of his race, warm love of souls, pure sentiments, natural piety, strengthened by thought and study, and illumined by revelation,—all of which invaluable gold was perhaps no better than rubbish to the seeker. (CE 1:130)

His disregard for these excellences was a more sinful part of his behavior than the intellectual presumptuousness which he shared with Rappaccini, the perfect type of the zealot of physical science: " '[T]here are few things,—whether in the outward world, or, to a certain depth, in the invisible sphere of thought,—few things hidden from the man who devotes himself earnestly and unreservedly to the solution of a mystery.' " (CE 1:75) Such a quest was frightfully impious, indeed, but more heinous was his diabolical disregard of the good which his inquest revealed.

There was no perfidy in Rappaccini of the sort that infected Chillingworth. Chillingworth cloaked his malevolence under the guise of friendship, working "in close design, by fraud or guile." (*PL* 1.1.646.)

> For neither man nor angel can discern
> Hypocrisy—the only evil that walks
> Invisible, except to God alone,
> By his permissive will, through Heaven and Earth.
> (*PL* 3.11.682–85.)

Such deceit was the legendary practice among agents of the Black Man:

> The Devil does insinuate his most Horrible *Temptations*, with pretence, of much *Friendship* and *Kindness* for us. . . . to salute men with profers to do all manner of Service for them; and at the same time to Stab them as *Joab* did *Abner* of old; this is just like the *Devil*, and the *Devil* truly has many Children that Imitate him in it.[16]

That Hawthorne considered secrecy evil, even though it was concealment of something innocent or merely venial, he had demonstrated in his tale "Roger Malvin's Burial." Much more censurable, then, was this concealment of a diabolical intent.[17] If the offence could be augmented, secrecy would be its augmentation.[18]

III

FATE AND FREE WILL

A consistent conception runs through all of Hawthorne's consideration of how far an individual is to be held responsible for the good and evil he does. To designate this conception, for which he employed no convenient brief term, I appropriate the term *karma*. I mean by it the conception that a human being defines his own character continuously and progressively through the tendency of his choices, great and small, and thus gradually fixes in his character a set of established inclinations and dispositions which are more potent determinants of his thought and action than any momentary volitions and impulses, however strongly supported by some temporary conjunction of special circumstances, can be. Character is destiny, but destiny accomplished by the lifelong process of repeated choices, both impulsive and deliberate. The effect of such a process is not eventually to destroy the power of free will entirely, but rather progressively to limit the possibilities of choice. The individual does exercise a real self-determining faculty; no single choice precludes the possibility of a later choice of contrary tendency; but tendencies of choice do become established through re-peated volitions consistent with each other until they are in effect stronger than "the will of the instant." Perhaps a profound insight into human motives would reveal that such tendencies of choice, even before they became established through successive volitions and acts, were predictable and inevitable in conse-quence of the individual's peculiar endowment of latent procliv-ities, but at least they do not become actualized without the seeming volition of the agent. Hawthorne apparently rejected the supposition that the agent has no real freedom, that in effect a man's character grows upon him like a fatality, unfolding a predestined pattern which the agent makes real through his acts, and consciously comprehends during this process of realization, but perhaps has no ultimate power to determine or alter. The human mind for him was neither Locke's blank sheet to be written on by experience, nor a sheet on which all the meanings were already traced in invisible writing to be rendered legible by experience; it was something in between, a something of which the power of selecting and determining what would be dominant was reserved to the agent.

But this is, after all, reserving more power and freedom to the individual than Hawthorne evidently believed in. Although there was a large *area* of undetermined possibility, what would be developed within it was only partially susceptible of deter-mination by the conscious will of the individual; the incomprehensible powers that environ man (the powers which Hardy calls "Hap") are at least as operative as the will of the agent in determining what shall be enacted and fixed within the area of theoretically free possibility.[19] The clearly implied explanation of how the acts he has performed may seem even to the agent himself a fatality lies in the difference between the conscious intent and immediate and evident consequence of a particular act, on the one hand, and the imperceptible tendency and ultimate collective consequence of a whole train of actions on the other hand. The individual may have never clearly grasped and consciously willed the remote collective consequence which nevertheless is an inevitable result of the successive particular actions he has consciously willed and performed, and which it has been in his power to refrain from willing and performing. When this remote, unforeseen, collective consequence is something he deplores, he may, repudiating responsibility therefor, explain it in either of two ways—as something predetermined; or as the fatal consequence of some particular act, probably the initial act of a consistent series. In either case, he will see in the result the operation of an adverse fate. If the individual supposes the result would have been the same with or without his cooperative decision, he is a thorough-going determinist. On the other hand, he feels just as certainly that he has been incapable of free and intelligent choice if he believes that the unwished consequence was a joker Fate had concealed up its sleeve to distribute as the necessary accompaniment of some innocent card which the agent was free to take or refuse. This latter is what might be called "the fatal misstep theory." It is the fixing upon some initial, or culminating, or otherwise conspicuous step in a long ambulation in a fixed direction, as being decisive; such a notion proceeds from our sense of willing particular acts and not realizing so consciously our settled and almost automatic determinations, so that we are too ready to attribute the result of a long-continued process to a single conscious portion of it.

The *karma* concept had been prominent in Hawthorne's ethical speculations, especially in his cogitations upon the connected subjects of free will and responsibility, for a long while. He had employed it in the character of the Angler, in *Fanshawe,* a man who advanced so gradually and imperceptibly in his career of horrid crime that, when he was awakened to the enormity of his crimes, "The sudden consciousness of accumulated guilt made him desperate." (CE 3:435) It was a motif of several of the *Twice Told Tales*:

> An influence beyond our control lays its strong hand on every deed which we do, and weaves its consequences into an iron tissue of necessity. (CE 9:136–37)
> ... Fatality, an emblem of the evil influence that rules your fortunes; a demon to whom you subjected yourself by some error at the outset of life, and were bound his slave forever, by once obeying him. (CE 9:307)
> "I keep up the search for this accursed stone because the vain ambition of my youth has become a fate upon me in my old age." (CE 9:153–54)
> Could the result of one, or all our deeds, be shadowed forth and set before us, some would call it Fate, and hurry onward, others be swept along by their own passionate desires, and none be turned aside by the PROPHETIC PICTURES. (CE 9:182)

Although there is an occasional suggestion in such passages of the "fatal misstep" theory (e.g., the second quotation above), the usual emphasis is that fate is the resultant of a cumulative sequence of a person's actions, and that it is voluntarily assumed by deliberate persistence in a certain course. Especially in the latter work is there apparent insistence upon the fact that fatal persistence is voluntary, that the compulsion which the individual alleges is merely supposititious. Thus, in explaining Hester's decision to remain in Boston, in *The Scarlet Letter*, Hawthorne wrote (my italics): "There is a fatality, a *feeling* so irresistible and inevitable that it *has the force of doom*, which almost inevitably compels human beings . . . " (CE 1:79) And in *The Marble Faun* Miriam replied to the sinister model, upon his insistence that their destinies were inevitably linked: "You mistake your own will for an iron necessity." (CE 4:96) Hawthorne held that the will is in a sense, a fatality, but he left the agent more freedom and responsibility than Jonathan Edwards had attributed to him. Edwards did not see a volition as an act of the mind in view of a motive, but looked upon volition and motivation as being scarcely distinct aspects of one act of the mind. Motivation was the movement of a consciousness toward an object; volition was the consciousness of a movement toward an object; their separation was scarcely more than a nominalistic delusion. Hawthorne's difference from this view seems to be an apparent distinction between the faculty of the will and the separate acts of will. The separate acts of the will give its determinate character and bias to the faculty of the will; so that, although the agent has sufficient control over his particular acts of will, they ultimately establish a kind of over-will which controls him and almost inevitably determines even his later acts of will. Thus, although what a man chooses may become a fatality, it is a fatality which he has progressively constructed; it has not been predetermined by any inner or outer compulsion, and is not the consequence of any particular fatal act which fixed a doom upon him.

The *karma* concept in Hawthorne's work is most thoroughly illustrated in the character of Chillingworth, who gradually debased his own character by deliberate persistence in a wrong course. The verbs Hawthorne used to designate his acts leave no doubt that they were self-determined. Hawthorne very frequently resorted to passive voice constructions to indicate the seeming inevitability of the actions of his characters, but not so with Chillingworth. "He *chose* to withdraw his name from the roll of mankind." (CE 1:118) (Hester was "*shut out* from the sphere of human charities.") (CE 1:81) "This unhappy man *had made* the very principle of his life to consist in the pursuit and systematic exercise of revenge." (CE 1:260) The guilty difference between Chillingworth and his victims was that pointed out by Milton as making the sin of Satan greater than that of Adam and Eve:

> The first sort by their own suggestion fell,
> Self-tempted, self-depraved; Man falls, deceived
> By the other first: Man, therefore, shall find grace;
> The other, none. (*PL* 3.11.129–32.)

His malice became a soul-destroying, sinful fatality gradually, through his persistence in it:

> He had begun an investigation, as he imagined, with the severe and equal integrity of a judge, desirous only of truth, even as if the question involved no more than the air-drawn lines and figures of a geometrical problem, instead of human passions, and

wrongs inflicted on himself. But, as he proceeded, a terrible fascination, a kind of fierce, though still calm, necessity seized the old man within its gripe, and never set him free again until he had done all its bidding. (CE 1:129)

Looking back upon his career of vengeance, he tried to evade responsibility by making use of the fatal misstep theory, eloquently declaring to Hester, in response to her vain plea that he abandon his purpose of revenge:

"By thy first step awry thou didst plant the germ of evil; but since that moment, it has all been a dark necessity. Ye that have wronged me are not sinful, save in a kind of typical illusion; neither am I fiend-like, who have snatched a fiend's office from his hands. It is our fate. Let the black flower blossom as it may!" (CE 1:174)

But his eloquent analogy of the inexorably germinating seed of evil should not persuade us, through its specious plausibility, to accept his view. Hester and Dimmesdale *were* sinful, and he *was* fiend-like. Hawthorne did not think that flowers of evil grew unless they were cultivated by human hands:

So spake the fiend, and with necessity
The tyrant's plea, excused his devilish deeds. (*PL* 4.39)

NOTES

1. I know that so general a distinction is rashly undiscriminating, but I hope that it will be accepted as accurate on the whole.

2. This may partially justify the eclecticism of my quotations, unavoidable in a brief treatment of so comprehensive a topic.

3. Hawthorne had read all of the authors quoted, some of them many times. The works mentioned are all recorded, as charged out to him on various occasions, in the "Charge Books" of the Salem Athenaeum Library. These have been transcribed and published: in *The Essex Institute Historical Collections* 68 (1932):65–87 (no editor given); and, more recently and more accurately, by Marion L. Kesselring in "Hawthorne's Reading, 1828–1850" *Bulletin of the New York Public Library* 53 (1949):55–71, 121–38, 173–94. See also Arlin Turner's "Haw-

thorne's Literary Borrowings," *PMLA* 51 (June 1936):543–62; and Austin Warren's "Hawthorne's Reading," *New England Quarterly* 8 (December 1935):480–97.

4. Thomas Fuller, *The Holy State and the Profane State*, ed. M. G. Walten (New York: Columbia Univ. Press, 1938), 2:212–14.

5. *Paradise Lost*, 4.506.—Later quotations will be identified parenthetically in the text.

6. Fuller, 2:169–70.

7. Rufus Suter, "The Concept of Morality in the Philosophy of Jonathan Edwards," *Journal of Religion* 14 (1934–35):268.

8. For Hawthorne's earlier consideration of the same phenomenon, see "Chippings with a Chisel."

9. Basil Willey, *The Seventeenth Century Background* (New York: Doubleday & Company, 1953), 42.

10. *Ibid.*

11. In the period of about a dozen years during which Hawthorne held a share in the Salem Athenaeum, Bacon's works were charged out to him three times, for periods ranging from two weeks to six months at a time. During the same years, he withdrew Montaigne six times; Montaigne's general attitude toward Nature was the same as Bacon's, although it was more in the spirit of Wordsworthian contemplation and enjoyment than of Baconian experiment and observation.

12. Wordsworth, *The Excursion*, 4.957–78. Hawthorne was intimately familiar with Wordsworth's work; and, although no major author was less given to direct quotation from or allusion to books than was Hawthorne, his own work is full of Wordsworthian reminiscences and echoes, somewhat disguised by being assimilated to Hawthorne's distinctive, consistent neo-seventeenth century style.

13. Hawthorne, *American Magazine of Useful and Entertaining Knowledge* 2 (November 1835):127.

14. Other doctors and scientists of the same type in Hawthorne's fictions are Septimius Felton, Dr. Heidegger, Aylmer ("The Birthmark"), Ethan Brand. Some of Hawthorne's artist characters (e.g. the artist of "The Prophetic Picture") likewise misuse their professional observations and insights.

15. For a discussion of Hawthorne's conception of the right relation between Man and Nature, see my article "Isolation in Hawthorne," *Personalist* 32 (January 1951):42–47.

16. Cotton Mather, *The Wonders of the Invisible World* (London: "Library of Old Authors," Reeves and Turner, 1862), 179.

17. The contortions of feature and frenzy of gesture which occasionally marked Chillingworth's demeanor were betrayals of his falseness, probably copied from the various disguises and frenzies of Satan

in *Paradise Lost* in his attempts to deceive Adam and Eve and their guardian angels. There is likewise an impression of Satanism masked behind a human front in Chillingworth's occasional malignancy of glance, which made the beholder "shrink and shudder" as if gazed at by an evil eye. His increasing deformity likewise visibly betokened the progressive perversion of his moral character.

18. "Roger Malvin's Burial" was first published in 1832. In Hurd's *Dialogues*, which Hawthorne read in 1829, Hurd remarks that Henry More had deplored Waller's attempts to defend "accommodation"—cloaking allegedly laudable purposes under deceitful acts and words, showing one face to the world and another to himself. More regarded any deceit as wickedness, even though the matter concealed was in itself innocent. Bacon distinguished three degrees of dissembling (in "of Simulation and Dissimulation") and gave conditional approval to all three, as being sometimes seasonable and politic.

19. Hawthorne's notion of this shadowy no-man's-land wherein innate human tendency, conscious will, and inscrutable circumstance join to define individual character and fate, is well conveyed in his comment on the Emperor Nero:

> I wish some competent person would undertake to analyze and develop his character, and how and by what necessity—with all his elegant tastes, his love of the beautiful, his artist nature—he grew to be such a monster. Nero has never yet had justice done him, nor have any of the wicked emperors: not that I suppose them to be any less monstrous than history represents them; but there must surely have been something in their position and circumstances to render the terrible moral disease which seized upon them so generally almost inevitable. (RE 10:288)

EIGHTEEN

Dimmesdale: Fugitive from Wrath

I

*High Stations in the church of God, lay men open to violent
and peculiar temptations of the Devil. . . . Men of high
Attainments, and Men of high Employments, in the Church of
God, must look, like* Peter *to be more* Sifted, *and like* Paul,
to be more Buffeted *than other men. . . . Especially such*
Ministers, *as move in the highest orb of Serviceableness.*
—*Cotton Mather,* The Wonders of the Invisible World

Critics of *The Scarlet Letter*
have frequently noted that, although Hester Prynne is a more
interesting character to modern readers, Arthur Dimmesdale's
role is the structural and thematic center of the romance. Henry
James observed, "The story . . . is in a secondary degree that
of Hester Prynne; it is not upon her the *dénouement* depends. It
is upon her guilty lover that the author projects most frequently
the cold, thin rays of his fitfully moving lantern."[1] Stuart P.
Sherman, although he sympathized more fully with Hester, conceded that Dimmesdale was the central figure: "His, apparently,
is the main tragic problem, and his is the solution of it."[2] But,
although "Arthur Dimmesdale is ordinarily considered the figure of primary importance,"[3] the bulk of critical comment has

dealt with Hester, and Dimmesdale's role has been comparatively neglected. This chapter will undertake to show in detail
that his is indeed "the main tragic problem" and that the "external evolution" and the "*dénouement*" of the romance depend
upon him. Further, it will explicate his role as an illustration of
Puritan conceptions of sinfulness and regeneration.

In the historic setting of seventeenth-century Boston, a
popular minister like Arthur Dimmesdale was the logical figure
to illustrate the theme that runs throughout all of Hawthorne's
fiction, that "in every heart, even the holiest, there is a germ of
evil." Dimmesdale's "was the profession, at that era, in which
intellectual ability displayed itself far more than in political
life; . . . it offered inducements powerful enough, in the almost
worshipping respect of the community, to win the most aspiring
ambition into its service." (CE 1:238) The devil's triumph over
such a man would show how desperate a warfare of good and evil
is waged in this moral no-man's-land of mundane life, and God's
claiming him despite the devil would impressively exhibit the
powerful operation of Divine Grace. The plot of *The Scarlet
Letter* consists of the struggle between God and the devil for the
soul of Arthur Dimmesdale.

The chief interest of the romance is not in the characters
"but in the situation, which is consistently kept before us,
though with a great deal . . . of a certain stable variation."[4] As
in all Hawthorne's fictions, the situation is presented, not in
dramatic progression, but in exposition and spaced scenes which
picture the positions that the exposition prepares. Hawthorne's
narrative does not have the dramatic continuity of a moving
picture; it has the static consecutiveness of a series of lantern
slides, with interspersed commentary.

> Passion and motive and character, having been brought together
> in given relations, begin to work toward a logical issue;
> but . . . the author does not, like a playwright, reflect the action
> swiftly while it passes, but rather arrests it and studies it, then
> lets it go by.[5]

Thus, "by using a minimum of physical movement, Hawthorne
invites attention to spiritual changes."[6]

Events directly presented in *The Scarlet Letter* cover about
seven years. The adulterous love affair between Hester and Arthur, the "postulate" of the romance, occurred during the two

years which preceded the opening scene of the book. The essential action is narrated in twenty-three chapters.[7] The first half of the book covers almost seven years; the second half, only a few weeks. The twelfth chapter is the midpoint of the book, but it is near the conclusion of the series of events which make up the story. That is to say, Hawthorne gave much more extended treatment to events near the climax of his narrative.

The main structural device of the romance is the scaffold of the pillory. It is the place where most critical action takes place, and it has an emblematic meaning too, for it is a standing reminder of the public accountability of wrongdoers. The main thematic device of the story is the scarlet *A*. Just as the scaffold integrates the events, the letter symbolizes the essential meanings of the romance. Through the succession of its various and timely manifestations, what Hawthorne elsewhere called "a stain upon the soul" (CE 9:220) becomes in "many guises" "flagrant to the common eye." The plot of *The Scarlet Letter* exhibits the protracted struggle between influences seeking to prevent the minister from ascending this emblematic scaffold and assuming this symbolic letter, and influences seeking to induce him to do so. In the course of this struggle, these engines which society has devised for publicizing and punishing sin are appropriated for its deeper purpose by a more powerful and more mysterious force.

My explication will analyze the principal scenes of the romance in relation to the exposition which accompanies them. In order to distinguish what these principal scenes are, and what narrative principle gives them a connected signification, I will employ a conception set forth by John Gerber which is, I think, basic to any valid account of the structure of the book:

> Form in *The Scarlet Letter* rises out of a basic division of the whole into four parts, each of which gains its distinctiveness from the character that precipitates or is responsible for the action that takes place within its limits. Furthermore, the order of the parts is determined by the desires and capabilities of the characters.[8]

In the action of *The Scarlet Letter* I distinguish the following "four parts": (1) that in which organized society is the "activating agent"[9], (2) that in which Roger Chillingworth is the activating agent, (3) that in which Hester Prynne is the activating agent, and (4) that in which God is the activating agent and is revealed to have been the ultimate activator in the three earlier parts which had other ostensible agents. In all stages of the action, Arthur Dimmesdale is the character mainly acted upon.

II

[I] to the place of judgment will return,
There with my cries importune Heaven, that all
The sentence from thy head removed may light
On me, sole cause to thee of all this woe.
                                        —Paradise Lost

The first section of *The Scarlet Letter* defines the opening situation and adumbrates the subsequent action of the story. The three chapters (1–3) of this section constitute one prolonged scene, lasting from morning till past noon of a sunny June day when the beauty and bounty of nature contrast with the sin and suffering of humanity. All the persons of the story are assembled at the scaffold of the pillory: the adulterous woman with her "sin-born infant"; (CE 1:63) the community, both populace and officials; the wronged and vengeful husband; an Indian, representative of the "wild heathen Nature of the forest"; (CE 1:203) and the minister who, though revered by his flock as a "heaven-ordained apostle," (CE 1:120) is a secret sinner. For three hours Hester is exposed to "the heavy weight of a thousand unrelenting eyes"; (CE 1:57) at the end of this ordeal she still stands erect "on her pedestal . . . with the hot mid-day sun burning down upon her face, and lighting up its shame; with the scarlet token of infamy on her breast; with a whole people . . . staring at" her. (CE 1:63)

In this initial scene, the community, or society, is the activating agent. Although the ostensible occasion is the chastisement of Hester, the actual narrative business of the scene is to do these three things: (1) to present the official demand of society that the secret sinner's identity be made known; (2) to place Dimmesdale in the foreground, and to draw varied and insistent attention to the "special responsibility" which he bears for Hester's spiritual condition and to his disordered state of mind; and (3) to prepare for the action of the second part of the book, in which Chillingworth is to be the activating agent.

Chillingworth's imminent role is prepared for early. Recognition passes between him and Hester; he signals to her his intention to keep secret his identity and his relation to her; then he expresses vehemently, but so privately that his purpose is not disclosed to Hester and the minister, that he is determined to discover and revenge himself upon Hester's paramour.

Thereafter, various demands that Hester name the sinner or that he name himself are made through, and ultimately to, Dimmesdale. Prompted by religious and civil authorities, the minister addresses Hester in words which are both a public communication that voices the official demand and a private communication that points out to her that Dimmesdale's demand is merely formal and compulsory: "Thou . . . seest the accountability under which I labor." His private communication furthermore calls attention to a qualification that justifies her refusal to speak out: "If thou feelest it to be for thy soul's peace, and that thy earthly punishment will thereby be made more effectual to salvation . . ." (CE 1:67) As Hester is unrepentant and resentful of her punishment, such qualification takes all force out of his appeal. Feeling that her wrongdoing was actually rightdoing, and that society is irrational and vindictive, she refuses to deliver to agony and shame the man she still passionately loves.

Nevertheless, the minister hears his conscience speaking in his own plea, though Hester is deaf to it. At this point, too, occurs the first of Pearl's instinctive pleas to Dimmesdale to give her that acknowledgment which would be tantamount to a confession. The Reverend John Wilson correctly interprets the reaching out of Pearl's "little arms" and her "half-pleased, half-plaintive murmur," (CE 1:67) in response to the minister's voice, as a Providential phenomenon, but he incorrectly interprets it as a sign to Hester. And at this juncture Chillingworth, hidden and anonymous in the crowd, "coldly and sternly" commands: "Speak, woman!" (CE 1:68) But Hester, "looking into the deep and troubled eyes" of Dimmesdale, replies only "Would that I might endure his agony as well as mine! . . . I will not speak!" (CE 1:68) This, too, is more than a public refusal of a public demand; it is Hester's private expression to Arthur of her undiminished passion and devotion; and he, who "with his hand upon his heart, had awaited the result of his appeal," sighs his appreciation: "Wondrous strength and generosity of a woman's heart! She will not speak!" (CE 1:68)

From this scene emerges most plainly the question of who is the unidentified sinner—sought by popular clamor and official inquiry; secretly pursued by the vengeful husband; instinctively recognized and appealed to by his child; passionately shielded by his paramour, "through mistaken pity and tenderness"; (CE 1:67) burdened with shame and horror of himself, but "kept silent by the very constitution of [his] nature." (CE 1:132) The unifying motif of the romance is announced in these varied and insistent demands that Hester's fellow-sinner step forth from his place among the company of righteous folk, ascend the scaffold, and assume his scarlet letter. The order in which these demands are made, and the attitudes toward the sinner revealed by persons who figure in these demands and appeals, adumbrate the order and attitudes to be developed in later sections of the book.

Therefore, not the open and prolonged punishment of Hester, in this scene and throughout the romance, but the dubious and unresolved situation of the unacknowledged sinner constitutes the dramatic central situation. Hester's vital principle is romantic love, and the whole dynamic operation of this (except for a brief, pathetic, and ineffectual resurgence to come, when she becomes again an "activating agent") took place in the years preceding the opening of the romance. "The scaffold of the pillory was a point of view that revealed to Hester Prynne the entire track along which she had been treading since her infancy." But this same scaffold scene was the beginning of the series of events which were to lead Dimmesdale tardily to take his place beside her—events which constitute the dynamic substance of the story.

III

A permission from God, for the Devil to come down and break in upon mankind, oftentimes must be accompany'd with a Commission from some wretches of mankind itself.
—The Wonders of the Invisible World

The second part of *The Scarlet Letter* shows the process by which Arthur Dimmesdale's "moral force was abased into more than childish weakness." (CE 1:159) That Roger Chillingworth had undertaken such a Devil's Commission, the people sensed, his victim suspected, and Chillingworth himself eventually admitted to Hester.

The traits chiefly emphasized in Hawthorne's initial characterization of the young minister are his learning, especially his theoretical knowledge of good and evil; his inexperience and ignorance of worldly things; his intense sensibility; and the apprehensiveness and discomposure of his manner. All of these visible traits and manners can be interpreted as signs of angelic other-worldliness (and his flock interprets them thus), but they are gradually shown to be hints of the failure of his theoretical knowledge of good and evil to cope with the realities of sin in his own nature and in the world. "It would always be essential to his peace to feel the pressure of a faith about him, supporting, while it confined him within its iron framework." (CE 1:123) Before his fall, his was the situation described in Emerson's poem "Grace": "How much, preventing God, how much I owe / To the defences thou has round me set." But "All these fences and their whole array / One cunning bosom-sin blows quite away."[10] When the "iron framework" of Dimmesdale's creed proved unable to confine his "strong animal nature," (CE 1:130) the surprising discovery of sin in his own heart and practice inhibited such powers of moral recuperation as he possessed, all the more because of his previous confidence in the efficacy of his professional safeguards against sin.

Thereafter he underwent a prolonged moral crisis. He could succumb to his sin or rise above it, but in either event there must be a period of tension and doubt while the issue was being decided. His almost fatal error was in regarding his failure to confess as merely a failure in duty to society, whereas it was in fact a failure in duty to God. He had a duty to exhibit the truth about himself. "Puritanism . . . demanded that the individual confront existence directly on all sides at once, that he test all things by the touchstone of absolute truth, that no allowance be made for circumstances or for human frailty."[11] God requires the sinner to confess his guilt to his fellows, not because men have authority to judge and punish (being themselves fallible sinners), but because a sinner's preference of an untruth which preserves the good opinion of men to a truth which, though it gains the forgiveness of God, might forfeit the good opinion of men, is a preference of a worldly deceit to a spiritual reality. Furthermore, undetected sin among men, especially in their spiritual leaders, exposes the whole society to the "contagion of sin." "Among the social conditions of piety the simplest and most evident is contagion. . . . The evil condition of one corrupts those about him."[12] Moreover, such confession as Dimmesdale was obligated to make is edifying as a demonstration of the power of righteousness, "adding to the glory of God."[13] Dimmesdale's cherishing of a false semblance of himself which men mistakenly reverenced as his real character threatened to destroy his truth, the life of his soul: "To the untrue man, the whole universe is false,—it is impalpable,—it shrinks to nothing within his grasp. And he himself, insofar as he shows himself in a false light, becomes a shadow, or indeed, ceases to exist." (CE 1:145–46) In the course of seven years of hypocrisy Dimmesdale became such a "shadow"; he was morally so obscured that he dimmed almost to nonexistence.

Roger Chillingworth, fully comprehending the minister's precarious moral situation and the debility of his will, became, as he said to Hester, "a fiend for [the minister's] especial torment." (CE 1:172) For seven years he agitated his victim's tender conscience with continual reminders of his sin; goaded him to the verge of confession and then dissuaded him from it, thereby enfeebling his will and contributing to the inveteracy of his moral inerita.[14] The tendency of Chillingworth's treatment of the minister "was, not to cure by wholesome pain, but to disorganize and corrupt his spiritual being." (CE 1:193)

The action of this second section occupies nine chapters (4–12) covering seven years. Most readers do not realize very clearly that this section of the book is supposed to convey a sense of the measured lapsing of seven years. Hawthorne was apparently aware that he could "not reflect the action swiftly while it passes,"[15] for after this time had elapsed he obtrusively and repeatedly (more than twenty times) in ensuing chapters *told* his readers that seven years had passed. The greater part of this section is expository rather than dramatic, but the positions which Hawthorne's exposition explains are pictured in three judiciously placed scenes.

The first of these scenes is at the beginning of the second section (chapter 4). Chillingworth is the activating agent. In this scene he accomplishes three things. First, he makes clear that he intends no revenge upon Hester and no injury to Pearl, thus obviating the reader's suspense regarding the possibility of such developments. Second, by securing Hester's promise not to reveal his identity, he makes sure that Hester will not be able to warn her paramour against him. (In fact, throughout this section Hester is to be so engrossed in making her own situation endurable, largely by turning all her affection toward Pearl, that she pays little attention to Dimmesdale.) Third, Chillingworth urges Hester to identify her fellow-sinner. He thus picks up the motivation prepared for in the opening section. When she refuses, he declares:

> "Not the less he is mine. . . . He bears no letter of infamy wrought into his garment, as thou dost; but I shall read it on his heart. Yet . . . think not that I shall interfere with Heaven's own method of retribution, or, to my own loss, betray him to the gripe of human law. . . . Let him live! Let him hide himself in outward honor, if he may! Not the less he shall be mine!" (CE 1:75–76)

This speech exactly forecasts the actions of Chillingworth which follow in this second section.

The second scene of the second section of *The Scarlet Letter* occurs at the precise midpoint of the seven years covered in this section. The scene assembles the chief characters, ostensibly to decide whether Hester should be allowed to retain Pearl. At this time Hester is still in so precarious a mental state that maintaining her saving connection with Pearl is her all-engrossing object, so that she has little present inclination to resume relations with Dimmesdale. She ambiguously threatens him with exposure if he does not support her claim to Pearl; accordingly he does support it, decisively. But the scene confirms that the love-relationship between the two is still suspended and inoperative; and, further, that at this time neither of the lovers thinks of resuming it in a "life together." The scene shows also that the community's cognizance of the now almost forgotten transgression of Hester and its interest in identifying her paramour are now perfunctory, even officially laid aside. The Reverend Mr. Wilson says it is best "to leave the mystery as we find it, unless Providence reveal it of its own accord." (CE 1:116)

Nevertheless, the main business of the scene is not to show that the community has dropped its inquisition into Hester's adultery, nor that Hester is not yet disposed to persuade Dimmesdale to a renewal of it, although both of these circumstances are to be noted because they leave Chillingworth alone as the activating agent at this point of the story. What the scene chiefly demonstrates is that Chillingworth, at this midpoint of the seven years of his "devil's office," has for a long time past been certain of his victim, and is now intimately fastened to him and battening upon his misery. There is scarcely concealed gloating in his ironic remarks to and about the minister throughout this central scene of the second section. When, two chapters later, the physician at last inspects the stigma on Dimmesdale's breast while the minister is in a drugged sleep, he gloats fiendishly over a result of his machinations concerning which he had never been in doubt.

The third and climaxing scene of the second section occurs in chapter 12. This is the midchapter of the book; it is also the central one of the three scaffold scenes in the book. It occurs, however, at the end of Chillingworth's seven years' torture of Dimmesdale, and shows the culmination and apparent triumph of the physician's course of vengeance. This middle scaffold scene is "mock-penitential"; it shows "Dimmesdale's Agony."[16] "He had been driven hither by the impulse of that Remorse which dogged him everywhere, and whose own sister and closely linked companion was that Cowardice which invariably drew him back, with her tremulous gripe, just when the other impulse had hurried him to the verge of a disclosure." (CE 1:148) Although Remorse makes him ascend the scaffold, Cowardice makes his ascension an empty and ghastly irony. He ascends it, not at midday, but at midnight. No multitude is present to view him. Hester and Pearl are not with him, and he wears no letter openly revealed on his breast. Yet one by one most of these conditions of publicity are providentially added to the scene.

Dimmesdale, involuntarily shrieking in anguish, awakens Governor Bellingham, asleep in his nearby mansion; but the Governor, peering into the darkness, fails to descry Dimmesdale on the pillory.

> If the same multitude which had stood as eyewitnesses while Hester Prynne sustained her punishment could now have been summoned forth, they would have discerned no face above the platform, nor hardly the outline of a human shape, in the dark gray of the midnight. (CE 1:147)

It is as if Dimmesdale, a moral shadow, had been dimmed into nonexistence. Then "the Reverend Mr. Wilson" passed by, on his way home from "the death-chamber of Governor Winthrop, who had passed from earth to heaven within that very hour." (CE 1:150) He, like Governor Bellingham, failed to see Dimmesdale. Thus the officials of society still pass undistinguishing by the guilty man.

Nevertheless, all those persons and powers who know his guilt will find him out in the darkness and manifest their claims. Soon Hester and Pearl appear, also returning home from Governor Winthrop's deathbed, and comply with the minister's request that they stand beside him. But when Pearl repeats her insistent question, "Wilt thou stand here with mother and me, tomorrow noontide?", he tells her that he will not do so until "the great judgment day. . . . But the daylight of this world shall not see our meeting!" (CE 1:153)

> But before the minister had done speaking, a light gleamed far and wide over all the muffled sky. . . . It showed the familiar scene of the street with the distinctness of mid-day. . . . And there stood the minister, with his hand over his heart; and Hester Prynne, with the embroidered letter glimmering on her bosom; and little Pearl, herself a symbol, and the connecting link between those two. They stood in the noon of that strange and solemn splendor, as if it is the light that is to reveal all secrets, and the daybreak that shall unite all who belong to one another. (CE 1:153–54)

Then, "the minister, looking upward to the zenith, beheld there the appearance of an immense letter,—the letter A,—marked out in lines of dull red light" in "awful hieroglyphics on the cope of heaven." (CE 1:155) This light from heaven "imparted a new expression" of undisguised diabolism to the features of Chillingworth, now described near the scaffold. "Then might Roger Chillingworth have passed . . . for the arch-fiend, standing there with a smile and scowl to claim his own." (CE 1:156) Pearl addresses to the minister a final reproach, in which there is still a hint of possible salvation: "Thou wast not bold!—thou wast not true!—Thou wouldst not promise to take my hand, and my mother's hand, tomorrow noontide!" (CE 1:157) But the fiend, approaching his victim with mock solicitude, leads him away in confident triumph. Dimmesdale "yielded himself to the physician, and was led away." (CE 1:157)

This section, in which Roger Chillingworth is the activating agent, leaves him in apparent triumphant ascendancy.

IV

Alas, by what sweet thoughts, what fond desire,
Must they at length to that ill pass have reached!
—Inferno *(Cary trans.)*

The third section of *The Scarlet Letter* shows how Dimmesdale, his "moral force . . . abased into more than childish weakness," (CE 1:159) became convinced that he was "irrevocably doomed" (CE 1:201) and "yielded himself, with deliberate choice, as he had never done before, to what he knew was deadly sin." (CE 1:222)

In this section the activating agent is Hester. The transition from Chillingworth to Hester as activating agent was prepared in the final scene of the preceding section, when Dimmesdale, "overcome with terror" (CE 1:156) of the physician, appealed to Hester to help him. Hester "remembered her oath, and was silent," (CE 1:156) but at the opening of the third section she had "decided that [Dimmesdale] had a right to her utmost aid." (CE 1:159)

The minister's moral state at this point of the story exemplifies the Calvinist distinction between man's propensity to sin (universal depravity) and his actual sinning—between his sinful nature and his sinful behavior. "There is evil in every human heart, which may remain latent, perhaps, through the whole of life, but circumstances may rouse it into activity." (CE 8:29) During his Liverpool consulship Hawthorne was fascinated by the situation of an American Doctor of Divinity who, having escaped the protective scrutiny of his flock at home, abandoned himself to a long drunken orgy in a Liverpool brothel. Of this reverend whoremaster Hawthorne wrote:

> I leave it to members of his own profession to decide whether it
> was better for him thus to sin outright, and so be let into the
> miserable secret of what manner of man he was, or to have gone

through life outwardly unspotted, making the first discovery of his latent evil at the judgment-seat. It has occurred to me that his dire calamity, as both he and I regarded it, may have been the only method by which precisely such a man as himself . . . could be redeemed. (CE 5:30)

This actual situation which Hawthorne came across in his later years parallels in its moral significance to him the situation of Dimmesdale in *The Scarlet Letter;* innocence is not purity, but merely ignorance. Sin is always tragic and perilous, but it is the only means by which man can realize his moral nature.

Therefore the minister's sin was not heinous primarily because it expressed his sensual nature. Hawthorne shared Puritan belief that "since God created the soul with affections, these must be fundamentally good, even though they are now corrupted by sin." (Miller, 253) Dimmesdale's fornication is not reprehensible because sexual love is evil, but because man's sexual love is tainted in its expression in consequence of his sinful nature. Such a sin is not irremediable; it animates the sinner's spiritual force to struggle against his upstart passions. The Puritans held that "in wicked men the conscience is at odds with the will, and because all men are compounded of spirit and matter they are torn by a never ending contention between the soul and the body." (Miller, 29) During this struggle of conscience Chillingworth's fiendish meddling had utterly enfeebled the minister's moral energies, so that his "moral force . . . grovelled helpless on the ground." (CE 1:159)

At this juncture Hester—with her abundant and already experienced sexual attraction, convinced that "lawless passion" had "a consecration of its own," (CE 1:195) "strengthened by years of hard and solemn trial" (CE 1:167) and animated by "desperate tenderness" (CE 1:194) toward her erstwhile lover—urged the morally abased minister to enter upon "a new life" with her. And he, asking "wherefore should I not snatch the solace allowed to the condemned culprit before his execution?", (CE 1:201) "yielded himself, with deliberate choice, as he had never done before, to what he knew was deadly sin." (CE 1:222)

This section, in which Hester's love apparently completed the work of moral destruction which Chillingworth's hate had so far advanced, comprises seven chapters (13–19). Chillingworth

had destroyed his victim's moral capability; Hester was to animate his "strong animal nature" (CE 1:130) and thus to make
his soul thrall to rebel powers. The first chapter of this section
is expository and transitional, and accounts for the passage of a
few days or weeks; the remaining chapters picture consecutive
scenes that take place on the final day of this period of time.

The first chapter of this section tells us of Hester's resolve
to renounce her oath of silence, and to warn the minister against
Chillingworth. It also shows that "the scarlet letter had not done
its office" (CE 1:166) of making Hester repent, and makes it
clear that her counsel and persuasion must therefore be more
dangerous than helpful to Dimmesdale. In Hawthorne's view, a
woman's faculty of judging and doing right is her intuition, animated by love, and Hester's straying passions had destroyed the
truth of her intuitions.[17] The minister saw clearly that her persuasions would carry him to perdition, but "in Hawthorne's novels, the strong characters are evil; the good are weak."[18]
Therefore Dimmesdale could not resist Hester, whose "seven
years of outlaw and ignominy had been little other than a preparation for this very hour." (CE 1:200)

Just as appropriately as the other scenes take place at the
scaffold, which indicates the availability of confession and the
possible victory of conscience, the scenes of this section take
place in "the dismal forest" (CE 1:187)—a veritable wood of
error—on a "chill and sombre day." (CE 1:183)

In the first of these scenes Hester tells Chillingworth that
she intends to warn the minister against him. The physician does
not remonstrate, for he is now confident that his victim cannot
escape, and probably foresees that Hester's interference at this
point is likely to complete the minister's ruin.

The next scene is symbolic preparation for the meeting in
which Hester means to persuade Dimmesdale to elope with her
and Pearl. In this scene she puts from her the two influences
which have had the talismanic effect of preventing her active
and final commitment to evil. First, she denies the moral significance of the letter; next, she dismisses Pearl, who had been in
attendance at every previous interview in the book between
Hester and Arthur. Hester has already admitted to Pearl that the
letter is the mark of the Black Man, but when Pearl now repeats

her persistent query about the letter's meaning, and connects it again with the minister's gesture of putting his hand over his heart, Hester says, "What know I of the minister's heart? And as for the scarlet letter, I wear it for the sake of its goldthread." (CE 1:181)

> In all the seven bygone years, Hester Prynne had never before been false to the symbol on her bosom. It may be that it was the talisman of a stern and severe, but yet a guardian spirit, who now forsook her; as recognizing that, in spite of his strict watch over her heart, some new evil had crept into it, or some old one had never been expelled. (CE 1:181)

Then, as the minister approaches, Pearl mistakes him for the Black Man who "haunts this forest" (CE 1:184) and is thereupon sent away by Hester. Thus Hester prepares herself for the role of seductress in the following scene.

In this ensuing scene Arthur and Hester are a Paolo and Francesca, an Adam and Eve made lustful by the shared apple. "So strangely did they meet, in the dim wood, that it was like the first encounter, in the world beyond the grave, of two spirits who had been intimately connected in their former life, but now stood coldly shuddering, in mutual dread." (CE 1:190) This scene, often held to be the most interesting in the book,[19] demands little explication, for it merely enacts a result already determined. At its climax, when Arthur has agreed to the elopement after only a feeble show of conscience, Hester unclasps the scarlet letter and throws it away. Then she unbinds her luxuriant hair, which, "primly confined" beneath her cap throughout the previous seven years, symbolized her repressed sexual passion. The lovers now view a world brightened by their passion. "Love . . . must always create a sunshine, filling the heart so full of radiance, that it overflows upon the outward world." (CE 1:203) "Guilt has its moment of rapture," (CE 4:176) and in this hour Dimmesdale has forsaken the pains of heaven to enjoy the blisses of hell.

But Pearl, "the living hieroglyphic in which was written the secret they so darkly sought to hide," (CE 1:207) refuses to consort with her parents in this moment of lawless rapture. She keeps her distance on the far side of the brook, which as "the sensitive minister" noted, "is the boundary between two worlds. . . . Is she an elfish spirit . . . forbidden to cross a running stream?" (CE 1:208)

At the close of the scene Hester resumes the letter and again confines her hair beneath her cap. Pearl then rejoins her parents, but asks concerning Dimmesdale: "Will he go back with us, hand in hand, we three together, into the town?" (CE 1:212) When told that he would not, "Pearl would show no favor to the clergyman" and washed away his "unwelcome kiss" (CE 1:213) in the running stream. "She then remained apart, silently watching Hester and the clergyman." (CE 1:213)

In this section Hester's effort to assume control over the minister is brief, intense, and apparently successful. At the conclusion of it, she believes that she has decided their common future. Chillingworth, too, is still confident that his mastership is unshaken. But, unknown to either of these agents, a third influence is now to become dramatically dominant and final.

V

How welcome should a Death in the Lord *be unto them that belong not unto the Devil, but unto the Lord! While we are sojourning in this World, we are in what may upon too many accounts be called* The Devil's Country: *We are where the Devil may come upon us in* great wrath *continually. The day when God shall take us out of this World will be,* The Day when the Lord will deliver us from the hand of all our Enemies, and from the hand of Satan.—The Wonders of the Invisible World

The fourth and final section of *The Scarlet Letter* shows Dimmesdale, apparently doomed to perdition, spectacularly saved by God's grace. God is the activating agent in this section, and is shown to have been responsible, through his "permissive" power, for the apparently pernicious but actually redemptive actions of Hester and Chillingworth. The minister's dying speech declares that God "hath proved his mercy, most of all, in my afflictions. . . . Had either [any] of these agonies been wanting, I had been lost forever." (CE 1:236–37)

This section (chapters 20–23) is the most artfully handled part of the book. Hawthorne carries forward the impression that evil influences on the minister must be decisive; read anticipatively, the account suggests that Dimmesdale is rapidly declining to perdition. At the same time, the narrative, retrospectively considered, affords evidence that his regeneration was in process. This section is therefore a good example of Hawthorne's famed ambiguity. Although this ambiguity makes explication difficult, it is appropriate for several reasons. It shows that God moves in a mysterious way His wonders to perform. By indicating the turbulence within the minister's mind at this critical time, it renders credible the routing of evil influences by good ones which transpires. By retarding explicit recognition of his regeneration, it effects a dramatic peripety at the end of the story.

The account of Dimmesdale's regeneration faithfully follows orthodox Puritan conceptions, in its specification of the sinner's state before regeneration, of the stages in the actual process of regeneration, and the attitudes invoked toward regeneration.

The sinner was unable to initiate and perfect his own reformation.

> It was obvious that men had contrived to bring upon themselves all the anguish they suffered; it was still more obvious that neither this awareness nor the anguish itself liberated them from the trammels of perversity. A being who brought such a destiny upon himself could hardly expect to find within himself the power to master it. (Miller, 25)

"No man can enact regeneration by his own exertion." (Miller, 27) God's speech in *Paradise Lost* (2.173–82) summarizes the orthodox Puritan view:

> Man shall not quite be lost, but saved who will;
> Yet not of will in him, but grace in me
> Freely vouchsafed. Once more I will renew
> His lapséd powers, through forfeit, and enthralled
> By sin to foul exorbitant desires:
> Upheld by me, yet once more he shall stand

> On even ground against his mortal foe—
> By me upheld that he may know how frail
> His fallen condition is, and to me owe
> All his deliverance, and to none but me.

Utter moral incapability is explicitly Dimmesdale's condition at the beginning of this section. "Deadly sin" is "diffused throughout his moral system. It had stupefied all blessed impulses, and awakened into vivid life the whole brotherhood of bad ones. . . . [His conduct] did but show his sympathy and fellowship with wicked mortals, and the world of perverted spirits." (CE 1:222)

The last and most ominous sign of the minister's moral degeneration is the pride with which he looks forward to his day of worldly exaltation, when he is to preach the Election Sermon. The conceit of his own piety was the danger most pernicious to an eminent clergyman: "The *Devil provokes* men that are eminent in Holiness unto such things as may become eminently *Pernicious*; he provokes them especially unto *Pride*."[20] Throughout the seven past years of Dimmesdale's ministry he had felt agony because in every pastoral performance "he had spoken the very truth and transformed it into the veriest falsehood." (CE 1:144) As he told Hester, "As concerns the good which I appear to do, . . . it must needs be a delusion." (CE 1:191) "Puritanism . . . demands that the individual confront existence directly on all sides at once, that no allowance be made for circumstances of human frailty." (Miller, 45) So long as Dimmesdale's heart acknowledged the truth, though he could not will his tongue to utter it, he retained an essential and saving truth in his character: "The only truth that continued to give Mr. Dimmesdale a real existence on this earth was the anguish in his inmost soul." (CE 1:146) But "no man, for any considerable period, can wear one face to himself, and another to the multitude, without finally getting bewildered as to which may be the true." (CE 1:216) And the minister now calls it "most fortunate" (CE 1:215) that his planned elopement with Hester will not take place until after he enacts what threatens to be his culminating hypocrisy, the preaching of the Election Sermon. Apparently the last stage of his "eternal alienation from the Good and True" (CE 1:193) is this displacement by pride of his anguished consciousness of moral truancy; having lost his moral will, he appears now to have lost the remorse which was its residue and the germ from which it might be revived.

The first event in a sinner's regeneration is "justification." "A change must be wrought in his status before any can be made in his nature." (Miller, 27) This change is neither conscious nor visible; it is known to have occurred only by the positive regeneration which eventuates. Following the sinner's justification, "divine grace reaches forth to the prostrate man in two ways: first it comes as a call to a new life, a summons from above—which was called 'vocation'." (Miller, 27) Hawthorne gives various ambiguous intimations that this call to a new life reached Dimmesdale during the three days between his meeting with Hester in the forest and the preaching of the Election Sermon. The first of these intimations is the composition of the sermon itself, on the night of his return from the forest. Before composing the sermon he still shows signs of the "unaccustomed physical energy" and "unweariable activity" (CE 1:216) which had so phenomenally marked the revival of his "strong animal nature." Before composing the sermon, "he ate with ravenous appetite." (CE 1:225) But "he wrote with such impulsive flow of thought and emotion that he fancied himself inspired." (CE 1:225) In this passage there are strong evidences of both animal vitality and spiritual influence; the composition of the Election Sermon apparently marks the meeting, interfusion, and transference of powers in Dimmesdale. When Dimmesdale appears in the procession, on the day of the Election Sermon, everyone remarks that he exhibits more energy than at any time since he "first set foot on the New England shore," (CE 1:238) and that he no longer holds his hand over his heart. Although readers will naturally explain this phenomenal energy as a continuation of the animal vitality aroused by his meeting with Hester, "yet, if the minister were rightly viewed, his strength seemed not of the body. It might be spiritual, and imparted to him by angelic administrations." (CE 1:238–39) To Hester and Pearl, he seems not the same man they had so recently conversed with. To Hester, "he seemed remote from her own sphere, and utterly beyond her reach. . . . She thought of the dim forest. . . . How deeply they had known each other then! And was this the man? She hardly knew him now!" (CE 1:239) Pearl asks, "Mother,

. . . was that the same minister that kissed me by the brook? . . . I could not be sure it was he; so strange he looked." (CE 1:240) This passage is the most crucial instance of that ambiguity I have already mentioned. Read anticipatively, with the knowledge given of the minister's moral history, he seems at this point to be a reinvigorated hypocrite; read retrospectively, he is shown to be a man inspired, who has received his "vocation."

The second way in which divine grace "reaches forth to the prostrate man" is by effecting an alteration of the sinner's nature. "It penetrates his being and there it generates—or, in view of Adam's original nature, 're-generates'—a power to respond." (Miller, 27) It is this power to respond which Dimmesdale becomes aware of when, passing from the church after the Election Sermon, he meets Hester Prynne at the scaffold and accosts her thus:

> In the name of him, so terrible and so merciful, who gives me grace, at this last moment, to do what—for my own heavy sin and miserable agony—I withheld myself from doing seven years ago, come hither now, and entwine thy strength about me! Thy strength, Hester; but let it be guided by the will which God hath granted me. (CE 1:253)

Then, "partly supported by Hester Prynne, and holding one hand of little Pearl," (CE 1:254) he ascends the scaffold, at midday, in the presence of the multitude, and reveals the scarlet symbol of sin on his "sainted" breast. The sentence in which Hawthorne announces this act of confession is the thrilling climax of the romance: "The sun, but little past its meridian, shown down upon the clergyman, and gave a distinctness to his figure, as he stood out from all the earth, to put in his plea of guilty at the bar of eternal justice." (CE 1:254)

This "power to respond" which completes the work of regeneration "comes through the impact of a sensible species or phantasm, . . . some spoken word or physical experience." (Miller, 281) "The means . . . may be experience, . . . but ordinarily they are the words of a sermon and the sacraments of the church." (Miller, 289) Hawthorne intimates that it is the minister's own sermon that works this final operation of grace:

> Never had man spoken in so wise, so high, and so holy a spirit, as he that spake this day; nor had inspiration ever breathed

through mortal lips more evidently than it did through his. Its influence could be seen, as it were, descending upon him, and possessing him, and continually lifting him out of the written discourse that lay before him, and filling him with ideas that must have been as marvellous to himself as to his audience. (CE 1:248–49)

Thus, at this crisis of utmost peril to his soul, the grace of God fills the faltering minister—an interposition of God which gloriously demonstrates how the mystery of good could overcome the logic of evil. "The moment of regeneration, in which God, out of his compassion, bestows grace upon man and in which man is enabled to reply with belief, was the single goal of the Augustinian piety." (Miller, 25) With his last breath, Dimmesdale praises God for thus enabling him "to die this death of triumphant ignominy before the people." (CE 1:257) "The apotheosis of Dimmesdale upon the scaffold is certainly intended as an unequivocal spiritual victory for him."[21] Compared to this experience of grace, mundane happiness was of little worth. "The burden of Calvinism was that man must find his happiness in the glory and service of God, and not that man may not find happiness. The essence of sin is that man should prefer lesser good . . . to 'true virtue'."[22] "The good which God seeks and accomplishes is the display of infinite being, a good which transcends the good of finite existence."[23]

Some critics, lacking full critical sympathy with Hawthorne and preoccupied with "the good of finite existence," look upon the minister's death as a calamity, and opine that "[if] he had conscientiously been able to flee with [Hester] to a new life on the western frontier, there would have been no tragedy."[24] But this would have been, from Hawthorne's point of view, the greatest tragedy possible for Dimmesdale, for Hawthorne did not identify physical "death and tragedy."[25] Dimmesdale told Hester, "Were I an atheist,—a wretch with coarse and brutal instincts,—I might have found peace, long ere now. Nay, I should never have lost it." (CE 1:191) To Hawthorne, not physical but moral death was tragic and terrible: "Death is the very friend whom, in his due season, even the happiest mortal should be willing to embrace. . . . were man to live longer on earth, the spiritual would die out of him." (CE 10:489) Death is always in due season when it comes at the right time to keep the spiritual from dying out in man. Even the most sanguine of Transcendentalists, Alcott, wrote, "It is not death but a bad life that destroys the soul."[26] Dimmesdale died in that state of triumphant holiness to which every wayfaring Christian aspires; to him as to Adam, "Death becomes / His final remedy" (*PL* 11.61–62).

VI

At the present time . . . we do not hear any voice of heroic
magnitude proclaiming that good is good and evil evil, that
man is a religious and moral being in a religious and moral
universe.—Douglas Bush, Paradise Lost in Our Time

A question persistently raised by Hawthorne's interpreters is whether Hawthorne believed the doctrines which his story exemplifies. Melville was convinced that Hawthorne "meant his meanings." To Melville, Hawthorne's "great power of blackness derives from its appeals to that Calvinistic sense of Innate Depravity and Original Sin, from whose visitations, in some shape or other, no deeply thinking mind is always and wholly free."[27] Henry James, however, held that Hawthorne had esthetic seriousness but not moral earnestness, and such later critics as Paul Elmer More have subscribed to this view. But contemporary critics are returning to Melville's opinion, and hold that, although Hawthorne had a manifest "lack of interest in technical theology," "there is no question that Hawthorne's religion had its facts as well as its values."[28] "Despite his rejection of formal theology, his brooding absorption in what was common to human experience revealed to him the kernel of reality beneath the decayed husks. . . . 'He saw the empirical truth behind the Calvinist symbols'."[29] Although he had "a more tender mind" than the Puritans, and "his belief in universal depravity was colored by an unPuritan sympathy for the sinner,"[30] he had what Maritain has called the "peregrinal" conception of earthly life as an ordeal of moral "tension and movement." Although some critics may dismiss as an "intentional fallacy" the question of whether Hawthorne meant his meanings, other readers are aware that literature which lives, and speaks with increasing power to after generations, can be written only by a writer who takes his thoughts and his art with equal seriousness—in Miltonic phrase, "thoughts that voluntary move / Harmonious numbers." I do not mean by this that a reader must accept as still valid Sophocles' or Milton's or Hawthorne's vision of life, but that the sincerity of each of these authors has informed his work with an impression of truth which makes it still an available insight to modern readers who hold other tenets than theirs.

NOTES

1. *Hawthorne* (New York: Macmillan, 1879), 109.
2. "Introduction," *The Scarlet Letter* (New York, 1919), xxiii.
3. *Ibid.*
4. James, 111.
5. G. P. Lathrop, *A Study of Hawthorne* (Boston: Houghton Miffin, 1899), 222.
6. Alexander Cowie, *The Rise of the American Novel* (New York: American Book Co., 1948), 339. Although Cowie is right in remarking that this is the effect of Hawthorne's narrative method, his method was evidently imposed upon him by his technical limitations; at best, he made a virtue of necessity.
7. This assumes that the "Introductory" essay ("The Custom House") and the "Conclusion" (chapter 24) are not integral parts of the plotted narrative. In this opinion about "The Custom House" I am in agreement with such excellent critics as Austin Warren and Edward Wagenknecht; and Hawthorne's conclusion has been almost universally held to be an awkward and implausible knotting up of loose ends of his narrative.
8. "Form and Content in *The Scarlet Letter*," *New England Quarterly* 17 (March 1944):26. Although this discerning observation of the structural principle of *The Scarlet Letter* is fundamental to my reading of the romance, I disagree with Gerber about most details of the interpretation, with one important further agreement: the "four parts" of the romance which he distinguishes approximate those which I make out.
9. Gerber's phrase.
10. George Herbert, "Sin."
11. Perry Miller, *The New England Mind* (Boston: Beacon Press, 1965), 45. Subsequent references to Miller, parenthetically identified in the text, are to this work.

12. Ralph Barton Perry, *Puritanism and Democracy* (New York: Vanguard Press, 1944), 328.

13. *Ibid.*, 372.

14. "Fancy's Show-Box," an early essay by Hawthorne on the psychology of guilt consciousness, throws much light upon the agitation of Dimmesdale's conscience during these seven years.

15. Lathrop, 222.

16. These characterizations are, respectively, from Rudolph Von Abele, " 'The Scarlet Letter': A Reading," *Accent* 11 (Autumn 1951):221; Q. D. Leavis, "Hawthorne as Poet," *Sewanee Review* 59 (Spring 1951):433.

17. See my article "The Theme of Isolation in Hawthorne," *Personalist* 32 (Winter and Spring 1951):45–47, 184–85.

18. Austin Warren, "Introduction," *Hawthorne* ("American Writers Series," American Book Company, 1934), xxxix.

19. See, for example, Gerber, "Form and Content in *The Scarlet Letter*," and W. D. Howells, "Hawthorne's Hester Prynne" in *Heroines of Fiction* (New York: Harper, 1901).

20. Cotton Mather, *The Wonders of the Invisible World* (London: "Library of Old Authors," Reeves and Turner, 1862), 55.

21. Von Abele, 227.

22. Joseph Haroutunian, *Piety Versus Moralism* (New York: Henry Holt & Co., 1932), 263.

23. *Ibid.*, 144.

24. Frederic I. Carpenter, "Scarlet A Minus," *College English* 5 (January 1944):177.

25. *Ibid.*

26. "Days from a Diary," *Dial* 2 (April 1842):437.

27. "Hawthorne and His Mosses," *Literary World* 7 (August 17 and 24, 1850):126.

28. Warren, xxv.

29. F. O. Matthiessen, *American Renaissance* (New York: Oxford Univ. Press, 1941), 199. The inner quotation is from Herbert Schneider, *The Puritan Mind* (New York: Henry Holt & Co., 1930). See also my article "Modes of Ethical Sensibility in Hawthorne," *Modern Language Notes* 68 (February 1953):80–86.

30. Barriss Mills, "Hawthorne and Puritanism," *New England Quarterly* 21 (March 1948):101, 102.

PART FOUR

The Other Major Romances

NINETEEN

The House
of the Seven Gables:
"A Long Drama of Wrong
and Retribution"

Admirers of *The House of the Seven Gables* have always been hard pressed to justify their admiration. Those who read it less as a work of literary art than as a social or moral treatise readily find in it a unity of theme which meets their slight demand for esthetic design. They read it to trace the "moral" with which Hawthorne said he had "provided himself" (CE 2:2) in order to conform to the current fashion; but he deprecated the supposition that this "moral" expressed, or could express, the essential significance of a work of fiction, which could be brought out only "gradually," "deepening at every step." The moral Hawthorne stated (and, be it observed, a moral is not, after all, a theme—the moral being a retrospective abstraction, the theme an anticipative and directive judgment which controls the author's representation of life) was that "the wrongdoing of one generation lives into successive ones, and divesting itself of every temporary advantage, becomes a pure

and uncontrollable mischief." (CE 1:2) One critic defined the
wrongdoing of the Pyncheons as a sin against democracy.[1] Although such a thesis can be plausibly maintained and contrib-
utes to our understanding of the book, it reduces it from a work
of art to a rambling and awkwardly handled exemplification of
truisms. Others, who make stricter esthetic demands of the
work, are likely to be more severe in their criticism. Of course
they can point to the charm of its atmosphere, which, as Henry
James said, "renders, to an initiated reader, the impression of a
summer afternoon in an elm-shadowed New England town."[2]
But fiction of book length must have design as well as "impression" if it is to endure as a classic, and even Hawthorne's
best-intentioned critics have been puzzled to make out any organizing principle in *The House of the Seven Gables*: they are unable to polarize its elements. It apparently lacks a single
consecutive action and a constant set of characters. The narrative leaps over whole generations with apparent arbitrariness.
The characters appear to have been prodded from repose, not
into life and action, but merely into momentary and aimless
liveliness; they appear to be posturing and gesturing rather than
acting out the inner necessities of their individual natures according to the exigencies and opportunities of an actual environment. The story appears to progress casually, even haphazardly,
rather than to advance toward a crisis determined by factors
inherent in the given situation.

Situation is what normally gives a novel its unity. The unity
of a long work of fiction usually derives from its being a sustained attempt to trace the release in action of the potential
energies in some interesting and typical human situation which
involves the fates of various persons. The situation may be local
and trivial, involving the petty though piquant vanities and am-
bitions of a few persons, as in *Barchester Towers*; or it may be vast
and momentous, involving the lives and fortunes of whole pop-
ulations, as in *War and Peace*; but in any case it treats of a crisis
in the relationship of a particular set of persons in a specific
place at a definite time. Clear distinction of this crisis provides
a center of interest in reference to which all the characters and
events of the story are seen to belong to one significant config-
uration of life.

Critics have looked vainly in *The House of the Seven Gables* for such a dynamic situation culminating in a crisis. They find instead a series of minor, quite static, situations, a discursive rather than a plotted development. They decide either that the book has no unifying principle, no *ensemble*, or that one of its several situations is significant and the others are extrinsic. Adopting the first of these opinions, George Woodberry, Hawthorne's first disinterested critic, pronounced *The House of the Seven Gables* not a single story but "a succession of stories bound together"[3] by a common motif. Preferring the alternative, Austin Warren, one of the most perceptive of present-day critics of Hawthorne, called the book "actually an expanded novelette" and proposes drastic "retrenchment'" in order to get at the "real plot," which he ascertained to be a demonstration of "the effect of pride, poverty and suffering upon two old aristocrats," Hepzibah and Clifford, "the central characters."[4]

Hawthorne himself, in his first enthusiasm for the finished book, thought it had "more merit than *The Scarlet Letter*" and was "more characteristic" of his powers.[5] It is strange that Hawthorne, one of the best self-critics among American writers, should have thought so highly of a work allegedly so defective. Shall we trust his judgment (with due allowance for the mood of relief with which an author views a fresh accomplishment) or that of his critics? In this dilemma we may well recall Coleridge's "golden rule" of criticism: "*Until you understand a writer's ignorance, presume yourself ignorant of his understanding.*"[6] Coleridge was admonishing a baffled reader to look further—not to assume that a book must yield his sense, but to search patiently for its sense.

Critical reprehension of *The House of the Seven Gables* evidently proceeds from fixed ideas about the substance and form proper to a long work of prose fiction. From the period when the novel first showed signs of emerging as a distinct literary genre, its usual subject has been "real life" and its technique "realism." Since the seventeenth century the trend of Western thought has been away from idealisms of whatever sort and toward materialism. Literature, especially prose fiction, while it has gradually perfected its techniques for giving adequate account of the various impressions made by the visible world upon man's senses, has correspondingly lost its techniques for giving the semblance of reality to imaginations of the ideal. During the last two centuries the novel has become a respectable and popular literary form because it is well suited to exhaustive reporting of the tangibilities of ordinary life. A modern reader's assumption about a novel is that it is primarily a more or less realistic though imaginary history of persons. Such histories may vary in scope from the introspective minutiae of *Ulysses* to the coarser and more conspicuous events in a more extended and overt range of life in *The Old Wives' Tale*. Despite striking differences of material, most novels still support Henry James's dictum in *The Art of Fiction*: "The novel is history."[7]

Hawthorne's distinction between the novel and the romance, which Henry James dismissed as "not answering to any reality," was an attempt to admonish readers that his books were not histories: they were less concerned with facts than with ideas, with persons than with human nature, with present circumstances than with the timeless influences which animate them. He agreed with Coleridge's dictum that "to remove the disturbing forces of accident is the business of ideal art."[8] In fact, Hawthorne's distinction between the novel and the romance was a diffident transcendentalist manifesto, declaring that he would write not realistic but transcendental fictions:

> When a writer wishes to call his work a Romance, . . . he wishes to claim a certain latitude, both as to its fashion and material, which he would not have felt himself entitled to assume had he professed to be writing a Novel.
>
> [The novel] is presumed to aim at a very minute fidelity, not merely to the possible, but to the probable and ordinary course of man's experience. (CE 2:1)

Hawthorne was anxious to avoid exposing *The House of the Seven Gables* "to that inflexible and exceedingly dangerous species of criticism" which insists upon "bringing his fancy-pictures almost into positive contact with the realities of the moment." (CE 1:3)

A modern critic would say that Hawthorne was protesting the application of canons of realism to his work. One of the ambiguities of the overworked word *realism* is that it means both a mode of expression and an assumption about the nature of ultimate reality. Indicating a mode of expression, it means concrete and circumstantial rendering of sensible things. Hawthorne aimed at this sort of realism in his fiction, although in an eclectic and subdued way. Indicating the nature of reality, realism means acceptance of the world of appearance as the "real" world. Hawthorne was not a realist in this sense. Although his notebooks are full of wonderfully vivid and precise delineations of actual persons, places, and events, in his fiction, as Henry James complained, "he never attempted to render exactly or closely the actual facts of the society that surrounded him."[9]

His whole endeavor, like that of his Artist of the Beautiful, was "to spiritualize matter" (CE 10:459)—to interpret what he called "the grand hieroglyphic" (CE 4:258) of the visible world, not as the sociologist does, by drawing from it abstractions which would have their whole truth grounded in the tangibilities from which they are derived, but as a transient projection of an ideal world beyond, as merely phenomenal. Nevertheless, he was not quite a transcendentalist, for he conceded more importance to the visible world than the Alcotts and Emersons seemed to; he mistrusted their tendency to abstract ideal truth from the body of fact which gave it life. To him, transcendentalists were "young visionaries" and "gray-headed theorists." The literature of American transcendentalism characteristically took aphoristic forms, because truths fished from the sky by intuition are too fragmentary and illusive to furnish materials for a substantial edifice of narrative: a transcendental novel is almost a contradiction in terms.

Persistent reading of his romances as novels despite his repeated insistence that they should not be so read has made it difficult to clear the ground for unprepossessed examination of the actual sense and form of his work. *The House of the Seven Gables* cannot be understood as a history of particular persons in a specific place at a definite time; it is, instead, a series of *tableaux vivants et parlants* showing phases and types of humanity embodied in different generations of two families which live in significantly revelatory relationship with each other within an ancient but changing tradition. In the explication which follows, the book is considered not as a narrative organized by strict concatenation of events, but as a kind of prose symphony organized in five stages or movements. Its devices will be taken as expedients to evade present and palpable circumstance and to reveal what lies beyond it. One of these devices is *eloignment*, an attempt to transport the reader into a province of the imagination midway between the historical and the ideal, where tests of realism are not too stringently applied. In the Preface to *The House of the Seven Gables*, he expressed a wish that "the book may be read strictly as a Romance, having a great deal more to do with the clouds overhead than with any portion of the actual soil of the County of Essex." (CE 2:3)

A second major device of Hawthorne's is his use of a kind of magic of agencies which have the power of opening a sensitive person's vision and imagination in rare moments, so that, in Wordsworthian phrase, he "sees into the life of things." Such talismanic power is in certain objects—the well in the garden, the Malbone miniature, and the portrait of the first Pyncheon. But Hawthorne's chief device of magic is an effect of certain conditions of light, especially of moonlight. This is the very device which Coleridge had proposed to himself as plausible for presenting the visions of a romantic imagination: to make use of "the sudden charm, which accidents of light and shade, which moonlight or sun-set diffused over a known and familiar landscape."[10] Hawthorne had used the "moonlight of romance" (CE 10:337) as an agency of imaginative vision throughout his earlier work in such tales as "Young Goodman Brown" and "My Kinsman, Major Molineux," and in *The Scarlet Letter*. He spoke in "Major Molineux" of "the moon, creating, like the imaginative power, a beautiful strangeness in familiar objects, [giving] something of romance to a scene that might not have possessed it in the light of day." (CE 11:221) This transforming power of moonlight, which opens to the imagination the ideal truth that lies behind everyday reality, is his principal device in the climactic scene of *The House of the Seven Gables*.

A third major device of Hawthorne's is his use of parallel repetitions which suggest that supposedly distinct realities are in fact recurrent assertions of an identical ideal life which continually manifests itself in changing forms. The Pyncheon portraits remind us that this is true of members of the Pyncheon family. The Pyncheon poultry echo this motif. The Pyncheon garden is identified with the garden of Eden. Various generations of Maules and Pyncheons re-enact the same roles. As Hawthorne puts it, "the future is but the reverberation of the past."

The fourth of Hawthorne's major devices is by far the most important: his establishment and continuous development of the symbolic aspects of all the objects in the romance—the central symbol of the Pyncheon house; the symbolism of environing things, garden, well, weeds, and flowers; the symbolism of articles, portraits, poultry, clothing, music, and photography.

The first "movement" in *The House of the Seven Gables*, especially the indispensable first chapter (which Austin Warren says should be discarded), establishes the key symbolism of the House—announces the dominant theme of the book. Although the House is necessarily first looked at at a particular time and under a particular aspect (specifically, in an ancient phase of its physical existence), it is, as any house philosophically considered must be, a projection of human ideas, an expression of tradition. As a physical fabric, Hawthorne points out that it is merely one of "the solid unrealities" that "we call real estate." (CE 2:263) But the physical edifice "seemed to constitute the least and meanest part of its reality." (CE 2:27) It exists more significantly to the moral consciousness as a projection of human character: the character of the persons who in building it expressed their own human natures, and of successive generations who have lived in it and have had their human development largely determined by it. "So much of mankind's varied experience had passed there . . . that the very timbers were oozy, as with the moisture of a heart. It was itself like a great human heart, with a life of its own, and full of rich and sombre reminiscences." (CE 2:27)

Hawthorne alters his simile to express a more extrinsic aspect of the symbol:

> The aspect of the venerable mansion has always affected me like a human countenance, bearing the traces not merely of outward storm and sunshine, but expressive, also, of the long lapse of mortal life, and accompanying vicissitudes that have passed within. Were these to be worthily recounted, they would form a narrative of no small interest and instruction, and possessing, moreover, a certain remarkable unity. (CE 2:5)

The last sentence in this quotation suggests that Hawthorne saw in the events of his narrative a unity which his critics have overlooked. The House's long continuance in the world symbolizes the remarkable unity of events during "the long lapse of mortal life," not, of course, the life of an individual, but a larger pattern of human life which includes individual lives. These events, "if adequately translated to the reader, would serve to illustrate how much of old material goes to make up the freshest novelty of human life." (CE 2:6) The House, visible and enduring, images the sameness of life during many generations. Man forms tradition, and tradition forms man. Although human institutions "grow out of the heart of mankind," (CE 10:26) as Hawthorne wrote in "The Old Manse," they are a matrix as well as a mirror of human character; in creating traditions, man fixes his own character by making a mold for himself to grow in.

Forming traditions is essentially a process of accommodating man's ideas to natural phenomena. Nature, including human nature, is somewhat plastic. Man has imposed his ideas on his own yielding nature and has given them a corresponding external form in his created objects and institutions. Mankind might show little continuity of character over a span of generations if it had not thus embodied its ideas in things external to itself and if it did not dwell so intimately within this external embodiment that its development is thereby determined. The natural objects long associated with the House symbolize the friendliness of Nature to tradition:

> In front grew the Pyncheon elm, which, in reference to such trees as one usually meets with, might well be termed gigantic. It had been planted by a great-grandson of the first Pyncheon, and although now fourscore years of age, or perhaps nearer a hundred, was still in its strong and broad maturity, throwing its shadow from side to side of the street, overtopping the seven gables, and sweeping the whole black roof with its pendent foliage. It gave a beauty to the old edifice, and seemed to make it a part of nature. (CE 2:27)

This passage suggests three things: Nature is friendly to tradition, which becomes a kind of natural fact itself through long continuance; tradition is nevertheless artificial and subordinate—Nature overtops it; Nature appears to have perennial youth, while the traditions which it harbors visibly fall into decay and need renovation.

There were also uglier growths on the Pyncheon property. In close proximity to the House flourished "an immense fertility of burdocks." (CE 2:27) "Such rank weeds (symbolic of the transmitted vices of society) . . . are always prone to root themselves about human dwellings." (CE 2:86) Other vegetation symbolized the beauty of human character transmitted through many generations:

> A crop, not of weeds, but flower-shrubs, . . . were growing aloft in the air, not a great way from the chimney, in the nook between two of the gables. They were called Alice's Posies. The tradition was, that a certain Alice Pyncheon had flung up the seeds, in sport, and that the dust of the street and the decay of the roof gradually formed a kind of soil for them, out of which they grew, when Alice had long been in her grave. (CE 2:28)

Thus, just as vegetable nature produces both weeds and flowers, human nature puts forth its flowers of good and evil in the humus of tradition. In this passage we see the elaborateness and thoroughness of Hawthorne's symbolism. The flowers grow in the air; the burdocks on the ground. The soil in which the flowers grow is formed partly of the dust from the street, partly of the decay from the roof—that is, partly from nature and partly from man.

The second movement of *The House of the Seven Gables* concerns the building of the House (establishment of tradition) and the defining of human relationships involved in its building. A tradition is fashioned by all the human beings whose existence it takes into account and belongs to all of them, even though it affords positions of privilege to some and deprives others. The House, then, although as a piece of "real estate" it is the legal property of the Pyncheons, belongs in a larger sense to both Pyncheons and Maules: as a tradition, it is oriented toward both the aristocratic and plebeian elements of humanity and indicates their relative status as members of one body.

Even as property, the moral right of the Pyncheons to exclusive possession of the House is more cloudy than their legal right. Morally, the story tells of a heinous violation of the Mosaic law forbidding murder and of the Christian law enjoining love. It is a modern version of the story of Naboth's vineyard, the contrived murder of a worthy poor man by his rich and great neighbor who coveted his small property. More specifically, the story illustrates certain utilitarian assumptions (variously expressed by Locke, Rousseau, Franklin, and Mill) about the just tenure of property. The small plot of ground which Pyncheon obtained through the contrived murder of Maule was the latter's by triple right:[11] (1) first occupancy: the land had belonged to no one before Maule occupied it, it was "primeval forest"; (CE 2:7) (2) improvement by labor of the occupant: "With his own toil, he had hewn out" (CE 2:7) his holding "to be his garden ground and homestead"; (CE 2:7) (3) use: Maule had appropriated only what satisfied his legitimate need—"an acre or two of earth," (CE 2:7) "small metes and bounds." (CE 2:7) Pyncheon's claim to this property was as specious as his means of getting it was iniquitous. He not only dispossessed the first occupant and deprived him of the fruit of his labor but seized in addition "a large adjacent tract of land" (CE 2:7) and vigorously pressed a claim "to a vast and as yet unexplored and unmeasured tract of eastern lands." (CE 2:18) Such inordinate appropriation of what Rousseau would have called "undivided property" belonging to all men in common was an ominous introduction into a new world of an inequitable way of life conveyed from a foreign tradition already moribund.

The traits of the Pyncheon family in this generation are all combined in the character of the Pyncheon founder, who was guilty of pride, covetousness, and luxury in their grossest forms. Colonel Pyncheon should not, however, be regarded as an incarnation of evil. Though not amiable, he was a strong and respectable character in terms of the tradition then valid. In private life he was capable of tenderness, as is indicated by mention of his feeling toward his young grandson; in public life, he was a respected embodiment of strict authority. The House of the Seven Gables, a House of tradition unfairly appropriated by Pyncheons to the deprivation of Maules, does not, as M. L. Étienne in a contemporary review fantastically suggested, represent the Seven Deadly Sins;[12] it represents the whole nature of man at a given time. In Hawthorne's view the forms of society were not good or evil according to the degree of their conformity to some contemplated ideal social pattern such as democracy, "the true moral order" for Hawthorne, as one critic opines; social forms and traditions were good and evil because of the good and evil of the human nature expressed in them. Hawthorne, haunted by a sentence from Bunyan's *Mr. Badman* ("From within, out of the heart of man proceedeth sin"), held that the heart of man is "the little yet boundless sphere wherein existed the original wrong of which the crime and misery of this outward world were merely types." (CE 10:403–4) Although the tradition embodied in the House expressed at the period of its first planting in the New World more of the evil of the human heart than of its good, it was a strong, full, and sufficient projection of the whole social nature of man at that time.

The third movement of *The House of the Seven Gables* represents the House in apparent prosperity still, but actually in incipient decay. The exclusiveness of the Pyncheons is having a fatal effect. The tradition which they have appropriated too much to their own uses and accommodated too much to their special character is disintegrating. It no longer has the vitality of humanity, but merely projects the isolated Pyncheon character. The Pyncheons, like the House in which they dwell, are undergoing a disintegration of character; specifically, the Pyncheon traits are becoming dissociated and intensified in individual members of the family. Gervayse Pyncheon possesses two traits of the old Colonel, his covetousness and his luxury. These traits have an appearance of refinement which is really a proof of their loss of vitality. The covetousness of the Colonel, a mere grasping for property, still persisted, but Gervayse looked upon property as the means of purchasing aristocratic position. The gross carnality of the Colonel was refined sybaritism in Gervayse. Such developments would be expected in a family that had inherited wealth and privilege through many generations. Alice Pyncheon embodies the arrogant pride of the Pyncheon founder, although in a more elegant form. Alice is an amiable but pathetic character because she combines with this pride a natural tenderness and sympathy which we are to understand that she has by right of feminine, not her Pyncheon, nature. Although her arrogance and her sympathy are not harmonious traits, her behavior is consistent, for her Pyncheon pride is stronger than her womanly sympathy.

All these significances are symbolically expressed in a little scene in which the current representative of the Maules, the carpenter Matthew, approaches the House and enters it on what he supposes is to be an errand of repair, and proffers during his stay a symbolic offer of reunion, which is rejected by the Pyn-

cheons. He ponders: "Does the House need any repair? Well it
may, by this time; and no blame to my father who built it." (CE
2:187) But no sign of dilapidation was evident, "though its style
might be getting a little out of fashion"; (CE 2:190) it looked,
"in the October sun, as if it had been new only a week ago."
(CE 2:190) Its sound exterior was matched by activity within:
"The house had that pleasant aspect of life which is like the
cheery expression of comfortable activity in the human countenance." (CE 2:191) Servants and slaves were energetically and
cheerfully plying their tasks, and the more favored inmates of
the mansion were diverting themselves pleasantly:

> At an open window of a room in the second story, hanging over
> some pots of beautiful and delicate flowers, exotics, . . . was the
> figure of a young lady, an exotic, like the flowers, and beautiful
> and delicate as they. Her presence imparted an indescribable
> grace and faint witchery to the whole edifice. (CE 2:191)

When she was not tending her flowers, beautiful and exotic Alice
stirred the listeners in the House with "the sad and sweet music
of her harpsichord, and the airier melancholy of her accompanying voice." (CE 2:200) Her father, Gervayse, was occupied with
equally elegant affairs. Magnificently dressed, he sat "sipping
coffee, which had grown to be a favorite beverage with him in
France." (CE 2:193) The pretentious splendor of the apartment
could not disguise that it expressed the taste of the old Colonel:
"Through all this variety of decoration, however, the room
showed its original characteristics." (CE 2:193) In this House
built by his father, Maule is rudely reminded by Gervayse that
his democratic assumption of equality is intolerable, but Maule's
encounter with Alice is more significant. Although "set apart
from the world's vulgar mass by a certain gentle and cold state-
liness," (CE 2:201) there was "the womanly mixture" in her
"tender capabilities." (CE 2:201) All the carpenter "required
was simply the acknowledgment that he was indeed a man, and
a fellow-being, moulded of the same elements as she." (CE
2:201) When this acknowledgment was withheld, he asserted
through his mesmeric power over Alice the fact that Maule and
Pyncheon were indeed formed of the same human clay.

The tradition at this stage still has beauty in it, though not
much strength. It is still no more an embodiment of evil than
when it expressed primarily the character of Colonel Pyncheon.

It has lost vitality, but has gained grace, the characteristic of an old but not yet thoroughly disintegrated tradition. Hawthorne was later to offer a similar judgment of the somewhat attractive decline of English tradition, in *English Notebooks*: there must have been "something very good" in such forms, "good for all classes—while the world was in a state out of which these forms naturally grew." (EN, 172) The bad was not inherent in the tradition, but in the fact that the tradition was getting out of adjustment with the current needs of humanity.

The fourth movement of *The House of the Seven Gables* represents tradition in a dangerously advanced stage of dilapidation. Servants and masters, industry and gaiety, have all died out of it. This phase of the House, when it must either be repaired or collapse, Hawthorne chose to designate as the present time, thus giving to his narrative something like the focus and proportion which an epic achieves by beginning *in medias res*. The latent decay in both House and Pyncheon family, threatening entire disintegration, has become open and perilous. In effect, the Maules have been thrust entirely into obscurity and out of the tradition. The House is ready to fall to pieces and shelters in its rickety vastness only two human wrecks. The Pyncheon character has undergone a further disintegration. The rapacity of Gervayse has passed to Judge Pyncheon and is intensified into mania; his sybaritism has passed to Clifford, enfeebled to imbecility. The aristocratic pride of Alice has descended to Hepzibah, impoverished to absurdity; her womanly feeling has found new expression in Phoebe and is in fact Phoebe's whole and sufficient principle of life. Pride and luxury are forms of inertia; the embodiments of these still inhabit the disintegrating House. Greed and love are energetic; the embodiments of these have both left the House to find the life which the House has lost. Judge Pyncheon retains his Pyncheon name and identity and still asserts his claim of ownership to the House, because he thinks it still holds deeds which will enable him to aggrandize himself further; he intends still to exploit it selfishly. Phoebe has lost both her Pyncheon name and family character; she significantly reminds Hepzibah: "I have not been brought up a Pyncheon." (CE 2:74)

The fifth movement of *The House of the Seven Gables* is the climactic continuation of the fourth. It sees the assembling within the House once more of all the elements of life associated

in its founding, which have been through generations undergoing a fatal dissociation. Maule has returned, having lost his
Maule identity under the name of Holgrave, and is admitted to
the House as a lodger by Hepzibah, who feels humanly drawn
to him and fairly abandons her pretensions of superiority in his
company. Phoebe has returned, and her love vitalizes the old
House. The climax of the romance is the courtship of Phoebe
by Holgrave, a symbolic repetition of Matthew Maule's overtures to Alice Pyncheon. The renovation of tradition is symbolized in a wonderfully delicate scene in the Pyncheon garden.
Comment on this scene calls for notice of some of the passages
which bring out the symbolic role of Phoebe as a reconciler and
renovator. The contrast between Phoebe and Hepzibah is
explicit.

> As to Phoebe's not being a lady, or whether she were a lady or
> no, it was a point, perhaps, difficult to decide, but which could
> hardly come up for judgment at all in any fair and healthy
> mind. . . . She shocked no canon of taste; she was admirably in
> keeping with herself, and never jarred against surrounding cir-
> cumstances. . . . Instead of discussing her claim to rank among
> ladies, it would be preferable to regard Phoebe as the example of
> feminine grace and availability combined, in a state of society, if
> there were any such, where ladies did not exist. There it should
> be woman's office to move in the midst of practical affairs, and
> to gild them all . . . with an atmosphere of loveliness and joy.
> (CE 2:80)

This concept of perfect womanhood is specifically contrasted
with the aristocratic concept of the lady:

> To find the born and educated lady, on the other hand, we need
> look no farther than Hepzibah, . . . in her rustling and rusty
> silks, with her deeply cherished and ridiculous consciousness of
> long descent. . . . It was a fair parallel between new Plebeianism
> and old Gentility. (CE 2:80–81)

But this contrast does not constitute censure of aristocracy and
absolute acceptance of democracy as "the true moral order." It
is the contrast of new plebeianism with old gentility; the gentility of Hepzibah is a grotesque shadow of that of Alice Pyncheon.
Hawthorne favored the vital over the moribund tradition.

Instead of Pyncheon hauteur, Phoebe diffused love. "Holding her hand, . . . you might be certain that your place was good

in the whole sympathetic chain of human nature." (CE 2:141) When she became the pulse of the machine in the House, it was transformed by her presence, although "no longer ago than the night before, it had resembled nothing so much as the old maid's heart." (CE 2:72) "The grime and sordidness of the House of the Seven Gables seemed to have vanished since her appearance there . . . [through] the purifying influence scattered through the atmosphere of the household by the presence of one youthful, fresh, and thoroughly wholesome heart." (CE 2:136) Nature in the vicinity of the House was reanimated by her presence. On the morning after her arrival, she discovered a rosebush in the garden, planted long before by Alice, which, though long afflicted with blight and mildew, was now so profusely covered with white blossoms that it "looked as if it had been brought from Eden that very summer," (CE 2:71) although the bush was growing in a soil "now unctuous with nearly two hundred years of vegetable decay." (CE 2:71) The fragrance of character of both Alice and Phoebe is compared to rose-scent, and Phoebe symbolically assumes the care of these roses, which stand for the continuing sense of beauty in her family. Music is also used to link the characters of Phoebe and Alice and to establish a repeated motif. Although Phoebe could not produce strains of beauty on Alice's harpsichord, that antique, exotic and genteel instrument, "she possessed the gift of song," (CE 2:138) which Hawthorne emphasizes was a gift of nature, not an effect of art and cultivation.

In effect, Phoebe was the perfection of modern womanhood, as Alice had been of ladyhood. Alice, Hepzibah, and Phoebe were distinct notes of a human melody which threaded with sweetness the darker strain of the Pyncheon fortunes. Through the feminine characters in *The House of the Seven Gables* Hawthorne shows that the qualities of a human type are not apparent in the span of a single life, but must be studied in a succession of human existences.

Phoebe as woman, then, not as Pyncheon, and Holgrave as man, not as Maule, are reconciled in the moonlight in the garden. In the course of the summer, they have been working "in this black old earth" (CE 2:91) together. On this fateful eve their working together in the garden, so reminiscent of Milton's picture of Adam and Eve's joint labors before the Fall, is in the nature of a farewell meeting. In the course of their talk, Holgrave declaims against the House, as expressive of "the odious and abominable Past, (CE 2:184) and says that it ought to be purified by fire. Later, as they are seated beneath an arbor, he reads to her his story of the disdain of Alice for Matthew and of Matthew's cruel revenge. As he reads, the family history repeats itself; his reading mesmerizes Phoebe, as his ancestor Maule had mesmerized Alice. But just as Phoebe had failed to show Pyncheon disdain for Holgrave, so does Holgrave refrain from showing Maule vindictiveness toward Phoebe. At this moment the world is magically transformed for Holgrave by the love within and the magic moonlight around him. He looks with new vision at the old House. As the moon shines out "broad and oval, in its middle pathway," (CE 2:213) its illumination of the old House is a revelation to his awakened sensibility:

> Those silvery beams were already powerful enough to change the character of the lingering daylight. They softened and embellished the aspect of the old house. . . . The commonplace characteristics—which, at noon tide, it seemed to have taken a century of sordid life to accumulate—were now transformed by a charm of romance. . . . The artist chanced to be one on whom the reviving influence fell . . . (CE 2:213)

Holgrave had inherited the Maule gift of insight into character and impulse to use it. His ancestor Matthew Maule claimed the power of attaining knowledge "through the clear, crystal medium of a pure and virgin intelligence," (CE 2:200) and he "was fabled to have a strange power of getting into people's dreams, and regulating matters there according to his own fancy, pretty much like the stage-manager of a theatre." (CE 2:189) These twin gifts of insight and curiosity were, according to Hawthorne, essential gifts of artists, but were liable to abuse if they were used to dominate others, as Matthew Maule had dominated Alice. Holgrave was tempted to use such a power over Phoebe: "To a disposition like Holgrave's, at once speculative and active, there is no temptation so great as the opportunity of acquiring empire over the human spirit; nor any idea more seductive to a young man than to become the arbiter of a young girl's destiny." (CE 2:212)

Holgrave resisted this temptation, and thus became a true artist; for he had entered Hawthorne's Hall of Fantasy and realized "that the dominions which the spirit conquers for itself among unrealities, become a thousand times more real than the earth . . ." (CE 10:58) The daguerreotypist, who had introduced himself to Phoebe as one who made "pictures out of sunshine," declaring "there is wonderful insight in Heaven's broad and simple sunshine," (CE 2:91) has had a revelation of spiritual truth more real to him than daylight reality:

> "It seems to me," he observed, "that I never watched the coming of so beautiful an eve. . . . After all, what a good world we live in! How good and beautiful! How young it is, too, with nothing really rotten or age-worn in it! This old house, for example, which sometimes has positively oppressed my breath with its smell of decaying timber! And this garden, where the black mould always clings to my spade, as if I were a sexton delving in a graveyard! Could I keep the feeling that now possesses me, the garden would every day be virgin soil, with the earth's first freshness in the flavor of its beans and squashes; and the house!—it would be like a bower in Eden, blossoming with the earliest roses that God ever made. Moonlight, and the sentiment in man's heart responsive to it, are the greatest of renovators and reformers." (CE 2:213–14)

This sentiment, so much an echo of Hawthorne's own feeling that the Old Manse had been for him an Eden, expresses the reality of tradition for Holgrave after he acquired "the deep intelligence of love." (CE 10:460) When, later on, he proposes marriage to Phoebe, the transforming power of love is again emphasized: "The bliss which makes all things true, beautiful, and holy shone around this youth and maiden. They were conscious of nothing sad nor old. They transfigured the earth, and made it Eden again." (CE 2:307)

With this Hawthorne's poem essentially ends, but in concluding chapters he ties up loose ends of the realistic level of his narrative in his usual arbitrary and inept fashion. Judge Pyncheon is disposed of by a providential stroke of apoplexy, and the Pyncheon evil is extinguished in him, for it had all been concentrated finally in his character. The survivors are left in comfortable enjoyment of his ill-gotten wealth.

The House of the Seven Gables is not a study of "the effect of pride, poverty, and suffering upon two old aristocrats"; that study is an incident in a much larger design. Neither is it a symbolic study of some particular sin, such as offense against "the true moral order" of democracy. Nor is it chiefly meaningful as a realistic "impression" of New England life. It is, and was intended to be, all of these things, but it is much more. It is an allegory of love versus self-love, of human tradition versus personal ambition and family pride, of imagination versus preoccupation with present fact. In each of these contrasts the faculty named in the first term of the pair is shown to embrace a larger and more valuable reality than the second. Above all, Hawthorne expressed in *The House of the Seven Gables* a conviction that the character of any distinct stream of human existence cannot be adequately scrutinized in individual lives—which, to him, were not distinct, separate, self-controlled manifestations of human reality: human character must be examined in larger configurations in which a succession of lives exhibits the prolonged development of human tendencies. Most men have a mistaken sense that each personal life can be appraised as an entity, but Hawthorne says, not so: though the individual tries to make life firmly his own, it is not a part of him; he is a part of it.

NOTES

1. See Lawrence Sargent Hall, *Hawthorne: Critic of Society* (New Haven: Yale Univ. Press, 1944), 160–67.

2. *Hawthorne* (New York: Harper & Brothers, 1879), 120.

3. *Nathaniel Hawthorne* (Boston: Houghton Mifflin, 1902), 209. See also Paul Elmer More, "The Solitude of Nathaniel Hawthorne," *Shelburne Essays, First Series* (New York and London: Putnam, 1904), 37; Newton Arvin, *Hawthorne* (Boston: Little, Brown, 1929), 192.

4. "Nathaniel Hawthorne," *Rage for Order: Essays in Criticism* (Chicago, 1948).

5. Horatio Bridge, *Personal Recollections of Nathaniel Hawthorne* (New York: Harper, 1893), 125–26.

6. *Biographia Literaria*, Shawcross, ed., 1:xii.

7. Quoted in "The Art of Fiction," *The Theory of the American Novel*, ed. George Perkins (New York: Holt, Rinehart and Winston, 1970), 178.

8. *Biographia Literaria*, Shawcross, ed., 2:9.

9. *Hawthorne*, 120.

10. *Biographia Literaria*, Shawcross, ed., 1:14.

11. These theories of property, first definitely set forth in Locke's *Two Treatises of Government*, are substantially those advanced in John Stuart Mill's *Principles of Political Economy*, first published three years before *The House of the Seven Gables*. It is probable, however, that if Hawthorne had been influenced by his reading to adopt them, he found them in Rousseau's *Social Contract*. The records of the Salem Athenaeum list twenty borrowings of Rousseau by Hawthorne. Franklin, frequently read and greatly venerated by Hawthorne, expressed the same views.

In England, shocked by the extreme disparity between the luxurious life of the rich and the miseries of the poor, as Melville had been in *Redburn* and *Israel Potter,* he wrote,

> There may come a time, even in this world, when we shall all understand that our tendency to the individual appropriation of gold and broad acres, fine houses, and such good and beautiful things as are equally enjoyable by a multitude, is but a trait of imperfectly developed intelligence. . . . (CE 5:306)

After viewing a wholesale pauper marriage in which a crowd of "the mere rags and tatters of the human race" were married in a joint ceremony, and "had execution done upon them in the lump," and later attending a splendid society wedding, he wrote,

> Is, or is not, the system wrong that gives one married pair so immense a superfluity of luxurious home, and shuts out a million others from any home whatever? One day or another, safe as they deem themselves, and safe as the hereditary temper of the people really tends to make them, the gentlemen of England will be compelled to face this question. (CE 5:307, 309)

12. "Nathaniel Hawthorne," *Revue Contemporaine* 31 (May 1857): 657.

TWENTY

The Blithedale Romance: "A Counterfeit Arcadia"

In the preface to *The Blithedale Romance* Hawthorne wrote that he had "occasionally availed himself of his actual reminiscences" of Brook Farm, where he had lived for a little more than half a year (from April to November 1841) a decade before writing the romance, "in the hope of giving a more lifelike tint" to his "fancy-sketch." But he stressed his "fictitious handling" of the subject and declared that the personages introduced were imaginary. He wrote also that he did not "put forward the slightest pretensions to illustrate a theory, or elicit a conclusion, favorable or otherwise, in respect to Socialism."

> In short, his present concern with the Socialist Community is merely to establish a theatre, a little removed from the highway of ordinary travel, where the creatures of his brain may play their phantasmagorical antics, without exposing them to too close a comparison with the actual events of real lives. (CE 3:1)

Critics have generally agreed that, as Henry James wrote, he treated Brook Farm "mainly as a perch for starting upon an imaginative flight."[1] Nevertheless, sketchy resemblances to ac-

tual persons have been suggested for most of his principal characters except Westervelt, who is the least realistic figure in the
romance. And Hawthorne's disclaimer that he intended any conclusion about socialism is unconvincing in view of remarks in his
letters from Brook Farm to his wife-to-be Sophia Peabody.

In fact, *The Blithedale Romance* is a hybrid production, half
romance and half social commentary, which is perhaps why
Henry James pronounced it an inconclusive "mixture of elements." "A number of objects and incidents touched with the
light of the profane world—the vulgar, many-coloured world of
actuality, as distinguished from the crepuscular realm of the
writer's own reveries—are mingled with its course."[2] The following interpretation discusses the elements in this mixture.
The method of the chapter will be, after establishing the artist
presence through which characters and events are observed and
related, to set forth first the contemporary concerns and character types that engaged Hawthorne's attention and provided subjects for his fiction, and following each such exposition, to
discuss his fictional treatment of these subjects as rendered
through the imagination of the poet-narrator, who is a surrogate
for the author.

I

COVERDALE: THE POET

The Blithedale Romance is the only one of Hawthorne's four
major romances written in the first person. Probably this is because so much of his material came from his experience and he
could not treat it objectively. The technical consequence of the
first-person mode is that it confers a doubtful authority on the
narrator—doubtful because events and characters are viewed
through "the colored, magnifying, and distorting medium of
[his] imagination." (CE 1:155) Furthermore, the narrator is recalling events that occurred many years earlier. He had been a
young man when he witnessed and took part in them, but is
now an "old bachelor" with an "unsatisfied retrospect" on his
past life. (CE 3:247) Consequently, his recollections have the
"dreamy consistency" that Hawthorne frequently said past
events had for him.

When Coverdale joined the Blithedale Community, it was not from an enthusiasm for social reform so much as the attraction of something that might be treated poetically. He said,

> "I hope. . . , now, to produce something that shall really deserve to be called poetry—true, strong, natural, and sweet, as is the life which we are going to lead—something that shall have the notes of wild-birds twittering through it, or a strain like the wind—anthems in the woods, as the case may be!" (CE 3:14)

His conception of his relation to his fellow communists at this juncture was that described in the early sketch "Sights from a Steeple":

> The most desirable mode of existence might be that of a spiritualized Paul Pry, hovering invisible round man and woman, witnessing their deeds, searching into their hearts, borrowing brightness from their felicity and shade from their sorrow, and retaining no emotion peculiar to himself. (CE 9:192)

Coverdale said he was "making my prey of people's individualities, as my custom was." (CE 3:84) He indulged his curiosity by peering into other persons' doings, himself unobserved, from such stations as his leafy treetop "hermitage" and the boarding-house window in town from which he could see into Zenobia's hotel room opposite; and by attending as unobtrusively as possible to dramatic scenes between other persons.

He excused such prying on the ground that he was sympathetic with persons scrutinized, and also by supposing that it was his duty as a poet to transform their doings by giving them the permanence of art:

> My own part in these transactions was singularly subordinate. It resembled that of the Chorus in a classic play, which seems to be set apart from personal concernment, and bestows the whole measure of its hope or fear, its exultation or sorrow, on the fortunes of others, between whom and itself this sympathy is its only bond. Destiny, it may be,—the most skilful of stage-managers,—seldom chooses to arrange its scenes, and carry forward its drama, without securing the presence of at least one calm observer. It is his office to give applause when due, and sometimes an inevitable tear, to detect the final fitness of incident to character, and distil, in his long-brooding thought the whole morality of the performance. (CE 3:97)

He said that his purpose was "to make pretty verses, and play a part, with Zenobia and the rest of the amateurs in our pastoral." (CE 3:43) He told Hollingsworth, "When we come to be old men, . . . we will look back to these early days, and make a romantic story for the young people. . . . In due course of ages, we must all figure heroically in an epic poem." (CE 3:129) Hollingsworth called this nonsense, and not unreasonably said, "Miles Coverdale is not in earnest, either as a poet or a laborer." (CE 3:68)

Zenobia was the principal subject of his almost voyeuristic observation and speculation. She was aware of his persistent scrutiny, and said, "What are you seeking to discover in me?" "She bent her head towards me, and let me look into her eyes, as if challenging me to drop a plummet-line down into the depths of her consciousness." (CE 3:47–48)

Coverdale not only watched her unceasingly but he quizzed her with impertinent and provocative questions about her relationships with Hollingsworth and Priscilla. She resented his inquisitiveness and rebuked him:

> "You know not what you do! It is dangerous, sir, believe me, to tamper thus with earnest human passions, out of your own mere idleness and for your sport. I will endure it no longer! Take care that it does not happen again! I warn you!" (CE 3:170)

Coverdale responded that he did so from an "uncertain sense of duty," and she brushed this aside as a "stale excuse."

> "I have often heard it before, from those who sought to interfere with me, and I know precisely what it signifies. Bigotry; self-conceit; and insolent curiosity; a meddlesome temper; a cold-blooded criticism, founded on a shallow interpretation of half-perceptions; a monstrous scepticism in regard to any conscience or any wisdom, except one's own; a most irreverent propensity to thrust Providence aside, and substitute one's self in its awful place—out of these, and other motives as miserable as these, comes your idea of duty!" (CE 3:170)

Despite this blistering indictment Coverdale continued his probing until Zenobia again made an exasperated protest: "This long while past, you have been following up your game, groping for human emotions in the dark corners of the heart." (CE 3:214) And at last, just before her suicide in desperation at her rejection by Hollingsworth, she resignedly told Coverdale, "You are turning this whole affair into a ballad. . . . By all means write this ballad, and turn your sympathy to good account, as other poets do, and poets must, unless they choose to give us glittering icicles instead of lines of fire." (CE 3:223, 224)

He tried to pry into the secrets of other characters as well, although not so persistently. Thus he said of Priscilla, "I could not resist the impulse to take just one peep beneath her folded petals," (CE 3:125) and he teased her with provocative remarks about Hollingsworth's apparent preference for Zenobia. It was not in her character to administer a stinging verbal rebuke like Zenobia's, but she told him imperiously to leave her, and "made a little gesture of dismissal." (CE 3:126)

Coverdale also pried out the secret history of Old Moodie, the father of the two sisters, and "tried to take his view of the world, as if looking through a smoke-blackened glass at the sun. It robbed the landscape of all its life." (CE 3:84)

The danger of such inquisitiveness to the artist, in making him cold-hearted, was something that Hawthorne often suspected in himself. He had defined it in his sketch of the artist in the tale "The Prophetic Pictures," published sixteen years before *The Blithedale Romance:*

> Like all other men around whom an engrossing purpose wreathes itself, he was insulated from the mass of human kind. He had no aim—no pleasure—no sympathies—but what were ultimately connected with his art. Though gentle in manner, and upright in intent and action, he did not possess kindly feelings; his heart was cold; no living creature could be brought near enough to keep him warm. (CE 9:178)

It was apparently Coverdale's appalled and guilt-stricken sense of responsibility for the tragic outcome of events into which he had pried and intruded that caused his later years to be "all an emptiness," as he confessed at the end of his narrative. (CE 3:246)

> It is not, I apprehend, a healthy kind of mental occupation, to devote ourselves too exclusively to the study of individual men and women.
> . . . My conscience has often whispered me, I did Hollingsworth a great wrong by prying into his character, and am

perhaps doing him as great a one, at this moment, by putting
faith in the discoveries which I seemed to make. (CE 3:69)

Hawthorne felt that his marriage had brought him near
enough to a living creature to keep him warm, and save him
from lapsing into the cold-heartedness that was a danger to the
artist. Significantly, when Coverdale recalls the Blithedale tragedy, he is still a bachelor, and intends to remain one. As Roy R.
Male remarks, "Coverdale is what Hawthorne feared he might
have become if he had not given himself in love and marriage."[3]

II

UTOPIANISM IN THE EARLY NINETEENTH CENTURY

The nineteenth century reformer was typically a person
who expected to make people happy by inducing them to conform their lives to some millennial scheme. He did not go so far
as Thoreau, who in his extreme individualism said that all human institutions are like "toadstools by the wayside"; but he
fondly contemplated substituting some heart's-desire scheme of
his own devising for the sorry scheme of things that had evolved
through long ages. This desire, so ardently cherished by nineteenth century rationalism, awaited a practical test of its theories
until the prosperity, comparative political quietude, fluid state
of society, and pragmatic zeal of the new century in America
made controlled social experiment feasible.

Although utopianism is an ever-present leaven in even the
most conventional of western societies, it is not at all times
uttered and acted on vigorously, two conditions being necessary
for its potent manifestation. The first is a negative condition—
the absence or breaking-up of too-rigid traditions and conventions; the second is positive—the impetus of some resurgent
idea that animates a new concept of the good society. From the
time of the earliest colonization of America it has been regarded
as an available territory for the realization of utopias; there was
a utopian aspect in the original settlement of the eastern sea-
board as well as in the later movement of westward expansion.
In the words of George Norlin, our ancestors

have been, for the most part, dissenters and nonconformists with
rebellion in their blood. They came overseas to these un-
preempted shores as refugees from the inhibitions and disabili-
ties of established orders in their home countries whose
oppressions they had not been able to shake off. Theirs was a
flight from restraint.[4]

And Frederick Jackson Turner remarked, in *The Frontier in American History*, that

> What the Mediterranean Sea was to the Greeks, breaking the
> bond of custom, offering new experiences, calling out new insti-
> tutions and activities, that, and more, the ever retreating frontier
> has been to the United States directly, and to the nations of
> Europe more remotely.[5]

But the merely negative impulse of a flight from restraint
can lead to anarchy, not to Utopia, unless a dynamic unifying
idea that can subdue and harmonize divergent wills is carried
along. As M. L. Étienne, a French contemporary and critic of
Hawthorne, observed, emigrants to America were not merely
refugees from facts; they were voyagers to ideas. "On peut in-
venter un état social dans la vieille Europe: il est si malaisé d'en
faire l'épreuve. En Amérique, l'épreuve est au bout de tous les
projets. . . . Imaginez une manière de vivre nouvelle: des
grands éspaces de terre sont là qui attendent des maîtres."[6] To
Europeans the concept of America as Utopia was a continuing
idea; to Americans it was a heritage.

Hawthorne's time was eminently a period in which utopia
was making vigorous assaults on tradition. Emerson, noting the
spirit of the time, remarked,

> It seems so easy for America to inspire and express the most
> expansive and humane spirit; new-born, free, healthful, strong,
> the land of the laborer, of the democrat, of the philanthropist, of
> the believer, of the saint, she should speak for the human
> race. . . . It is a country of beginnings, of projects, of designs, of
> expectations.[7]

The specific conditions for resurgent utopianism were
abundantly present. Calvinism, which, because of its pessimistic
and deterministic aspects had, despite a conscious intention to
found a new Jerusalem in America, been on the whole unfavorable to the humanistic attempt to construct an earthly paradise,

gave way to a colorless and neutral utilitarianism that signalized the decline of the old tradition but failed to supply an inspiriting idea in its place. Transcendentalism arose exuberant and optimistic from this disintegration of the old faith. At the same time, the political outlook was favorable to endeavors at social reconstruction; the election of Jackson to the presidency in 1828 apparently marked the ascendancy of democracy over the social and intellectual aristocracy that had flourished since colonial times. Philanthropic projectors like Robert Owen, who had early discovered signs that the "reign of ignorance rapidly approaches to dissolution, its terrors . . . already on the wing," were ready to announce that "the destruction of ignorance and misery is to be effected, and the reign of reason, intelligence, and happiness, is to be firmly established,"[8] and turned to America as the land of millennial promise.

The European concept of Utopia in that era was primarily engendered by revolt *against* something—economic and social inequities—and envisaged external changes in the social pattern. The native American concept was oftener aspiration *toward* something—a liberation of mind more than an amelioration of material circumstances (for this seemed assured on a continent rich in unexploited resources), and was animated by the hope of inspiring individuals to a larger life through establishing conditions favorable to their intellectual and moral self-improvement. O. B. Frothingham, the historian of the American Transcendentalist movement, wrote:

> New England furnished the only plot of ground on this planet, where the transcendental philosophy had a chance to show what it was and what it proposed. The forms of life there were, in a measure, plastic. There were no immovable prejudices, no fixed and unalterable traditions. . . . No orders of men, no aristocracies of intellect, no privileged classes of thought were established. . . . A feeling was abroad that all things must be new in the new world. There was call for immediate application of ideas to life.[9]

Although such faith in systematic reform was the beginning stage in the evolution of opinion of most humanitarians of the period, their confidence was soon shaken by the results of their schemes of reform. The failure of such projects as those of Robert Owen at New Harmony, Indiana, Frances Wright at Nashoba, Tennessee, and Brook Farm convinced the most reasonable of these over-sanguine projectors that man's condition could not be improved merely by tinkering with the social framework in which he lived. It was early apparent that Brook Farm, established late in 1840, was a failure. Margaret Fuller confessed her disillusionment with such utopian projects: "The author, beginning like the many in assault upon bad institutions, and external ills, . . . sees at last that the only efficient remedy must come from individual character."[10] Emerson likewise declared that mere reform of institutions accomplished nothing: "The criticism and attack on institutions, which we have witnessed, has made one thing plain, that society gains nothing whilst a man, not himself renovated, attempts to renovate things around him."[11] Emerson was too much an individualist to expect much from a collective experiment which should do nothing more than reorganize the material circumstances and outward relations of life: "These benefactors hope to raise man by improving his circumstances," he said in his "Lecture on the Times"; "by combination of that which is dead they hope to make something alive. In vain."[12] Therefore he was from the beginning a skeptical, though benevolent, observer of the Brook Farm enterprise; "[he] never refers to Brook Farm," wrote Lindsay Swift, the historian of Brook Farm, "without conveying to the finest sense the assurance that someone is laughing behind the shrubbery."[13]

There were two antagonistic principles inherent in American utopianism that made the failure of communistic enterprises inevitable. One was the romantic individualism of the time; the other was the collectivist mystique that required individuality to be submerged in an ant-like social organism. Emerson said that the members of a socialist community must be "fractions of men, because each finds that he cannot enter it without some compromise."[14] Charles Lane, an English crank who financed and joined in Bronson Alcott's pathetic Fruitlands "Con-Sociate Family," which expected to be a "New Eden," said of Brook Farm, "It is not a community; it is not truly an association; it lacks oneness of spirit."[15] Emerson found fault with Brook Farm because members lost their individuality in it; Lane, because they did not. In the final, declining phase of Brook Farm, after

Hawthorne had left, George Ripley and the other leading spirits of the enterprise tried to revive it by seizing the collectivist horn of the dilemma and converting it to Fourierism, an attempt that was bound to fail. Emerson's final estimate of the reform movement of his times reiterates his conclusion that such schemes try to impose an intolerably arbitrary pattern upon desirable human diversity:

> We could not exempt [Fourierism] from the criticism we apply to so many of the projects with which the brain of the age teems. Our feeling was that Fourier had skipped no fact but one, namely Life. He treats man as a plastic thing . . . skips the faculty of life, which spawns and scorns systems and system-makers; which eludes all conditions; which makes or supplants a thousand phalanxes and New Harmonies with each pulsation.[16]

III

HAWTHORNE ON SOCIAL REFORM: BLITHEDALE AND BROOK FARM

The common motive of the Blithedale colonists was a flight from restraint. "We had individually found one thing or another to quarrel with in our past life, and were pretty well agreed as to the inexpedience of lumbering along with the old system any farther." (CE 3:63) This was the "Come-Outer" principle that has impelled dissent ever since the first settlement of the continent, and is still active in these latter years of the twentieth century. The Blithedale colonists felt that they had to put themselves outside of the established system to reform their lives. "We had stept down from the pulpit; we had flung aside the pen; we had shut up the ledger." (CE 3:19) "We had left the rusty iron framework of society behind us; we had broken through many hindrances that are powerful enough to keep most people on the treadmill of an established system." (CE 3:63)

The colonists hoped to reform society, not by action from within the system, but by removing themselves from it and furnishing an example to less innovative persons who felt its "irksomeness almost as intolerable as we did." (CE 3:19)

> It was our purpose . . . to give up whatever we had heretofore attained, for the sake of showing mankind the example of a life

governed by other than the false and cruel principles, on which human society has all along been based. (CE 3:19)

The better principles that they advocated were humanitarianism, a classless society, and economic cooperation and mutuality of goods instead of economic competition and selfish appropriation:

> We meant to lessen the laboring man's great burthen of toil, by performing our due share of it at the cost of our own thews and sinews. We sought our profit by mutual aid, instead of wresting it from an enemy, or filching it craftily from those less shrewd than ourselves, . . . or winning it by selfish competition with a neighbor. (CE 3:19)

But Blithedale was flawed from its inception, by the individualism and eccentricity of its members, and by its anti-establishment posture. Constituted as it was of the dissenters and failures of society, it lacked cohesion.

> On the whole, . . . it was a society such as has seldom met together; nor, perhaps, could it reasonably be expected to hold together long. Persons of marked individuality—crooked sticks, as some of us might be called—are not exactly the easiest to bind up into a faggot. . . . We were of all creeds and opinions, and generally tolerant of all, on every imaginable subject. Our bond . . . was not affirmative, but negative. (CE 3:63)

Such a collection of misfits could not expect to be taken as an example by conformists within the system they had repudiated. "[A]s regarded society at large, we stood in a position of new hostility, rather than new brotherhood. . . . Constituting so pitiful a minority as now, we were inevitably estranged from the rest of mankind, in pretty fair proportion with the strictness of the bond among ourselves." (CE 3:20–21)

After some months in Blithedale, and after the disillusionment of his break with Hollingsworth, Coverdale "determined to remove [himself] to a little distance, and take an exterior view of what [they] had all been about." "Such fermentation of opinions as was going on in the general brain of the Community" was "a kind of Bedlam."

> I was beginning to lose my sense of what kind of a world it was, among innumerable schemes of what it might or ought to be. . . .
> No sagacious man will long retain his sagacity, if he live exclu-

sively among reformers and progressive people, without periodically returning into the settled system of things, to correct himself by a new observation from that old standpoint. (CE 3:140–41)

Coverdale's retrospective comment on the delusive optimism of the Blithedale drop-outs has the skeptical tone of Hawthorne's comments on the failure of Brook Farm. Coverdale concluded that

by projecting our minds outward, we had imparted a show of novelty to existence, and contemplated it as hopefully as if the soil beneath our feet had not been fathom-deep with the dust of deluded generations, on every one of which, as on ourselves, the world had imposed itself as a hitherto unwedded bride. (CE 3:128)

The various sketchily indicated objects of the Blithedale Community were all shown in the romance to be failures. The attempt to harmonize labor and thought was unsuccessful. There was no true equality of persons, and the colonists were supercilious toward outsiders. The endeavor to promote the happiness and material well-being of members by bringing them in intimate association in a unit larger than family ended in tragedy.

Hawthorne, who had spent seven months as an active member of the Brook Farm Association, decided before the end of his stay that the project was impracticable. *The Blithedale Romance*, although written more than a decade after his Brook Farm experience, is an accurate expression of his opinion. He agreed with Emerson and Fuller that institutional reform tries to adapt men to theories instead of adapting circumstances to individuals. Such projects were too inflexible to suit the infinitely various emotional and material needs of persons.

He acknowledged that persons appeared, though rarely, who had insight into the designs of Providence, although they were not likely to be regarded as prophets in their own country and generation. "It often happens that the outcasts of one generation are revered as the wisest and best of men by the next." (CE 6:27) But his consistent view was that a man was always in error in supposing that "it mattered anything to the great end in view whether he himself should contend for it or against it." (CE 2:180) The man who appeared to achieve something for the world's betterment was merely a human lever through which great forces were acting. "Great men have to be lifted up on the shoulders of the whole world, in order to conceive their great ideas, or perform their great deeds." (CE 8:501)

He believed that the providential scheme advanced despite, not because of, human projects of reform, for "the world, and individuals, flourish upon a constant succession of blunders." (CE 5:30) He explained this flourishing upon a succession of blunders by supposing that there was design in the world, including men's blunders, but not design comprehended and directed by men. He even took the paradoxical position that providential purpose was advanced through the acts of persons whom he considered villains and enemies of mankind, as well as through the cooperation of good persons. He remarked of the persecutions of Archbishop Laud, that drove the Puritans to America, that "Liberty would have had no cradle, and the world would have been injured in its march perhaps for centuries, but for the timely aid of the Archbishop."[17]

It was his skepticism about human wisdom and capability that led Hawthorne to stand aloof from the various reforming enthusiasms of his time. He disapproved of abolitionist agitation, not because he condoned slavery, but because he looked upon such agitation as an attempt to hurry Providence. He felt sympathy for "the Negro," and looked with sorrow on "the cotton field where God's image becomes a beast of burden," (CE 10:216) but he declared himself "rather more of an abolitionist in feeling than in principle." His fullest expression of his views upon the subject occurs in his biography of Franklin Pierce, in which he says that slavery is

> one of those evils which divine Providence does not leave to be remedied by human contrivance, but which, in its own good time, by some means impossible to be anticipated, but of the simplest and easiest operation, when all its uses shall have been fulfilled, it causes to vanish like a dream. There is no instance, in all history, of the human will and intellect having perfected any great moral reform by methods which it adapted to that end; but the progress of the world, at every step, leaves some evil or wrong on the path behind it, which the wisest of mankind, of their own set purpose, could never have found the way to rectify. (RE 12:417)

This is not merely campaign rhetoric; he confirmed the opinion in a private letter to Horatio Bridge, his closest friend. It accounts for his profound pessimism about the Civil War (which may have been a contributing cause of the phenomenal decline of his health and depression of his spirits which ended in his untimely death before the war ended). He looked upon war as an actual evil of immense magnitude undertaken to effect a problematical good. "No human effort, on a grand scale, has ever yet resulted according to the purposes of its projectors. The advantages are always incidental." (RE 12:332)

Mistrusting efforts "on a grand scale," he thought that the right mode—that is, the only certainly efficacious one—of doing good in the world was to bestow kindness and benefit on persons individually. "Charity, to be truly efficient, should have a personal feeling; for, if it embrace too many objects, it will probably become meagre and unsubstantial, like a soup for six thousand paupers."[18]

He thought of progress as a slow process of renovation and innovation within the rusty iron framework of society, not as a radical restructuring:

> All human progress is in a circle; or . . . an ascending spiral curve. While we fancy ourselves going straight forward, and attaining, at every step, an entirely new position of affairs, we do actually return to something long ago tried and abandoned, but which we now find etherealized, refined, and perfected to its ideal. The past is but a coarse and sensual prophecy of the present and the future. (CE 2:259–60)

He did not expect a perfect society to evolve in America in his lifetime as the utopians hoped, but he thought the times provided conditions for the gradual evolution of a better society based on traditional forms. The feeble efforts of individuals and organizations to hasten this slow progress were unavailing. Conservatives who sought to perpetuate modes of exclusion based on ancient inequities of wealth and privilege, and radicals who sought to abolish all distinctions in a human fraternity based upon collective ownership of property, were equally at odds with the spirit of progress. So he depicted Blithedale as a "counterfeit Arcadia," whose denizens were deluded persons each of whom had an eccentric notion of goods to be pursued and tried to bend the others to his will and desire.

IV

HOLLINGSWORTH: THE REFORMER

Hollingsworth, the focal male character of *The Blithedale
Romance*, had admirable native traits and good intentions, but
was so narrowed by inadequate education that he lacked appreciation of intellectual and artistic matters valued by his more
cultivated associates. He was a superior and attractive representative of the same class of good-natured materialists of which
Robert Danforth, the blacksmith foil to the Artist of the Beautiful, was an earlier specimen. "Hollingsworth's figure was not
tall, but massive and brawny, and well befitting his original oc-
cupation, which . . . was that of a blacksmith." (CE 3:28) He
had no "external polish" and "courtesy of manner," but there
was "a tenderness in his voice, eyes, mouth, in his gesture, and
in every indescribable manifestation, which few men could resist, and no woman." (CE 3:28)

His cherished project of establishing an institution for the
reformation of criminals, which became narrowed and intensified to fanaticism, was the perverted outgrowth of his ten-
der-heartedness. It was evident in his solicitous attendance at
Coverdale's sick-bed in an early scene; but after Hollingsworth's
fanaticism had spoiled his relationships with his closest associates, Coverdale wondered "whether it were possible that Hollingsworth could have watched by my bedside, with all that
devoted care, only for the ulterior purpose of making me a pros-
elyte to his views." (CE 3:57)

Convinced of the probity of his intentions, Hollingsworth
urged his project with such vehemence, such intolerance of difference of opinion, that his virtue became vice. His rise from
toil and obscurity, although it gave him compassion for the la-
boring poor, had been a cultural deprivation; so he made no
distinction between the arts and graces that beautify life and
elevate thought and the sybaritic self-indulgence that debases it.
Thus he condemned Coverdale's poetry as idle frippery, and
was impatient with him and Zenobia for being interested in
matters beyond his imagination.

This failure of imagination is Hawthorne's way of indicating
that philanthropic optimism is more likely to be a characteristic

of unenlightened, half-educated persons than of those with cultivation and greater knowledge of life. His Brook Farm experience had convinced him that a life of manual toil was incompatible with intellectual and artistic activity. At one time he had shared the opinion that Bronson Alcott expressed in an "Orphic Saying," that "labor exalts and humanizes the soul."[19] "To insure a more natural union between intellectual and manual labor than now exists"[20] was one of the objects of the Brook Farm Association. But after months of physical drudgery he concluded that "labor is the curse of the world, and nobody can meddle with it without becoming proportionably brutified." (LL 2:25) Coverdale is represented as coming to the same conclusion.

A wider cultivation would have prevented Hollingsworth's ruin through excess of humanitarian zeal and optimism. The dark side of his extreme partiality for his particular scheme of reform was a denial of merit in other, perhaps more rational and comprehensive, plans of social improvement. Although a member of the Blithedale Community, and aware of how many of his fellow communists were deeply in earnest, he privately called Blithedale "a wretched, insubstantial scheme," (CE 3:130) and scoffed at Coverdale's faith in its desirability and practicability: "I neither have faith in your dream, nor would care the value of this pebble for its realization, were that possible." (CE 3:131) He coolly contemplated turning his friends off Blithedale Farm in order to establish there his institution for the reformation of criminals. Although he intended to marry Zenobia in order to use her money to finance his project, he was equally scornful of the feminism that she advocated, and scornfully contradicted her assertion and Coverdale's that equality of the sexes was just and possible. He said that "woman is a monster . . . without man as her acknowledged principal," and declared that if there were any prospect of woman's insisting upon equality with man, "I would call upon my own sex to use its physical force, that unmistakeable evidence of sovereignty, to scourge them back within their proper bounds." (CE 3:122–23)

Such firm conviction that one sees the whole truth clearly, and such willingness to force compliance with the supposed truth that one sees, are ugly traits of ignorant zealotry that are still dangerously threatening in the present time. Hawthorne had long been interested in the paradox of the good man whose philanthropy was so narrow that it injured all around him. "When a good man has long devoted himself to a particular kind of beneficence—to one species of reform—he is apt to become narrowed . . . and to fancy that there is no good to be done on earth but that selfsame good to which he has put his hand." (CE 10:217)

Emerson noted the same characteristic in reformers:

> They are partial; they are not equal to the work they pretend. They lose their way; in their assault on the kingdom of darkness they expend all their energy on some accidental evil, and lose their sanity and power of benefit. It is of little moment that one or two or twenty errors of our social system be corrected, but of much that the man be in his senses.[21]

The disillusioned Pantisocrat Coleridge earlier remarked the same fault in philanthropists:

> I have never known a trader in philanthropy who was not wrong in heart somewhere or other. Individuals so distinguished are usually . . . men not benevolent or beneficent to individuals, but almost hostile to them, yet lavishing money, and labour and time on the race, the abstract notion.[22]

Hawthorne had often drawn portraits of men with too much intellect in proportion to their heart; in Hollingsworth he portrayed a man with too little. Zenobia accurately observed that he was "not so much an intellectual man . . . as a great heart." (CE 3:21) More intellect would have shown how poor a comprehension of life had engendered "the cold, spectral monster which he had himself conjured up, and on which he was wasting all the warmth of his heart." (CE 3:55) His ignorant fanaticism corrupted his "great and rich heart." (CE 3:219) "He had taught his benevolence to pour its warm tide exclusively through one channel; so that there was nothing to spare for other great manifestations of love to man." (CE 3:55)

The worst effect of his monomania was that it made him a tyrannical egotist in his personal relationships. He cast off his dearest friend Coverdale "for no unworthiness, but merely because he stands upon his right as an individual being, and looks at matters through his own optics." (CE 3:135) When his fiancée Zenobia's wealth proved unavailable to finance his philanthropic scheme, he discarded her. He ruined his own life as well, for when he finally saw the tragic consequences of his conduct, he lapsed into impotent despondency.

Hawthorne could never have approved without strong reservations Emerson's injunction "Trust thyself"; for he did not believe, as Emerson wrote in "Self-Reliance," that "When we discern justice, when we discern truth, we do nothing of ourselves, but allow a passage to its beams." Zenobia speaks for him in her final impassioned accusation of Hollingsworth: "Self, self, self! You have embodied yourself in a project. You are a better masquerader than the witches and gipsies yonder; for your disguise is a self-deception." (CE 3:218)

V

FEMINIST THEORIES

Hawthorne's generation was familiar with and influenced by doctrines of feminist reformers on the other side of the Atlantic. Charles Fourier had attacked marriage as an oppression of both sexes, but especially the female. He asserted that woman would be superior in accomplishment to man if she were not victimized by "the oppressive system necessitated by the conjugal bond." "Woman in a state of liberty will surpass man in all the faculties of mind and body which do not depend upon physical strength." He called marriage anti-social and contrary to human nature, which he regarded as incapable of perpetual fidelity in love. His remedy is what has since been called free love, somewhat regulated by a set of classifications that his inveterate Gallic love of neat order impelled him to devise:

1. *The Constant*, united in permanent marriage . . .
2. *The Capricious*, enjoying the liberty of divorce.
3. *The Gallant*, having statutes less rigorous still.[23]

This arrangement would allow admirably for the variability of human inclinations and would enable everyone, particularly women now doomed to be unsatisfied old maids, to obtain sexual satisfaction. During their passionate youth women would be gallant, or at least capricious, and would enter constant relationships only when their passions had cooled with age and they began to seek peace and security. Abridging Bacon's epigram,[24] Fourier looked upon wives as being mainly nurses to old men. Although women were to be "emancipated" at eighteen, "people would not marry till late in life, at the age when passions are calm, and marriage would be restored to its true function, which is to be the support and solace of old age."[25]

William Godwin advanced similar theories without the fantastic systematization of Fourier. He too called marriage oppressive, "the most odious of all monopolies," and contrary to human nature, and like "the systematizing Frenchman" (Hawthorne's characterization of Fourier) proposed its legal abolishment: "The intercourse of the sexes will in such a state fall under the same system as any other species of friendship."[26]

Hawthorne's not very settled opinion about improving the status of woman appears to be that it cannot be done merely by changing the laws and conventions governing sexual relationships, and certainly not by rebellions of individuals chafed by restrictions, but rather by the development of a wider sympathy and provision of a fuller opportunity for women somehow within the framework of the old conventions.

This moderate view is that which his feminist acquaintances shared. Sophia Ripley wrote, in the *Dial*, "Woman is educated with the understanding, that she is only half a being, and an appendage. . . . Let her not lean, but attend on . . . her husband as a watchful friend."[27] And Margaret Fuller, in *Woman in the Nineteenth Century*, evidently advocated no changes in laws and conventions, if I interpret her correctly, but only a change in the spirit of the relationship between the sexes:

> Woman, self-centred, would not be absorbed by any relation; it would be only an experience to her as to a man. It is a vulgar error that love, *a* love, to Woman is her whole existence; she also is born for Truth and Love in their universal energy.[28]

This is like Zenobia's plaint: "How can [a woman] be happy, after discovering that fate has assigned her but one single event, which she must contrive to make the substance of her whole life? A man has his choice of innumerable events." (CE 3:60) Coverdale replied to this with a flippant innuendo ("A woman, I suppose, . . . by constant repetition of her one event, may compensate for her lack of variety" [CE 3:60]), but he felt the full force of her poignant question, and after her suicide feelingly declared that "the world should throw open all its avenues to the passport of a woman's bleeding heart." (CE 3:241)

VI

ZENOBIA, PRISCILLA, AND FEMINISM

In *The Blithedale Romance* it is evident that Zenobia had been an advocate of advanced views like those of Fourier and Godwin—apparently capricious and perhaps gallant in her conduct. In her amours she had been unfortunate, having lavished her "dewdrops" on the cynical and false materialist Westervelt, a man incapable of making a spiritual response to her passion. As, in Hawthorne's opinion, a woman's passions properly exercised are her mode of intelligence, this frustration had the unfortunate effect of making her sentiments and judgments untrustworthy thereafter.

Zenobia's feminist doctrines were apparently less genuine convictions than rationalizations of her error and passion, unlike Hester Prynne's, whose "native energy of character, and rare capacity" enabled her to overcome the bitterness of her troubled and passionate history and to attain to "a firm belief, that, at some brighter period, when the world should have grown ripe for it, in Heaven's own time, a new truth would be revealed, in order to establish the whole relation between man and woman on a surer ground of mutual happiness." (CE 1:263)

Coverdale remarked of Zenobia's feminist zeal, "Women, however intellectually superior, . . . seldom disquiet themselves with the rights and wrongs of their sex, unless their own individual affections chance to lie in idleness, or to be ill at ease." (CE 3:120–21) Zenobia confessed in her last speech to Coverdale that her moral judgment had been perverted by her sexual aberration. "The woman who swerves in a hair's breadth . . . out of the beaten track . . . with that one hair's breadth, . . . goes all astray, and never sees the world in its true aspect afterwards." (CE 3:224) Because she was not disinterested and sincere, she was an ineffectual advocate of feminine liberty. Having forfeited her chance of conventional satisfactions, and taken up an attitude in defiance of the censorious world, she tried in vain to retrieve what she had lost. The "gentle parasite" (CE 3:123) Priscilla, docilely—even abjectly—accepting woman's conventional role, won the prize of marital felicity that her proud, voluptuous sister contended for.

Hawthorne's fictional treatment of feminism in *The Blithedale Romance* is generally consistent with his views as examined in chapter 14, and with his ideas about woman's proper status and relation to man as developed in the two earlier romances. If there is a difference, it is in Coverdale's compassionate understanding of the problem of female dependency. He apparently felt the injustice of Hollingsworth's fierce diatribe against Zenobia's assertion of the rights of women. He did not, however, openly disagree with Hollingsworth, but merely wondered at Zenobia's meek and tearful acceptance of the rebuke.

> "Women almost invariably behave thus!" thought I. "What does the fact mean? Is it their nature? Or is it, at last, the result of ages of compelled degradation? And, in either case, will it be possible ever to redeem them?" (CE 3:124)

These queries imply Coverdale's disposition to admit the justice of equality of the sexes; and in fact Hawthorne seems to have been divided in mind on the question, just as Coverdale was. For he was attracted to two different ideas of womanhood: the sensuous, passionate type that aroused his deepest susceptibilities, and the spiritual, virginal type that his conventional prudishness approved. These types appear over and over again in his fiction, sometimes paired in what Melville called a diptych, as in John Inglefield's daughters, in Zenobia and Priscilla, and in Miriam and Hilda; sometimes singly, as the passionate type in Hester or the spiritual type in Sylph Etherege. Phoebe Pyncheon, a spirit yet a woman too, is perhaps an attempt to combine the two, as apparently Hawthorne thought they were combined in his wife, his "Phoebe." In his love letters to her before their marriage he ecstatically praised Sophia's spirituality, but after their marriage, while she was absent from him, he wrote in his notebooks that he longed to have her in bed with him.

These different ideas of womanhood reflect the division between the author's conservative thought and his deeper feeling. His conscious conventionalism, inherited from his Puritan ancestors and confirmed by his upbringing, was at odds with his urgent but unacknowledged sexuality. He had tasted with gusto Eve's luscious apple, but the Calvinistic taint in his conscience made him feel guilty. He projected his guilt on the temptress figures in his romances—Hester, Zenobia, and Miriam—and punished them for his libidinous urges. He also set up in Westervelt a figure that represented the rejected impulses of his own nature, and directed censure and contempt toward this "moral and physical humbug," this "wizened little elf." (CE 3:95) By these unconscious scapegoat subterfuges Hawthorne repudiated what was deepest in his nature and eased his guilt-obsessed consciousness.

His strategy of making Zenobia and Priscilla half-sisters succeeds brilliantly as a method of dealing with his dilemma of choice between ideals of womanhood according to his moral picturesque mode. His deep preference is for the Zenobia type. Coverdale's constant peeping at Zenobia was prompted as much by prurience as by what he tried to believe were the requirements of his role as Chorus to the Blithedale drama, and he dwelt with evident enjoyment on lascivious fantasies about her. Her "words, together with something in her manner, irresistibly brought up a picture of that fine, perfectly developed figure, in Eve's earliest garment." (CE 3:17)

> Zenobia was a magnificent woman. . . . She should have made it a point of duty . . . to sit endlessly to painters and sculptors, and preferably to the latter; because the cold decorum of the marble would consist with the utmost scantiness of drapery, so that the eye might chastely be gladdened with her material perfection, in its entireness. (CE 3:44)

Here Coverdale attempted to disguise his libidinous urges as artistic appreciation (as the author himself did in his musings on the Venus di Medici afterwards). Coverdale had a casual impulse to "take just one peep beneath [Priscilla's] folded petals," but he fantasized repeatedly on his supposition that Zenobia was "a woman to whom wedlock had thrown wide the gates of mystery. . . . There is no folded petal, no latent dewdrop in this perfectly developed rose!" (CE 3:47)

On her first appearance, in a snowstorm, Priscilla appeared to be one of Hawthorne's snow-images—that is to say, a purely fanciful figure.

> The fantasy occurred to me, that she was some desolate kind of a creature, doomed to wander about in snow-storms, and that, though the ruddiness of our window-panes had tempted her into a human dwelling, she would not remain long enough to melt the icicles out of her hair. (CE 3:27)

"Stout," "grim," and "grisly" Silas Foster, an earthly foil to the Blithedale dreamers, recommended the same kind of vivifying treatment of her that the hardware merchant Lindsey adopted for the snow-girl in "The Snow-Image": "Give the girl a hot cup of tea, and a thick slice of this first-rate bacon. . . . That's what she wants. Let her stay with us as long as she likes, and help in the kitchen, and take the cow-breath at milking time; and, in a week or two, she'll begin to look like a creature of this world." (CE 3:31)

Priscilla's physical frailty and spirituality are repeatedly described. She was "pallid and slender, and with unaccountable nervousness." (CE 3:186) She was "a tremulous little creature . . . There was lack of human substance in her; it seemed as if, were she to stand up in a sunbeam, it would pass right through her figure. . . . But, nevertheless, the child had a heart." (CE 3:185)

Hawthorne took care to furnish a realistic explanation of her frailty, however, to counter the snow-image fantasy. Her drab life of poverty in the city, in unwholesome conditions, where she earned a pittance in the characteristic feminine toil of a seamstress, sufficiently explained her wan and meager aspect. "As I first saw her, she had reminded me of plants . . . doing their best to vegetate among the bricks of an enclosed court, where there is scanty soil, and never any sunshine." (CE 3:27) During her stay in Blithedale the girl did acquire bloom and substance, as much because of the love of her associates and a healthful life in sunshine and fresh air as because of Silas Foster's prescriptions. Priscilla "still kept budding and blossoming. . . . So unformed, vague, and without substance, as she had come to us, it seemed as if we could see Nature shaping out a woman before our very eyes." (CE 3:72)

The complement of her physical frailty was her spirituality. "Hidden things were visible to her, . . . and silence was audible." (CE 3:187) It was the rumor of these occult powers that brought Westervelt to her and put her under his mesmeric control as the Veiled Lady. Coverdale told her, "You have spiritual intimations respecting matters that are dark to us grosser people," (CE 3:142) but Zenobia scoffed at Coverdale's fancies about Priscilla: "As she has hardly any physique, a poet . . . may be allowed to think her spiritual." (CE 3:34)

In the rivalry of the passionate and willful Zenobia with feeble Priscilla, who "was only a leaf floating on the dark current of events," (CE 3:168) Coverdale expected Priscilla's "fragile thread of life . . . inextricably knotted . . . with other and tougher threads [to] be broken," (CE 3:100) but Hollingsworth rejected Zenobia for Priscilla. The author's reward to the spiritual woman is correspondent to his punishment of the sexually experienced woman. In the last line of the romance Coverdale (hence his author) confirmed the justice of this by his "confession." "I myself—was in love—with—Priscilla!" (CE 3:247)—a pious declaration that put the stamp of approval on conventional morality.

VII

COVERDALE'S PRIVATE THEATRE

Near the beginning of *The Blithedale Romance* someone asked, "Have we our various parts assigned?" (CE 3:16) This question set the stage for Coverdale's ballad that turned into a tragedy.

Zenobia's dramatic presence encouraged his inclination to view all the characters and events with illusive credence.

> The presence of Zenobia caused our heroic enterprise to show like an illusion, a masquerade, a pastoral, a counterfeit Arcadia, in which we grown-up men and women were making a play-day of the years that were given us to live. (CE 3:21)

Before the train of dramatic events was set in motion, Coverdale established his role as spectator of the performance: "It was impossible not to be sensible that, while these three characters [Hollingsworth, Zenobia, and Priscilla] figured so largely on my private theatre, I . . . was but a secondary or tertiary personage with either of them." (CE 3:70) He defined the tense situation whose dramatic development he awaited with eager attention:

"For a girl like Priscilla, and a woman like Zenobia, to jostle one another in their love of a man like Hollingsworth, was likely to be no child's play." (CE 3:72)

When Priscilla's "air, while perfectly modest, delicate, and virginlike, denoted her as swayed by Hollingsworth, attracted to him, and unconsciously seeking to rest upon his strength," (CE 3:77) she was jealously observed by Zenobia, who in turn was under Coverdale's scrutiny.

> It would have made the fortune of a tragic actress, could she have borrowed it for the moment when she fumbles in her bosom for the concealed dagger, or the exceedingly sharp bodkin, or mingles the ratsbane in her lover's bowl of wine or her rival's cup of tea. Not that I in the least anticipated any such catastrophe. . . .
> . . . [Yet] it might chance, between Zenobia's passionate force, and [Hollingsworth's] dark self-delusive egotism, to turn out such earnest as would develop itself into a sufficiently tragic catastrophe. (CE 3:78)

He watched the progress of this development with intense interest and anticipation:

> I had wondered a thousand times . . . how Hollingsworth meant to dispose of these two hearts, which he had engrossed into his own huge egotism.
> There was likewise another subject, hardly less fruitful of speculation. It was whether Zenobia was so entangled with Westervelt that she was free to give her affections to Hollingsworth. (CE 3:126–27)

The characters enacting this drama in Coverdale's private theatre resented his prying and showed their resentment in cold behavior. He was fretfully aware of "that dreamlike and miserable sort of change that denies you the privilege to complain, because you can assert no positive injury." (CE 3:138–39)

Finally, mulling over possible developments, Coverdale became impatient for a resolution and

> began to long for a catastrophe. If the noble temper of Hollingsworth's soul were doomed to be corrupted by the too powerful purpose, which had grown out of what was noblest in him; if the rich and generous qualities of Zenobia's womanhood might not save her; if Priscilla must perish by her tenderness and faith, so simple and so devout;—then be it so!

. . . As for me, I would look on, as it seemed my part to do, understandingly, if my intellect could fathom the meaning and the moral, and, at all events, reverently and sadly. The curtain fallen, I would now pass on with my poor individual life. (CE 3:157)

Immediately following this, when Zenobia, as a deliberate rebuff, let down the curtain at the window through which he had been peering in on her meeting with Priscilla and Westervelt, on the eve of Zenobia's betrayal of her sister by delivering her into Westervelt's hands to be mesmerized as the Veiled Lady, Coverdale saw this as a stage gesture. "It fell like the drop-curtain of a theatre, in the interval between the acts." (CE 3:159)

At this point he was uncertain about what the true character of Zenobia might be beneath the various roles she assumed so easily. He could not decide whether her character of a proud, luxurious woman of the city or that "in which she presented herself at Blithedale" were the truer one. "In both, there was something like the illusion which a great actress flings around her." (CE 3:165) So he provoked her with prying questions.

I determined to make proof if there were any spell that would exorcise her out of the part that she seemed to be acting. She should be compelled to give me a glimpse of something true; some nature, some passion, no matter whether right or wrong, provided it were real. (CE 3:165)

She warned him, "it is dangerous . . . to tamper thus with earnest human passions, out of mere idleness, and for your sport." (CE 3:170)

Zenobia's "radiant presence" (CE 3:244) gave vivid interest to Coverdale's sport, and even after her suicide he was

affected with a fantasy that Zenobia had not actually gone, but was still hovering about the spot and haunting it. . . . It was as if the vivid coloring of her character had left a brilliant stain upon the air. (CE 3:228)

After the final curtain had fallen on the drama that had so engaged his attention in his private theatre, Coverdale realized that in adopting the life of a spiritualized Paul Pry he had forfeited any real existence of his own. "I have made but a poor and dim figure in my own narrative, establishing no separate interest, and suffering my colorless life to take its hue from other lives." (CE 3:244)

It seems fair to conclude that of all Hawthorne's fictions *The Blithedale Romance* is the most "inward," the most revealing of the author's unconscious as well as his conscious nature.

NOTES

1. *Hawthorne* (New York: Harper & Brothers, 1879), 133.

2. *Ibid.*, 128.

3. *Hawthorne's Tragic Vision* (New York: Norton Library, 1964), 151.

4. *The Quest of American Life* (Boulder, CO: Univ. of Colorado Press, 1945), xi.

5. (New York: Henry Holt and Co., 1920), 38.

6. "Nathaniel Hawthorne," *Revue Contemporaine* 31 (May 1857): 645.

7. "Historic Notes of Life and Letters in New England," *Works* (Boston: Houghton, Mifflin and Co., 1883), 10:352.

8. *A New View of Society: or, Essays on the Principle of the Formation of Human Character, and the Application of the Principle to Practice,* "Essay Third" (London, 1813), 25, 27.

9. *Transcendentalism in New England: A History* (New York: Putnam, 1876), 105–6.

10. *Writings of Margaret Fuller,* ed. Mason Wade (New York: Viking Press, 1941), 150.

11. "New England Reformers," *Works* (Boston: Houghton, Mifflin and Co., 1903), 3:261.

12. "Lecture on the Times," *Works* (Boston: Houghton, Mifflin and Co., 1903), 52.

13. *Brook Farm, Its Members, Scholars and Visitors* (New York, 1900), 52.

14. "New England Reformers," *Works,* 3:264.

15. *Autobiography of Brook Farm,* ed. Henry Sams (Englewood Cliffs, NJ: Prentice Hall, 1958), 90.

16. "Historic Notes of Life and Letters in New England," *Works,* 10:352.

17. Arlin Turner, *Hawthorne as Editor* (Baton Rouge, LA: Louisiana State Univ. Press, 1941), 236.

18. *Ibid.*, 259.

19. "Orphic Sayings," *Dial* 1 (January 1841):354.

20. *Autobiography of Brook Farm*, 6.

21. "New England Reformers," *Works*, 3:261.

22. *Table Talk and Omniana* (London: George Bell & Sons, 1884) 244.

23. *The Social Destiny of Man*, trans. Henry Clapp, Jr. (New York: R. M. Dewitt, 1857), 133, 129, 130, 127.

24. "Wives are young men's mistresses, companions for middle age, and old men's nurses." *Bacon's Essays and Wisdom of the Ancients* (Boston: Little, Brown, and Company, 1884), 86.

25. Fourier, 128.

26. *An Enquiry Concerning Political Justice and its Influence on General Virtue and Happiness*, edited and abridged by Raymond A. Preston (New York: Alfred A. Knopf, 1926), 271, 272, 273.

27. "Woman," *Dial* 1 (January 1841):364–65.

28. *Writings*, ed. Wade, 216.

TWENTY-ONE

The Marble Faun: "A Masque of Love and Death"

A century ago *The Marble Faun* rivaled *The Scarlet Letter* in popularity. It used to be admired as an elegant guidebook to Italy, but readers now agree with Henry James that the impression it gives of Italy is "factitious."[1] Parvenu Americans of the Gilded Age relished its comments on Italian art, but these are now deplored as mere decorative embellishments that clog the narration. Nineteenth-century readers prized *The Marble Faun* chiefly for its cloudy allegorical suggestiveness; they delighted to read it as an edifying puzzle, a Christmas pie full of moral sugarplums. It was, as E. P. Whipple said, "a labyrinth of guesses,"[2] in which biased interpreters followed such different clues that they were led to discoveries of meaning sometimes flatly contradictory to each other. Thus, Father A. F. Hewitt, writing in *The Catholic World* in 1885, found in the romance a record of Hawthorne's being "brought face to face with Catholicism, having his mind freed to a considerable extent from Protestant prejudices";[3] whereas Jessie K. Curtis, writing in *The Andover Review* a few years later, asserted that the book represents "Protestantism facing Popery."[4] (These apparently conflicting views are perhaps not irreconcilable, as we shall see, although such opinions are so explicit that they express merely part truths about the romance.)

Because the book was thus overvalued for its genteelism and didacticism, it is now seldom read; such extrinsic attractions are no longer thought to be the proper ground of interest in fiction, and nineteenth-century moral precepts and art appreciations have slight appeal for twentieth-century readers.

Academic critics, however, continue to give the romance some attention, but not to expound its moral teaching and art commentary. Modern criticism is mainly of two sorts: either it is what Hawthorne called "that inflexible and exceedingly dangerous species of criticism" which insists upon "bringing his fancy-pictures almost into positive contact with the realities of the moment," (CE 2:37) "exposing them to too close a comparison with the actual events of real lives"; (CE 3:1) or it is an explication of *The Marble Faun* as symbolic narrative, moral but not moralistic in the narrow sense of the older criticism, presenting a moral vision of life, but not pretending to any specific moral utility or practical tendency in influencing conduct.

Criticism of the first sort is a relentless pursuit of particularity, which, as Hawthorne complained, "looks too closely at the wrong side of the tapestry" (CE 4:455)—that is, endeavors to find a literal meaning for the book by seeking a factual reference for its characters and events. This attempt to force Hawthorne's romances to an extreme of particularity is as misguided as the attempt of nineteenth-century moralists to force them to an extreme of abstract generalization.

Criticism that interprets *The Marble Faun* as symbolic narrative follows Hawthorne's intention. He said that the romance was designed to bear "a certain relation to human nature and human life," (CE 4:465) but this design is far different from the intention of a novelist (Hawthorne refused to accept the label) who attempts circumstantial transcription of chapters of actual life. He felt that essential significances are implicit in the facts that are the ground of their manifestation: "A high truth, indeed, fairly, finely, and skilfully wrought out, brightening at every step, and crowning the final development of a work of fiction, may add an artistic glory, but is never any truer, and seldom any more evident, at the last page than at the first." (CE 2:2–3) This chapter will explore the symbolism of characters in *The Marble Faun* and will examine the implications of the situation in which the characters are involved.

I

Hawthorne was an habitual idealist, who apparently saw the world as the projection of an idea in the mind of God; in "The Hall of Fantasy," for example, he envisaged the possibility that Heaven would consist of immediate union with the divine idea—that is, of emancipation from physical modes of perception which require the material world as an object of contemplation. Although he thought that the world substantially existed independently of the human, if not of the divine, mind, man's perception of the world he considered to be not merely passive and recipient, but imaginative—that is, subjectively creative. Man's attention selects from various phenomena elements that correspond to and reflect the images with which his imagination is filled. Thus the visible world, although its real existence does not depend upon man's recognition of it, exists to an individual only as a construct of his private consciousness. This explains Hawthorne's fondness for mirror devices in his stories, and his favorite metaphor of the heart as a cavern which man explores and from which issue the figures that people his moral world.

He characteristically, then, treats the visible world, the projection of divine idea and the object of human cognition, as a set of symbols of a spiritual or ideal world beyond it: "Everything has its spiritual meaning, which to the literal meaning is what the soul is to the body." (RE 11:330) He handles visible reality plastically, to reflect the varying states and conditions of perception of his different characters, each of whom lives literally in a world of his own unique apprehension. These various worlds are of course very much alike, so that human beings share much of reality, although different persons can never apprehend an identical reality. A sympathetic person, disinterested and intellectually agile, can assume by turns the perspectives of different characters involved in a common situation and can successively grasp their quite different but all relatively valid apprehensions of the world.

Hawthorne uses three kinds of characterization (often in combination in one of his characters):

> *persons*—individual human beings (humanity individuated);
> *types*—representatives of categories of humanity (humanity classified);

symbols—simplified and intensified embodiments of distinct human traits (humanity analyzed).

Personal and typical characters are usual in novels, but symbolic characters are less common and not so readily understood. Hawthorne's symbolic characters are somewhat like the characters of a medieval morality play, each being not primarily a complex, unique, and "real" person, but an embodiment of a possible human trait. In order, however, to make his characters less general, flat, and pallid than the characters of a morality, he endows them with enough distinctness and accidentality to make them appear to be possible and actual human beings, although many of his characters—for example, Pearl in *The Scarlet Letter* and Donatello in *The Marble Faun*—seem to be more diagrams than characters.

His settings support the effect of his characterizations; they are local and solid enough to seem actual; possessed of natural features that can be used as symbols to reinforce the implications of the narrative; and plastically handled to project the states of mind of the characters who view them subjectively, and to give intimations of powers working behind them and through them. They are not impermeable objects of which the whole reality is in their visible and stable momentary appearance, but are like Melville's "pasteboard masks."

Hawthorne's techniques of handling character and setting were apparently developed by synthesis of elements from seventeenth-century allegory, Coleridgean theories of the romantic imagination, and the strain of narrative realism that has given the modern novel its definitive tendencies (Scott's influence on Hawthorne has, however, been exaggerated).

II

Donatello, "the very Faun of Praxiteles," (CE 4:7) is an almost completely symbolic character. He symbolizes the Natural Man. He is "in a high and beautiful sense, an animal," (CE 4:78) and enjoys "the warm, sensuous, earthy side of nature . . . as mankind did in its innocent childhood." (CE 4:13) Thus "linked . . . with what we call the inferior tribes of being," (CE 4:71) he conversed with birds and animals (as did Milton's Adam and Eve, and Pearl in *The Scarlet Letter*), who "dreaded

him no more in his buoyant life than if a mound of soil and grass
had long since covered his dead body, converting it back to the
sympathies from which human existence had estranged it" (CE
4:75)—a hint that even the sentient life of animals is a step away
from the vital center of natural existence. Though infra-human,
the Faun's character was yet "the more perfect within itself."
(CE 4:78) "He made no impression of maimed or stinted nature." (CE 4:14)

The Faun communicated with his world and participated in
its life almost solely through his instincts. He expressed his
reality best in movement—gestures, the animated play of limbs
and features, and, most of all, dancing, the spontaneous utterance of his whole sensibility in joyous action. "Little caprioles
in the air . . . are characteristic of his natural gait." (CE 4:102)
More intellectual modes of awareness and expression he prac-
ticed imperfectly: his gesticulation "doubtless was the language
of the natural man, though laid aside and forgotten by other
men, now that words have been feebly substituted in the place
of signs and symbols." (CE 4:77)

The world as it exists to the apprehension of Donatello, the
Natural Man, is a Garden. Monte Beni, his ancestral home, is a
Paradisal Hill. The paradisal aspects of even the artificial
Borghese gardens become distinct and vivid when he enters
them, and the ruins of man's operations upon nature there are
seen to be superficial and temporary obscurations of the underlying reality.

The Faun significantly lacks some traits regarded by civilized men as essential to human nature. His inability to intellec-
tualize his world made him seem a "simpleton," with "hardly a
man's share of wit." (CE 4:7) He had no conception of time, of
the distinction between now and not now. He could hardly
"send his mind back into the past," (CE 4:81) and "it perplexed
him even more to think of the future than to remember the
past." (CE 4:81) That is, he was so engrossed in the reality of
the moment that the reality of time past was difficult to recall
and the reality of time to come was unimaginable.

His inability to distinguish between immediate reality and
remote possibility, either past or to come, made him not only
unconscious of time but also unconscious of self. He had no idea
of his individual reality which had a definite character in his own
contemplation and duration in time. He had no idea, either, of

an order of things distinct from himself that existed independently of his own existence. The transition from nature and instinct to mind and thought is an emergence, an alienation, a sophistication that he had not learned; so he did not habitually distinguish the immediate realities of *Now* and *I* from the distant ones of *Then* and *Other*.

Lacking conceptions of a temporarily distinct self and of an enduring order of things distinct from self, he lived a life spontaneous and simple, not calculated and complex. His motives were sympathy and antipathy, not purpose and endeavor. He acted according to the attractions and repulsions of the immediate objects of his consciousness, and poured his whole being into the pulsations of each instant.

This simple but full sensuousness of his life made him ageless, by exempting him from considerations of his personal history and destiny, of what had been and will be. "It is equivalent to being immortal on earth." (CE 4:15) Besides this personal agelessness resulting from his unconsciousness of time, he exhibited the agelessness of the human species, through the immemorial persistence in him of the essential Monte Beni character "from a period beyond memory or record." (CE 4:234) This striking persistence of human type is emphasized not only in its reincarnation in widely separated generations of his ancient family, but also in the striking resemblance of Donatello to the antique Faun of Praxiteles, which suggests that the sculptor's conception "may have been no dream, but rather a poet's reminiscence." (CE 4:10–11)

Another defect of the Faun, from the point of view of sophisticated mankind, is his amorality. Making no distinction between self and not-self, now and then, he necessarily had "no conscience, no remorse, no troublesome recollections of any sort, no dark future either." (CE 4:13–14) Recognizing his utter incomprehension of the abstractions by which sophisticated persons try to direct their lives consistently (or at least intelligibly), his friends "habitually and instinctively allowed for him, as for a child or some other lawless thing, exacting no strict obedience to conventional rules." (CE 4:14)

Although the Faun could not be moral, he was spontaneously honest. Instead of moral responsibility, he had candor. "The being here represented is endowed with no principle of virtue, and would be incapable of comprehending such; but he would be true and honest by dint of his simplicity." (CE 4:9) Every moment of his existence was an unreserved self-revelation, and therefore truth; but he could not have the kind of moral virtue that consists in making one's life conform by self-control to an idea. He was incapable of reflection, pre-meditation, intention, or will in any meaningful degree, and no more controlled his own conduct by conscious purpose than does the leaf falling from the bough or the pollen alighting on the pistil of a flower. This prelapsarian, subrational innocence is quite different from the innocence usually attributed by Haw-thorne to his characters before their initiation into sin—although little Pearl in *The Scarlet Letter* has a similar innocence, her incip-ient humanness is more evident. Hawthorne's earlier innocents were usually persons who, before their involvement in sin, shared the tainted nature that Calvinism attributed to all of Adam's children, and whose sins were therefore inevitable acts of self-realization.

To judge rightly the character of Donatello, one must regard him as a presentment of one element of human nature, not as an attempt at realistic delineation of a human individual. He is the simple embodiment of an element of human reality that Haw-thorne recognized in all human beings, although sophisticated and modified out of recognition in many. He made his Faun as much an idealization as he took Praxiteles' Faun to be, and he succeeds in his own terms. Henry James's misguided criticism, that "it is a pity that the author should not have made him more definitely modern, without reverting so much to his mythologi-cal properties and antecedents, . . . which belong to the region of picturesque conceits, much more than to that of real psychol-ogy,"[5] offers a canon of judgment utterly inapplicable. Haw-thorne was not interested, as James was, in individual psychology and psychological particulars especially, but in the general and typical psychological and moral patterns that seemed to him to be fundamental and recurrent in human experience.

III

Just as the Faun is a symbol of man's instinctive presence in nature, so is the Spectre of the Catacomb (Miriam's model) a symbol of man's beguilement into a world of abstractive thought. Instead of joyous participation in the instant life of nature, his existence is a gloomy isolation in an introspective egoism, his consciousness peopled by phantoms from a remembered past. The Faun and the Spectre are at opposite extremes in the range of sophistication. In Hawthorne's figure of the human heart "allegorized as a cavern; at the entrance . . . sunshine and flowers . . . Within, . . . a terrible gloom and monsters," (CE 8:237) which occurs in an early entry in his notebooks, these expressionistic characters are figured. The Faun is human nature among the sunshine and flowers at the entrance to this unexplored cavern of the heart; the Spectre is a monster that haunts the terrible gloom within. The Faun expresses man's delight in a vivid present that insistently solicits the senses; the Spectre man's sorrow over a shadowy past that irrepressibly haunts the mind. The world as it exists to the apprehension of the Spectre is a Tomb. He is one "to whom midnight would be more congenial than noonday." (CE 4:30) He is associated with darkness, as the Faun is with sunshine.

The Spectre distinguishes his reality through the faculty of memory; the past determines the character of the present and future for him, so that his characteristic activity is following someone. His relentless pursuit of Miriam typifies what Hawthorne described in "Monsieur du Miroir" as "the hopeless race that men sometimes run with memory, or their own hearts, or their moral selves." (CE 10:169) Memory perpetuates every evil and error enacted in life, and extends their operation through time to come. Ugliness that in the natural course of events would be purged from the system of things is carried along by memory as the determining principle in emergent actuality. The Spectre would "gratify his fiendish malignity . . . by perhaps bringing some old pestilence or other forgotten and long-buried evil on society; or, possibly, teaching the modern world some decayed and dusty kind of crime which the antique Romans knew; and then would hasten back to the catacomb." (CE 4:33)

The concepts of memory and time combine to give an individual self-consciousness and age—for age is the appreciable duration in time of an individual thing. The Faun, as we have remarked, was ageless because he lacked the conception of his distinct identity through a past, a present, and a future. The Spectre, in contrast, was aged. The Faun's life was a perpetual renovation of humanity, but the Spectre's exemplifies the persistence of the ego. Instead of submitting himself to being converted "back to the sympathies from which human existence had estranged" him, and rising again to sentience as a fresh manifestation of vital reality, he has resisted death and thereby paradoxically resisted life and prolonged his mortality. He pursued other human beings in order to "beguile new victims into his own misery" (CE 4:33)—that is, to withdraw them from life (which includes death) and nature into his dismal condition of self-love and sterile introspection. This is one of Hawthorne's several treatments of the Wandering Jew legend that had struck his fancy indelibly.

IV

Hilda as a character is both a symbol and a type, in the senses in which these modes of characterization were defined earlier in this chapter. She is a symbol of Puritanism and a type of the naive nineteenth-century American. Also, less important, she typifies Victorian womanhood.

Her world is the Tower, which symbolizes a state of heavenward aspiration. Although Hawthorne remarked in speaking of Donatello that everyone either "ascends to truth or delves down to reality," (CE 4:262) Hilda's tower was the emblem of a spiritual exaltation to which she had never had to ascend, and she was incapable of delving down to reality. Her spirit had never had to "struggle through the incrustation of the senses" (CE 4:381) as the Faun's did before he attained the summit of *his* ancient tower. "Hilda does not dwell in our moral atmosphere." (CE 4:121) She is "a partly ideal creature, not to be handled, or even approached too closely" (CE 4:63)—that is, such spirituality as hers cannot stand contact with mundane realities. Her womanhood "is of the ethereal type." (CE 4:128)

In short, Hilda's moral goodness was that of a person who avoided the world, not that of one who made trial of the world and found out through experience the good and evil of one's own nature. Her worship of the Virgin, which Hawthorne felt obliged to apologize for as a suspiciously Catholic practice, merely symbolized her devotion to an immaculate purity. Her shrine, her white doves, and her white garments all betoken spotlessness. The shrine was "at a height above the ordinary level of man's views and aspiration." (CE 4:52) As one ascended her tower, the street cries "grew faint and died away; as the turmoil of the world will always die, if we set our faces to climb heavenward." (CE 4:53)

But most persons must live in the turmoil of the world and find their reality there. Hawthorne in fact thought it desirable that they should do so. He called himself "a man whose definition of happiness it is to live throughout the whole range of his faculties and sensibilities" (CE 1:40)—a fullness of self-realization that Hilda never experienced. She represented a point of view so narrow and exclusive that it automatically condemned experienced mankind, who had delved to depths of reality that such a fugitive and cloistered virtue could not justly measure. Hilda being so self-righteous, there is irony in her telling the priest whom she compels to listen to her "confession" that mortal man has no authority either to censure or forgive sinners.

Although Hilda as a "saint" was "cruel" and "merciless," (CE 4:209) her instinctive human and feminine sympathies made her capable of a compassion that her rigorous orthodoxy suppressed. Her first impulsive judgment of Beatrice Cenci, on viewing Beatrice's portrait, was that the girl pictured there was innocent of any essential stain of sin; but upon being reminded of the Calvinist creed to which she was committed, she asserted instead the judgment appropriate to the Puritanism that was her second, and stronger than human, nature—that Beatrice's guilt was inexpiable.

In fact, we may agree with Calvinist interpreters of *The Marble Faun* that Hilda does represent Puritanism, but her character and role in the romance do not constitute the tribute to Calvinism that such interpreters suppose. For all the purity and delicacy that Hawthorne discerns in the Puritan ideal, he finds it inadequate to cope with the reality of the human situation. Although Hilda in her sketchy character as *person*, as lovely New England girl, was made perfunctorily to descend from her virgin shrine to domestic life, she could never comprehend to the full what moral struggle is—she had a morally incomplete nature, a freakish innocence incapable of stain.

As a type, Hilda stood for the naive nineteenth-century American who ventures among older and more fully developed conditions of humanity and offers naive and uncomprehending judgments of it, like a bud innocently disdainful of the full-blown flower.

V

Kenyon symbolizes the artistic approach to life. The world as it exists to his apprehension is a studio.

Hawthorne held that art is the perception and exhibition of an ideal reality that the artist's insight discerns through the particulars and accidents of the concrete world. The creative artist penetrates to a changeless ideal nature that underlies changeable appearances. This penetration is the perceptive aspect of art. On its creative side, art constructs durable images, or at least suggestive reminders, of those ideal things which delight persons who have insight. These images then exist independently of their makers and serve as vivid prompters to the more torpid imaginations of less gifted persons. Julian Hawthorne, in his memoirs, said that his father evolved the ideas for *The Marble Faun* from his musing over the meaningful mystery of the bust of the Faun and the portrait of Beatrice Cenci, works which impressed him profoundly with suggestions of what he felt to be permanent elements of human possibility, whose truth is attested to by manifestation of the same qualities in actual persons of every generation.

Hawthorne supposed that the definitive trait of the artist was his faculty of insight, not his power of execution—for example, see "Drowne's Wooden Image" and "The Artist of the Beautiful." He remarked that the sculptor's assistants use their "merely mechanical skill" to relieve the artist of "the drudgery of actual performance." The assistants "free from its encumbering superfluities" the "figure embedded in the stone." The artist's "creative power has wrought it with a word." (CE 4:115)

The sculptor in *The Marble Faun* is an ideal artist in this conventional romantic sense. Other persons in the romance produce various works of pseudo-art, which tend to define by contrast what the nature of the true artist is. Miriam's painting, instead of being a revelation of the ideal, is too self-expressive;

she projects her own desires and anxieties on canvas, and obstructs inspiration with her own imperious passions. Hilda's art is simply another mode of her spiritual intuition and sympathy with holiness, and practically speaking is a form of devotion. She is merely an unusually gifted copyist, incapable of creative insight herself, but able to sympathize with, reproduce, and clarify the insights of true artists.

The problems of self and time which we remarked in connection with other characters are settled in a different fashion by the artist. He is a fully sophisticated man, but, although he has realized self fully, he is able to escape from egoism by detachment. He is completely disinterested in his role of seeing into the life of things, and he reveals the qualities of his vision with as little mingling of self-consciousness as possible. It is the general recognition of the artist's disinterestedness, his detachment, his capability of viewing things from all angles and accepting the special reality of each view, that makes other characters turn to Kenyon as a confidant.

The problem of time is likewise solved in a sophisticated way by the artist. Grecian urns, golden nightingales, and marble fauns exist outside of time. The test of any art's significance is the continued existence, under whatever change of guise, of the things it reveals and defines for mankind. Thus the observation of the same character in Donatello and the bust of the Faun animates the whole gallery. "The realization of the antique Faun, in the person of Donatello, gave a more vivid character to all these marble ghosts. Why should not each statue grow warm with life!" (CE 4:17) For the persons sharing such an experience, so long as they were caught up in it, time had ceased to be; they experienced an illusion that the "long Past" was living in "the narrow foothold of the Present." (CE 4:411)

Kenyon as ideal artist was made a sculptor because Hawthorne regarded sculpture as art *par excellence*, in its ideality, its apparently heightened detachment from particulars of representation, its greater resistance to the ravages of time than other forms of art. Although Kenyon had done some portrait busts, he took little pride in them for they were attempts to give enduring visibility to temporal things, rather than to give temporal visibility to enduring things. Hawthorne dismissed such productions as "concretions and petrifactions of a vain self-estimate." (CE

4:118) But, as Miriam said of Kenyon's ideal figures, they "turn feverish men into cool, quiet marble." (CE 4:119) This coolness and quietness of marble, its not lending itself so well to the rendering of particulars that painting achieves, makes it the medium most suggestive of artistic detachment. The material he works in makes the sculptor's art so enduring that it is suitable for expression of ideal things. As Kenyon says, "Sculpture, and the delight which men naturally take in it, appear to me a proof that it is good to work with all time before our view." (CE 4:119)

These attributes of Kenyon, the artist, make him a pre-Jamesian example of the "register"—a character who has the simple but rare gift of disinterested perception. The register sees things disinterestedly; the artist reveals them to others; and the confidant furnishes disclosure of the thoughts and motives of other characters.

VI

Miriam is the most ambiguous and at the same time the most significant character in *The Marble Faun*. Although "nobody knew anything about Miriam," her mystery was not an effect of vagueness but of richness. Her general character is one of complex variability. Her comment on the jointed figure in her studio is a significant self-description: "It is a lady of exceedingly pliable disposition; now a heroine of romance, and now a rustic maid; yet all for show; being created, indeed, on purpose to wear rich shawls and other garments in a becoming fashion. This is the true end of her being, although she pretends to assume the most varied duties and perform many parts in life." (CE 4:41) Various conjectures supposed Miriam to be the heiress of a rich Jew, a German princess, the partly negroid daughter of a wealthy American planter, and an English nobleman's lady. In the course of the narrative she appeared in numerous guises and disguises: as an artist, a woodland nymph, the thrall of a "nameless vagrant" who dragged her whither he would "fettered and shackled more cruelly than any captive queen of yore following an emperor's triumph," (CE 4:108) a village girl, and a female penitent. She resembled the portraits of Cleopatra and Beatrice Cenci, and, even more strikingly, certain vengeful Old Testament heroines whom she sketched, expressing in her representations an elusive suggestion of her own character of all-inclusive feminine possibility. Thus she is identified with many characters of womanhood in different epochs of history.

Near the end of *The Marble Faun* Kenyon met her, resplendent in attire and equipage, driving through the wintry Roman dusk. He had seen her playing many parts but had never learned her true identity, and now, he thought, "after a masque in which love and death had performed their several parts, she had resumed her proper character." (CE 4:397) But she herself was more in doubt about what constituted her proper character. "My reality! What is it?" (CE 4:82) she asked herself. She was as much an enigma to herself as a mystery to others. The traits repeatedly emphasized in her are passion, intelligence, and worldly experience. Although she was bewildered by the multiplicity of her own phases, they are all equally her real nature, for she is not an individual at all but a symbol of intelligent, passionate human nature that has experienced vicissitude and still vehemently pursues the hope of a happy personal life.

Miriam is the key figure of the romance. She is more human than any of the others, not because she is individualized or "realistic," but because she combines so many elements of human reality. In a sense, the other characters are all expressionistic embodiments of different parts of her broad humanity. It is their common association with her that brings the other characters into a pattern of relationship in the romance. Each one communicates with her on that level of her reality which his more specialized kind of awareness makes real for him. Or, to express the connection in another way, she finds part of herself in each one, but all of herself in none of her companions. In fact, the elements of Miriam's reality are inconsistent with each other and therefore incapable of full simultaneous realization. She sought detachment in the studio, but her painting was more a projection of her personal wishes and recollections than an artist's detached imagining of ideal things. She attracted the Spectre from the tomb—that is, she was overwhelmed by a recurrent and irrepressible conviction that her existence was fatally corrupted and dominated by a sinful past. She reverted briefly to nature, dancing with the Faun in the Garden, but such reversion to innocence could never be complete or long-enduring for an experienced person, and the Spectre invariably intruded and assumed ascendancy over her in spite of the Faun. She visited the saint in her tower, but passionately exclaimed that the saint was withdrawn from human realities. Her most impressive and real appearance was that of a worldly woman in the streets of Rome, which is itself Hawthorne's symbol of humanity in its completest stage of realization, with nature, art, saintliness, sin, and personal vanity and ambition all most fully realized.

Miriam also appears to stand for Catholicism. Just as Hilda stands for the American present of the nineteenth century, in which Calvinism still seemed a plausible if not adequate accommodation of man's moral nature to his worldly situation, so Miriam stands for the more sophisticated reality of Europe, older, more self-conscious—humanity full-blown rather than in the bud—for which Catholicism was a more adequate morality because it acknowledged and accommodated itself to good and evil, growth and decay, squalor and beauty, egotism and devotion, as operable within the Providential scheme. The hints about Miriam's Jewish origin, the traits of age expressed in her visage of youth, her assumption of garbs and guises appropriate to different local and temporal sets of circumstances, her frequent ostentations and as frequent humilities, all symbolize the ancient, experienced humanity of Catholicism.

VII

The action of the romance is designed to exhibit the characters I have distinguished. Through their association with Miriam, all the other characters enact their roles. That is, we see what happens when worldly experience enters the lives of nature and instinct, of egotism and the conviction of sin, of innocence and Puritan orthodoxy, and of art. The natural man becomes a moral man through experience. The conviction of sin haunts experience like a shadow. The Spectre is never really destroyed or suppressed—in fact, he enters into the consciousness of the Faun and continues his existence there, giving the Faun that duality which makes him moral. The saint rejects experience. The artist views it as objectively as possible.

The roles of Hilda and Kenyon in *The Marble Faun* are largely spectatorial. It is necessary to distinguish between what a Hawthorne character is as a symbol and what he does as an actor. As symbols of the modes of viewing reality of sainthood and art, respectively, Hilda and Kenyon represent more than they act out significantly. They look on and comment upon the actions of others. They suggest no such interesting uncertainties as the anomalous infra-humanity of the Faun, the "dusky, death-scented" (CE 4:36) preternaturalness of the Spectre, or the complex variability of Miriam, to add a larger dimension to their symbolic roles. They complete Hawthorne's diagram of possible modes of viewing the world of experience. Also, they exhibit two possible American points of view toward European realities, the absolute and the relative. Hilda judges from the standpoint of a rigorous absolutism, which measures human conduct simply and severely according to definite, inflexible standards. Kenyon has a more skeptical tendency (no doubt nearest to the author's); he observes the complicated play of human thought and passion, with its apparent elements of free will perplexed by fatality, and questions whether any hard and fast criterion can be reliable which sunders right from wrong as sharply as a cold-steel blade. The relativism that Kenyon speaks for is a more unmistakable element of the thought of *The Marble Faun* than of Hawthorne's earlier work because it was written from his fresh first experience of a Catholic, non-Anglo-Saxon culture.

At the close of the romance Hilda and Kenyon are what they were at the beginning. Hilda has seen the whole masque enacted, but has not set aside her prepossessions enough to comprehend it. Kenyon has comprehended it, but his marriage to Hilda signifies a deliberate commitment to the New England point of view that was his birthright, but from which his artistic detachment had hitherto enabled him to stand apart. Hilda is America and Miriam Europe, and Kenyon is, like Hawthorne, a voyager from an innocent and severe America to a sinful and sophisticated Europe that still somehow preserves its essential goodness and has learned morality through loss of innocence. Although the traveler rather dubiously clings to the simple, familiar verities of his New England, he is reluctant to judge ancient, sophisticated Europe by his alien and provincial standards. Perhaps Kenyon's betrothal to Hilda was a consciously symbolic action for Hawthorne himself.

VIII

The Marble Faun is Hawthorne's most imperfect romance because it is his most ambitious attempt to grapple with the central obsession of his life—the warfare between self and a transcendent good. He had no urge to philosophize—that is, to abstract, define, and systematize the diverse phenomena of experience into some sort of comprehensible scheme that the mind might rest upon as an exposition of the nature of reality. But he had one trait of the philosopher, which might be called an expanding consciousness: he never touched the limits of the reality he sought, and although he had no urge to think his way through infinity, he had an urge to feel his way through it. His temperament was that of the artist, seeking to represent life in striking similitudes addressed to the pulses more than to the intellect. His literary techniques admirably served his constant literary intention—vivid exhibition of the moral struggles of mankind.

Considered as a whole, Hawthorne's moral picturesque fictions show a large consistency of development. Beginning with the most immediate data of consciousness, he gradually extended his consideration of moral problems to the largest observable patterns of life, and finally pushed his speculations even beyond those limits.

In the introspective tales written in the secluded early years of his career occur his most subtle psychological analyses of sin as it is present to individual consciousness both in contemplation and in action that reveal to the agent what the proclivities of his own nature are.

Hawthorne's work as a civil servant, his Brook Farm experience, and his marriage and parenthood led him to consider moral problems in less subjective and individualistic terms. Observation combined with introspection furnished the data for his three American romances. The aspects of sin that engaged his attention in *The Scarlet Letter* are the tragedy of man's mixed nature, which leaves his moral fate in doubt throughout his earthly pilgrimage, and the pathos of the intermingling of human destinies, which exposes the innocent as well as the guilty to the consequences of sin. *The House of the Seven Gables* and *The Blithedale Romance* show the further enlargement of his consideration of moral problems. Going beyond his view of sin in individual consciousness and in intimate personal relationships, in *The House of the Seven Gables* he considered how the evil of particular persons, places, and times may perpetuate itself by being embodied in patterns of society and tradition transmitted from generation to generation. *The Blithedale Romance* complements this exhibition of the transmitted evil in tradition by pointing out that venerated human conventions are the product of the accumulated wisdom of ages, and contain man's cherishable good as well as his evil, and that well-intentioned efforts to eradicate social evil may have disastrous consequences. The present should criticize the past and attempt to improve upon it, but should not repudiate it and heedlessly destroy its immemorial and valuable arrangements.

The fruit of Hawthorne's half-dozen years of European residence, *The Marble Faun*, shows his increasing awareness of the fact that probably no actual system of society ever embodies anything but relative moral values. The substance of *The Marble Faun* is neither introspection nor detached observation, but the unhopeful speculation of a mind that had found evil in the heart of man, in the associations of men, and in the generations and nations of mankind. A scene in *The Marble Faun* shows Miriam, the Faun, and the Spectre as black shadows thrown by the moon on the sparkling waters of the Fountain of Trevi—and this is Hawthorne's final simile of human life. This is a world, he said, in which the desires of the heart must feed on shadows. The masque of love and death in which his characters play their parts "begins in mystery and ends in mist"[6] because it was the author's purpose to suggest that a shadow-play of antithetic influences is perpetually repeated in the history of the generations of men, and he will not localize and temporize his story to the point of obscuring this principle of recurrence.

The motif of life as a never-ending dance of sinister and mirthful figures is reiterated in the visible properties that surround the characters in his story: the procession of life represented on vases and sarcophagi, friezes and murals, in the grotesqueries of the Carnival, in funeral ceremonies and the ritual practices of monks and penitents, in the daily bustle of Roman streets, and the festivity and frolic of country life. Individual characters show the same variability: "Faces change so much from hour to hour, that the same set of features has often no keeping with itself." (CE 4:18) Miriam, recognizing her spectral persecutor in the dead Capuchin, reflected that the phenomenon "resembled one of those unaccountable changes and interminglings of identity, which so often occur among the personages of a dream." (CE 4:188–89)

In *The Marble Faun*, picturing a world in which the only intelligible and constant principle was the recurrence of identical patterns, Hawthorne defined the conclusion that he had groped for throughout his literary career—that the personal ego was the villain of the cosmic tragedy. The will of the part to resist the whole is bodied forth in all his early writing, and the counsel to submit is plainly written in *The Marble Faun*. The egoistic will confines man to the limitations of time, which puts death as a terminus to all he prizes, but the moment he is resigned to annihilation of ego he is ready to be resumed into the large eternal processes of life. Time stands between a momentless present and eternity, and attempts to perpetuate a succession of days. The personal self stands between unconscious participation in the life of nature and the resumption of all separate things into the universal process, and attempts to maintain its fleeting identity. The will stands between the instincts that prompt the impulses of each instant and the cosmic laws that compel all things through all eternity, and attempts to resist and coerce them both. All insufficiency, defeat, and pain come from the resistance of the part to the whole, and the anguish of the sufferer can be assuaged only by his yielding.

Struck by the presence of evil in all human conditions and systems, and by the sufficient appropriateness of all systems to their own apparent circumstances, Hawthorne tried in *The Marble Faun* to disengage the problem of evil from the matrix of any particular society and to view it under the aspect of eternity. In pondering ways to reduce evil to a fact tolerable to moral consciousness, he considered and rejected four solutions: the substitution of art for reality, the abandonment of morality for a life of frank naturalism, the acceptance of evil as a fatality that made man an irresponsible victim, and the Puritan repudiation of evil and evil-doers as essentially outside the system of moral reality and therefore merely aborted, factitious, or phantasmal appearances. Perceiving the inadequacy of each of these attitudes, he rested at last in the stoic view that contemplative detachment from the world's vicissitudes is the nearest approach man can make to a moral vision of life.

NOTES

1. *Hawthorne* (New York: Harper & Brothers, 1879), 160.

2. *Character and Characteristic Men* (Boston: Houghton, Mifflin & Company, 1882), 242.

3. "Hawthorne's Attitude Toward Catholicism," *Catholic World* 42 (1 October 1885):22.

4. *"The Marble Faun.* An Interpretation," *Andover Review* 18 (August 1892):141.

5. *Hawthorne*, 164.

6. *Character and Characteristic Men*, 240.

INDEX

Abrams, Meyer H., 37
Alcott, Amos Bronson, 246, 255, 278, 285
Allen, Ethan, 122
American Magazine of Useful and Entertaining Knowledge, 31, 223
Ariadne, 146–47, 160
Aristotle, 73, 172
Arvin, Newton, 268

Bacon, Francis, 17–18, 212–13, 223–24, 288, 297
Bacon, Roger, 212
Bellingham, Governor Richard, 234–35
Bennett, Arnold, 254
Bergson, Henri, 78
Berkeley, Bishop George, 139
Blake, William, 209
Bloomer Girl, 171
Bremer, Frederika, 116
Bridge, Horatio, 29, 49, 68–69, 74, 138, 268, 283
Brook Farm, 49, 82, 87, 163, 270–71, 278, 281, 296–97, 314
Browning, Elizabeth Barrett, 150
Browning, Robert, 5, 150
Browning, Robert, Jr., 150
Bunyan, John, 260
Bush, Douglas, 246
Byron, Lord (George Gordon), 75

Calef, Robert, 141
Calvinism, *See* Puritanism
Carpenter, Frederic I., 181, 248
Carrier, Martha, 133, 141
Cassirer, Ernst, 21, 92, 99–100
Cenci, Beatrice, 308
Channing, Ellery, 12, 16, 29, 86
Cleopatra, 310
Clotho, 146
Cloyse, Goody, 133

Coleridge, Samuel Taylor, 23, 31, 39, 41, 53, 75, 78, 89–90, 103–4, 134, 155, 159, 197, 253–54, 256, 286, 301
Comstock, Anthony, 66
Concord, Massachusetts, 1, 74
Conway, Wales, 2
Cowie, Alexander, 247
Cranch, Christopher P., 41
Crane, Maurice A., 49
Curtis, Jessie K., 298

Dante, 236
Davidson, Edward, 123
Democratic Review, 142
Descartes, René, 18, 20, 212
Dial, 248, 288
Dryden, Edgar, 15, 18
Duston, Mrs. Hannah, 168

Eden, 11, 209, 215, 256, 267
Edinburgh, Scotland, 71
Edwards, Jonathan, 210, 220
Emerson, Ralph Waldo, 1, 21, 37–39, 41–42, 69, 231, 255, 278–79, 281, 286–87
Erskine, John, 189
Étienne, M. L., 260, 276

Fairbanks, Henry G., 67
Farquhar, George, 47
Faulkner, William, 177
Faustus, 212
Fechner, Gustav Theodor, 20
Feidelson, Charles J., Jr., 97, 105, 140
Felt, Joseph B., 97
Fénelon, Abbé François, 17–18
Fields, James T., 98
Fleming, Standford, 205
Fogle, R. H., 43, 106
Fontenelle, Bernard, 17

Fourier, François, 182, 279, 287–89
Franklin, Benjamin, 260, 269
Frost, Robert, 21, 140
Frothingham, Octavius B., 277
Fruitlands, 278
Fuller, Margaret, 61, 147, 163–79, 189, 192, 278, 281, 288
Fuller, Bishop Thomas, 209
Furness Abbey, 35, 57

Galileo, 18
Gerber, John, 227, 247–48
Godwin, William, 182, 288–89
Goldsmith, Oliver, 18
Gollin, Rita K., 26, 106
Gothicism, 94, 109
Great Chain of Being, 9, 18, 27
Gross, Seymour L., 179
Gustavus Adolphus, 170

Hall, L. S., 268
Hardy, Thomas, 140, 186, 219
Haroutunian, Joseph, 189, 205, 248
Hawthorne, Julian, 178, 308
Hawthorne, Nathaniel: artist character, 26–29, 64–65, 142, 200, 272–75; artistic intention, 54–55, 63, 308; artist presence, 4–5; characterization, 45, 59, 123–24, 198, 300–301; dramatic sense, 44–49, 293–96; dream and fantasy, 78–82, 135; epistemology, 19–23, 39–42, 65–66, 69, 137–40; feminine and masculine traits, 116, 142–48, 163–79, 185–86, 189, 193–95, 291; feminism, 287–90; good and evil, 28, 38, 211, 246, 316; idealism, 37, 54, 58, 108, 111, 148–50, 157–59, 214, 291, 300; imagination, 30, 34–35, 53–66, 72, 85–91, 96, 113–15, 150–54, 200, 255–56; language, 99–104; life-giving touch, 84, 154–55, 158; metonymy, 118–23, 125–35, 140; moral picturesque defined, 1–3; nature, 10–13, 41–42, 54–55, 190–92, 195, 197, 250, 301–4; neutral territory, 48–49, 58–62; novel and romance, 254; organic theory, 93–94; painting and sculpture, 54–58, 64–65, 111, 309–10; perception, 69–74, 77–79; property, 259–60, 269; Providence, 12, 14, 16–17, 31, 44, 72, 126, 170, 196, 229, 281–82, 312; realism, 62–63, 68–76, 114–15, 200, 254–55; spiritualism, 80–84; symbolism, 21, 41–43, 82–83, 97–98, 103–5, 142–48, 155–58, 189, 203, 227, 235, 257–58; systems of reality, 9–18; time and eternity, 108–11, 309; tradition, 46; transcendentalism, 37–43, 93, 255; truth of impression, 95; utopianism, 275–83

—— CHARACTERS: Adam, 14, 15, 31, 142–43, 152; Alice (in *Ancestral Footstep*), 171; Angler, 219; Aylmer, 17, 53, 55, 223; Brand, Ethan, 9, 28, 33, 223; Brown, Goodman, 100, 130–41; Bullfrog, Mrs. Laura, 167–69; Capuchin. *See* Spectre; Chillingworth, Roger, 100, 117, 146, 182, 194, 203, 207–24, 227–37, 240; Coverdale, Miles, 5, 40, 46, 61, 145, 178, 272–96; Danforth, Robert, 144, 149, 283; Digby, Richard, 33; Dimmesdale, Arthur, 14, 118, 125–41, 146, 152, 181, 183, 186–87, 202–4, 208–9, 211, 222, 225–48; Donatello, 14, 27, 101, 108, 301–17; Dorcas, 100; Drowne, 150; Elinor, 148; Elsie, 148; Ernest, 40, 108, 192; Etherege, Sylph, 100, 149, 167–68, 290; Eve, 14–15, 31, 142–43, 152, 291; Faith, 130–41; Fauntleroy. *See* Moodie; Feathertop, 158; Felton, Septimius, 223; Foster, Silas, 292; Georgiana, 53, 149, 167; Heidegger, Dr., 116, 123; Helwyse, Gervase, 27; Hibbins, Mistress, 202; Hilda, 5, 147, 169, 290, 304–17; Holgrave, 4–5, 14, 46, 100, 124, 144, 146,

204, 265–67; Hollingsworth, 5, 149, 273–96; Hovenden, Annie, 143; Hovenden, Peter, 143, 158, 167; Inglefield, John, 116, 149, 290; Josiah, 100; Kenyon, 5, 55, 96, 147, 160, 308–17; Lindsey, 157–59, 167, 292; Lindsey, Mrs., 152–53, 155–57, 159; Ludlow, Walter, 148; Maule, Matthew (the first), 260; Maule, Matthew (the second), 261–62, 264, 266; Miriam, 5, 15, 49, 100–101, 147, 163, 169, 220, 290–91, 308–17; Moodie, 100, 274; Old Collector, 122; Old Inspector, 149; Ossoli. *See* Fuller, Margaret; "P.," 44, 109–10; Pansy, 54; Pearl, 4, 27, 62, 114, 116, 128, 144, 146, 152, 155, 187, 190–206, 229, 233–35, 238–40, 243–44, 301–4; Peony, 152–59; Perseus, 138; Phoebe, 5, 15, 27, 34, 62, 100, 102, 116–17, 124, 144–45, 169, 263–67, 290; Priscilla, 5, 27, 40, 100, 145, 149, 169, 273–96; Pry, Paul, 272, 295; Prynne, Hester, 4, 16, 102, 117–18, 127–28, 144, 152, 163, 169–77, 180–89, 195, 198–99, 202–3, 208–10, 221–22, 225–31, 233–40, 242–45, 289–91; Pyncheon, Alice, 116, 258, 261–66; Pyncheon, Clifford, 4–5, 34–35, 72, 91, 115–17, 123–24, 156, 158, 253, 263; Pyncheon, Colonel, 57, 149, 261; Pyncheon, Gervayse, 261; Pyncheon, Hepzibah, 14, 34, 102–3, 116–17, 156, 263–65; Pyncheon, Jaffrey (Judge), 4, 33–35, 110, 124, 149, 158, 167, 263, 267; Queen Christina, 170–71; Quicksilver, 138; Rappaccini, Beatrice, 215; Rappaccini, Dr. Giacomo, 215–17; Robin, 100; Rochcliffe, Lady Eleanore, 27; Rigby, Mother, 46, 158; Spectre, 304–17; Toll-Gatherer, 112; Violet, 53, 152–59; Wandering Jew, 28; Warland, Owen, 144, 255, 283; Westervelt, 5, 40, 145, 271, 291,

295; Wigglesworth (tombstone carver), 31, 33; Zenobia, 5, 11, 33, 61, 83, 116, 145, 163, 169, 177–78, 272–96

—— WORKS: "Alice Doane's Appeal," 48, 141, 154; "The Ambitious Guest," 192; *American Notebooks*, 77, 80, 89, 98, 149, 154, 167; *The Ancestral Footstep*, 2, 171; "The Artist of the Beautiful," 33, 55, 143, 158, 167, 308; "The Birthmark," 17, 55, 167; *The Blithedale Romance*, 4–5, 11, 27, 33, 40, 46, 83, 100, 113, 116, 118, 145–46, 177, 270–97, 314; "Browne's Folly," 119; "Buds and Bird Voices," 86; "The Canterbury Pilgrims," 103; "The Celestial Railroad," 36, 38; "Chippings with a Chisel," 31, 223; "The Christmas Banquet," 197; "The Custom House," 48, 82, 90, 98, 110, 122, 149, 154; "David Swan," 36; *Doctor Grimshawe's Secret*, 148; "Drowne's Wooden Image," 96, 148, 154, 308; "The Duston Family," 169; "Earth's Holocaust," 110, 192; "Edward Fane's Rosebud," 114, 116; "Edward Randolph's Portrait," 148; "Endicott and the Red Cross," 179; *English Notebooks*, 19, 154, 263; "Fancy's Show-Box," 248; *Fanshawe*, 219; "Feathertop," 40; "Fire-Worship," 124; "Footprints on the Seashore," 77, 146; "Graves and Goblins," 79; "The Great Stone Face," 40, 108, 148, 192; "The Hall of Fantasy," 45, 72, 300; "The Haunted Mind," 89; "The Hollow of the Three Hills," 117–18, 154; *The House of the Seven Gables*, 4, 14, 17, 27, 33–34, 45–46, 57, 62, 71, 83, 91, 100, 102–3, 105, 109–10, 115, 123, 144–45, 156, 158, 251–69, 314; "Howe's Masquerade," 71; "The Intelligence Office," 13;

Hawthorne, Nathaniel—(*cont.*)
  "The Journal of a Solitary
    Man," 29; "Lady Eleanore's
    Mantle," 27; "Main Street," 15,
    60, 116, 120; *The Marble Faun*,
    4–5, 14, 19, 23, 27, 33, 47–49,
    55, 60, 96, 100–101, 105, 108,
    147, 149, 160, 220, 298–317;
    Mosses from an Old Manse, 110;
    "Monsieur du Miroir," 148,
    305; "Mrs. Hutchinson," 132,
    160, 164–67, 173–77; "My Kins-
    man, Major Molineux," 89, 154,
    256; "The New Adam and
    Eve," 10, 142–43, 152, 187;
    "The Old Apple Dealer," 124;
    "The Old Manse," 2, 16, 28,
    37, 76–77, 154, 258; "Old Ti-
    conderoga," 120; "An Old
    Woman's Tale," 154; *Our Old
    Home*, 15, 47, 69, 82, 88; "P.'s
    Correspondence," 44, 149; *Pas-
    sages from the American Notebooks*,
    164; "The Procession of Life,"
    13, 124; "The Prophetic Pic-
    tures," 49, 113, 148, 223, 274;
    "Queen Christina," 169; "Rap-
    paccini's Daughter," 38, 125;
    "A Rill from the Town Pump,"
    120; "Roger Malvin's Burial,"
    42, 146, 217; *The Scarlet Letter*,
    4, 16, 27, 33, 42, 46, 48, 62, 66,
    75, 87, 90, 97–100, 102, 114,
    116, 118, 120, 122, 125–41, 146,
    173–77, 180–248, 314; "A Select
    Party," 58, 77; *Septimius Felton*,
    45, 94, 130; "The Seven Vaga-
    bonds," 113; "Sir William
    Phips," 111; "The Snow-Im-
    age" 142–60, 167, 292; *The
    Snow-Image and Other Tales*, 25;
    Tanglewood Tales, 146; "The
    Toll-Gatherer's Day," 36, 111,
    113, 146; *Twice-Told Tales*, 28,
    65, 220; "The Village Hall," 83;
    "The Village Uncle," 113, 192;
    "A Virtuoso's Collection," 28,
    57, 113; "The Wives of the
    Dead," 88, 154; "Young Good-
    man Brown," 19, 66, 130–41,
    256

Hawthorne, Rose. *See* Lathrop
Hawthorne, Sophia Peabody, 62,
    79, 83, 86–87, 94, 96, 145, 155,
    163–64, 178, 271, 290
Hawthorne, Una, 29, 115, 199–201
Herbert, George, 247
Hercules, 168
Hewitt, Fr. A. F., 298
Hibbes, Richard, 136
Howe, Julia Ward, 29
Howells, William Dean, 248
Hudson, W. H., 102
Hurd, Bishop Richard, 224
Hutchinson, Mrs. Anne, 172–77

International Magazine, 151

Jackson, Andrew, 277
James, Henry, Jr., 3, 19, 23, 25,
    60, 66, 115, 139–40, 145, 171,
    188, 225, 246–47, 252, 254–55,
    271, 298, 304, 310
James, Henry, Sr., 29
James, William, 19–21, 23–24, 99
Jarrell, Randall, 140
Johnson, Samuel, 18, 47, 69, 149
Joyce, James, 254

Kant, Immanuel, 22
Karma, 218–21
Keats, John, 23
Kermode, Frank, 22, 92–93
Kesselring, Marion L., 18, 222
Kesterson, David B., 42

Lane, Charles, 278
Lathrop, George P., 247
Lathrop, Rose Hawthorne, 106
Leamington, England, 94
Laud, Archbishop William, 282
Leavis, Q. D., 248
Leibniz, Baron G. W., 18
Lesser, Simon O., 23, 104, 141
Levin, David, 138, 141
Lincoln Cathedral, 94
Literary World, 248
Liverpool, England, 29, 82, 88,
    96, 236
Locke, John, 218, 260, 269
Lorenzo di Medici, 64
Lovejoy, Arthur O., 17–18

Malbone, Edward G., 116, 255
Male, Roy R., 36, 93, 142, 144, 146, 275
Manchester Cathedral, 76
Maritain, Jacques, 206–7, 246
Marks, Alfred, 23
Martin, Terence, 48
Mather, Cotton, 132–33, 141, 217, 223, 225, 240, 242, 248
Mathews, J. W., 18
Matthiessen, F. O., 189, 248
Melville, Herman, 19, 21, 23, 29, 38, 93, 177, 208, 246, 269, 301
Merrill, L. T., 189
Mesmerism, 83
Michelangelo, 50, 64–65
Mill, John Stuart, 260, 269
Miller, Perry, 135–36, 140–41, 237, 241–45, 247
Mills, Barriss, 248
Milton, John, 18, 109, 145, 186, 211, 213, 221, 223, 228, 241–42, 246, 265, 301
Minotaur, 146
More, Henry, 18, 224
More, Paul Elmer, 246, 268
Mount Graylock, 73

Naboth's Vineyard, 259
Nero, 110, 224
Newton, Sir Isaac, 147
Nietzsche, Friedrich W., 19–22, 24, 78
Norlin, George, 275
Normand, Jean, 69
North Adams, Massachusetts, 60

Oates, Joyce Carol, 22
The Old Manse, 11–12, 71, 74, 76, 86–87, 96, 111, 142, 163, 267
Othello, 134
Oversoul, 1, 43, 81
Owen, Robert, 277–78

Paracelsus, 212
Parcae, 145, 160
Pascal, Blaise, 18
Peabody, Elizabeth Palmer, 178
Perkins, George, 269
Perry, Ralph Barton, 248
Perugia, Italy, 94

Pierce, Franklin, 47, 282
Plato, 54–55
Plotinus, 31
Poe, Edgar Allan, 19, 146
Pope, Alexander, 18, 214
Powers, Hiram, 83
Prospero, 108–24
Puritanism, 16, 28, 38, 47, 66, 173, 184, 193–94, 205, 207–11, 226, 231, 237, 241–46, 252, 276, 304, 307, 312, 317

Ragan, James F., 160
Raphael (angel), 145
Raphael (artist), 56
Rembrandt, 77
Ripley, George, 279
Ripley, Sophia, 288
Rousseau, Jean-Jacques, 260, 269

Saint Peter's Cathedral, 73
Salem Gazette, 177
Salem, Massachusetts, 77, 87, 97–98
Salisbury Cathedral, 94
Sand, George (Mme. A. A. Dudevant), 180
Santayana, George, 22, 91–92
Schlegel, Friedrich, 18
Schneider, Herbert, 248
Shakespeare, 23, 147, 168
Sherman, Stuart P., 186, 225
Shroeder, John W., 124
Sophocles, 247
Spengler, Oswald, 110
Spenser, Edmund, 114, 151
Stovall, Floyd, 38
Suter, Rufus, 223
Swift, Lindsay, 278

Tennyson, Alfred Lord, 189
Theseus, 146–47
Thompson, G. R., 23
Thoreau, Henry David, 12, 29, 35, 38, 86, 110, 177, 275
Ticknor, William, 29, 88, 96
Tolstoi, Count Leo, 252
Trollope, Anthony, 96, 252
Tupper, Martin, 61
Turner, Arlin, 24, 38, 222, 297
Turner, Frederic Jackson, 276

Twain, Mark (Samuel Clemens), 19

Uffizi Gallery, 36, 54
Undine, 197

Vaihinger, Hans, 92
Venus, 168–69, 291
Venus di Medici, 35–36, 54, 56, 111
Von Abele, Rudolph, 248

Wade, Mason, 163, 177
Wagenknecht, Edward, 247
Waggoner, H. H., 189
Waller, Edmund, 224
Warren, Austin, 223, 247–48, 253, 256
Warren, Robert Penn, 67
Westminster Abbey, 30

Westminster Hall, 94
Whipple, E. P., 298
Whitehead, Alfred North, 22, 24, 137
Whitman, Walt, 31, 117, 177
Whitnash (England) Church, 73
Wigglesworth, Michael, 133, 195
Wilberforce, William, 30
Willey, Basil, 223
Wilson, Reverend John, 120, 127, 133, 173, 195, 229, 233, 235
Winthrop, Governor John, 120, 126, 133, 235
Woodberry, George, 253
Wordsworth, William, 85, 93, 145, 155, 160, 190–93, 204–6, 214, 223
Wright, Frances, 278

Yates, Norris, 124